Human Being, Bodily Being

Chakravarthi Ram-Prasad is Distinguished Professor of Comparative Religion and Philosophy at Lancaster University, and a Fellow of the British Academy. He is the author of six books and some fifty papers. *Divine Self, Human Self* (Bloomsbury) won the Society for Hindu-Christian Studies Best Book Award 2011–15.

Human Being, Bodily Being

Phenomenology from Classical India

Chakravarthi Ram-Prasad

OXFORD
UNIVERSITY PRESS

OXFORD
UNIVERSITY PRESS

Great Clarendon Street, Oxford, OX2 6DP,
United Kingdom

Oxford University Press is a department of the University of Oxford.
It furthers the University's objective of excellence in research, scholarship,
and education by publishing worldwide. Oxford is a registered trade mark of
Oxford University Press in the UK and in certain other countries

First published 2018
First published in paperback 2021

Published in the United States of America by Oxford University Press
198 Madison Avenue, New York, NY 10016, United States of America

British Library Cataloguing in Publication Data
Data available

Library of Congress Cataloging in Publication Data
Data available

ISBN 978–0–19–882362–9 (Hbk.)
ISBN 978–0–19–285692–0 (Pbk.)

Contents

Acknowledgements

No academic book can be written without accruing many debts, and certainly not one in which each chapter is on a different genre of classical Indian writing with its own scholarly literature, and which engages with a different set of contemporary Western philosophical materials. I would like to thank audiences that have heard presentations on one or more of the topics in this book, at Amherst College, Cambridge University, Chapman University, University of Copenhagen, University of Erfurt, Pedagogical University of Kraków, the Mind and Life Institute, California State University Northridge, Oxford University, University of Roehampton, Smith College, Uppsala University, and University of Wolverhampton. Audiences at various meetings of the American Academy of Religion, and Sanskrit Traditions in the Modern World offered many interesting responses to presentations based on research for this book. Seminars in my department at Lancaster University also proved very useful.

I have had many helpful conversations on the themes of this book with colleagues at Lancaster University, especially Brian Black, Gavin Hyman (as always), and Kim Knott. I am especially grateful to Shuruq Naguib and Alison Stone for discussing Chapters 2 and 4 with me, in particular on questions of gender, sexuality and body.

I have also benefited from conversations and discussions with Charlie Hallisey, Steve Heim, Jacqueline Hirst, and Sthaneshwar Timalsina.

My study of Sulabhā began with a typically animated discussion with Jessica Frazier. Anthony Cerulli wrote back encouragingly about my ideas on Caraka in Chapter 1.

Two anonymous readers for the Press offered sympathetic readings of the book and its articulation of the notion of ecological phenomenology; their comments helped clarify crucial aspects of the book.

Monika Kirloskar-Steinbach was extremely generous with her time, and I am very grateful to her for having read the entire manuscript, offering helpful suggestions throughout; at several points, my arguments have benefited from her precise observations and questions. Deepest thanks also to Laurie Patton, who incredibly carved out time from her schedule as a college president to likewise go through the whole manuscript. Her lively, witty, and subtle reading both helped me and cheered me up.

Chapter 4 derives from the many wonderful hours I spent reading the *Naiṣadhacarita* with Godavarish Misra: I am deeply appreciative of and grateful for his scholarship, patience, friendship, and good humour.

During fruitful conversations with Maria Heim, we developed together the idea of an 'ecological phenomenology'. I gladly acknowledge her critical role in enunciating this idea, which we have utilized in our respective projects and in our ongoing collaboration. I would also like to thank her specifically for helping me think through the works of Buddhaghosa, both in Chapter 3 of this book and in a joint paper we published recently.

As always, my family has provided the environment in which I have been able to work in contentment. Florence kept her customary intelligent silence on many a dog walk on which I thought through the details of this book. My parents, father-in-law and brother have been warm and supportive of yet another complicated project. Judith, who continues to make so many things possible, commented on my (feeble) attempts to articulate ideas from this book more intelligibly. Krishnan has directed his own interests into many a lively conversation on (and off) topic. And Nalini has kept me aware at all times about the really important stuff in life.

Introduction

Situating Ecological Phenomenology

Bare Outline of Chapters

In this book, I study explorations of experience that bring to the fore the nature and role of body. There is now well-established scholarship which demonstrates that the rich Indian philosophical traditions have paid close attention to questions of self, consciousness, agency, intention, motivation, and many other aspects of the human being. But there has been surprisingly little attention paid to the question of how 'body' is a persistent theme of many different genres of ancient and classical literature. It is worthwhile studying the texts because here, as in so many other areas of thought, the material throws up a dazzling variety of ideas about how we should treat 'body' (translated as such from words like *kāya*, *kuṭi*, *tanus*, *deha*, *pudgala*, *budhna*, and *śarīra*, to list just the simplest, and leaving out the endless number of poetic, metaphorical and other more elaborate terms). With its own ultimate concerns, a broad set of consensually recognized concepts, commensurable epistemological methods, and a vocabulary at once fluid and mutually comprehensible across styles, genres, centuries, and even languages (Sanskrit, Pali, various Prakrits and their successors, even post-classical Tamil), the literary world of Indic culture offers an exceptional range of materials—not just 'philosophical' texts—for anyone wishing to make the discussions of ideas a global conversation.

The chapters in this book are offered as case-studies for a particular methodological approach (described below) which enables us to understand afresh the many ways in which the human being is conceived as bodily being. They make a case cumulatively, even if not (strictly speaking) sequentially. (They need not be read in order, although there are some elements of progression across the book; and they are arranged in roughly chronological order.) I have deliberately chosen from very different genres precisely in order to demonstrate the generality of my argument. At the same time, this study is programmatic. I could have chosen other texts and genres, but I hope that these studies will lead to or prompt further examination of other works for their utilization of the notion of bodiliness.

'Body' is present as a conceptual category in the understanding of experience in a myriad of ways in Indian texts, and I hope to open up study of them to contribute to a wider, cross-cultural conversation about the human condition. Each chapter, in its way, deals with its own conception of body, specifically in terms of how subjectivity is expressed through intrinsically bodily modes—what I call 'bodily being'. But each conception is located within a particular framing concern and expressed through different literary modalities and tropes.

The first case is from the first medical compendium of classical India, the *Caraka Saṃhitā*, which was compiled in the first few centuries CE. I focus on the chapter on The Ordinary Person (*katidhāpuruṣa*), within the Section On Body (the *Śārīrasthāna*, one of eight sections in the book, each with between eight and thirty chapters of uneven length). Philosophical discussions occur in a chapter in the first section, On Rules *(Sūtrasthāna)*, concerning especially the epistemology of medical training and diagnosis; but it is in this chapter, The Ordinary Person, that the text steps back from actual medical issues to explore exactly who the human being is that is the subject of treatment. The text's explicit objective is the healthy and long life, and in this chapter and in other abstract passages, while it strives to articulate the nature of illness and health it perforce expresses what it is to be a (healthy or ill) person. In that expression is contained a view of the human being as a bodily being.

The second is a tightly nested episodic passage within the epic composition that is the *Mahābhārata* (composed around the start of the CE and redacted in the following centuries). To be specific, it is now given as chapter 308 of Book 12 (the *Śāntiparvan*, The Book of Peace) of the constituted edition (generally treated as the critical edition). It can also be seen as the fifty-eighth of sixty-three texts in the anthology called the *Mokṣadharma* ('the rules and ways of emancipation'), which is one of the three 'sub-books' of Book 12. This particular chapter narrates the encounter between a spiritually powerful yet protean almswoman, Sulabhā, and a King Janaka. Normally their dialogue is read as the confrontation between his claim that the highest form of emancipation (which both agree is a form of supreme equanimity) can be attained even while engaged in the world (the normative ideology of the 'householder'), and her argument that one must renounce all social life first (the normative ideology of the 'renunciant'). This episode also contains a great deal on the relationship between any emancipatory project and gendered power; and it becomes clear that bodily presentation and self-conception are integral to this relationship; it is hermeneutically significant that the renouncer here is a woman—not unknown but a relatively rare figure in the tradition. I follow this hermeneutic in inquiring what Janaka's declamation says about recognizable masculinist ideas of gender, body, and normativity, and how Sulabhā's powerful responses lay out different considerations about gender—how her bodily appearance determines her reception, an account of being human that accepts but renders contingent the bodily marks of sex, an outline of spiritual transcendence that is deliberately universalistic (and therefore a challenge to the normative limits Janaka would place on Sulabhā), and finally, a tantalizing glimpse of how she has worked with and through her gendered bodily presence to attain a socially significant emancipation from those normative limits. The framing within the story, which is sympathetic to her and leaves her unambiguously victorious, also prompts certain considerations about the potential for this story about gendered experience to contribute to contemporary discussions about body and gender.

The third chapter follows the process by which a highly detailed account of the human being as bodily being emerges through a series of contemplative practices described in the fifth century by Buddhaghosa in The *Visuddhimagga* (The Path of Purification), the Theravada Buddhist text that guides the monk through stages of practice to the attainment of perfection. I look primarily at four sections of the book. In the first three, meditation practices are described that are meant to disrupt an unthinking intuition about the stability of subject and objects, because it is that intuition that is held to lead to entanglement in suffering. Out of these practices, the monk comes to become attentive of the way that an apparent sense of isolation of human from environment and of separation of subject from material body is dissolved. This dissolution of ordinary intuitions occurs through both an expansion of personal self-awareness into the ambient environment of contemplation, and a phenomenological reduction of the body as a material given. The fourth and most elaborate practice addresses the constitution of experiential content, through a sustained analysis of the components of experience through the *abhidhamma* categories taught by the Buddha. What results is a creative destabilization of any fixed tripartite ontology of subject–body–world, leaving a methodologically sustained practice of treating the human as a dynamic system of experience explicable through analytic categories.

Finally, the fourth chapter focuses on Canto XVIII of Śrī Harṣa's great twelfth-century court poem, the *Naiṣadhacarita*, which is an exuberant celebration of the post-marital lovemaking of Nala and Damayantī, the hero and heroine whose courtship constitutes the main part of the composition. The piquant fact that this highly elaborated, emotionally dense, and vividly earthy poem was written by one of the most formidable dialectical metaphysicians of the Advaita Vedānta system has prompted commentators to search for its hidden spiritual depths, but I approach it philosophically in a completely different way, seeing this particular canto as a joyful narration of 'erotic phenomenology'. The lovers are robustly themselves and yet re-formed by the other; affect is generated by the hidden and deeply personal motivation of the two people, and yet also runs across and between them, drawing us another map of subjectivity and the limits of bodiliness altogether. The prefigured body is integral to the conventional depiction of heterosexuality; and yet, even within its conventions—most strikingly, perhaps, for working within such conventions—Śrī Harṣa leads us to ponder the (nearly) everyday changes to bodily sense and boundaries. Of the four cases, this is the one perhaps without a self-conscious philosophical programme to which I can harness my interpretation; but I present it as an effort to expand the horizons of the interpretive framework I offer below.

Preliminary Considerations about Comparison

In what follows, those who are familiar with modern Western philosophy may well be tempted to skim over my description of how Phenomenology comes to articulate its position as a response to a philosophical programme initiated by Descartes. (Throughout the book, I use 'Phenomenology' with a capital 'P' to refer to the pluralistic but nonetheless coherent tradition arising in twentieth-century Western philosophy. By contrast, 'phenomenology' can have a wide range of contextualized meanings.) However, there is a set of interlocking reasons for why I have framed my cross-cultural study in this way.

The first is that it is only by historicizing Descartes that I can deliberately estrange the reader from the presupposition that mind–body dualism (and its overcoming) is the only way to approach the analysis of bodily experience. This is important if we are to see the fruitfulness of studying those classical Indian texts that are oriented to bodily experience. The second is a different, countervailing comparativist consideration: while the use of phenomenology as a general approach to Indian materials is very productive, we can thematize that approach only by acknowledging the historical specificity of Phenomenology's emergence as a philosophical programme in the West. The particular use to which I put the phenomenological approach then becomes clear; otherwise, the reader may rightfully query the origin and utilization of 'phenomenology' as a comparativist category. Thirdly, I need to reassure the reader that my way of using phenomenology as a methodology that bypasses ontology does not push my use of it so far outside the concerns of Western philosophy that no meaningful cross-cultural study can be undertaken: for was not Phenomenology specifically a response to the ontological problem of the subject (as mind-and-body)? So I delineate Phenomenology's own native development of a methodological approach that eschews ontology, while admitting that it is much the less well-known reading of the purpose of phenomenology.

For these three reasons, I approach the outline of ecological phenomenology through these comparativist considerations. It is through them that the case is made for it: (i) It emerges from a study of classical Indian materials that deal with experience and draw on analytic conceptions of body and mind, but without the Cartesian problematization of mind and body that informs philosophical language today (and has even come to seem like a folk psychological intuition). (ii) It obviously draws on the terminology made possible only through the Western Phenomenological tradition, even while pertaining to texts quite innocent of the Phenomenological tradition's puzzlement. (iii) It develops an approach that is not lacking—albeit less common—in the Phenomenological tradition. When we combine these aspects, what we have is a philosophical position that emerges from classical Indian texts but is of quite general, cross-cultural value and application, at once rooted in the Indian material but conceptually recognizable from a Western perspective. As such, ecological phenomenology as it is developed here is expressive of a model of global philosophy.

With this preliminary explanation given, I turn to a series of interconnected and cross-cultural philosophical issues.

Body: Western Philosophy and the Cartesian Shock

In the philosophical culture of classical India as well as Western traditions (by which I mean the Greek but also the Judeo-Christian and Islamic), there appears to have been a widespread intuition that the human being was a subject of experience that bore a relationship with the body through which it was enworlded.[1] (By 'enworlded' I mean here the concept which conveys the recognition that, for the subject seeking to understand the world, the world is always already there; the subject's presence to itself is also the pre-given presence of the world of the subject. It is not part of my concern here to engage with the challenge this poses to Husserl's famous project of transcendental phenomenology.[2]) Consequently, we have a variety of pre-modern writing in these traditions, in which the body has some location within theories of the human being. There is therefore no lack of awareness in these materials, no absence of conceptually sophisticated terminology, regarding the significance of body-talk within any account of experience. But a sense that there might be a peculiar problem in accounting for the human being in terms of body and world is not yet articulated until the birth of modern, Western philosophy, in the exemplary meditations of Descartes. As every student of philosophy knows, we encounter in Descartes the idea that, to even begin to have an epistemology out of which an account of the human being may be built, we must confront what he asserted was a fundamental metaphysical divide between the human subject and its body/world.[3] Hitherto, in India and the West, if the body was a problematic, it was for ethical reasons or for the sake of developing a comprehensive ontology of reality: a thinker had to conceptualize it in terms that permitted properly determined human action, or in terms that assimilated the different dimensions of human existence—subjectivity, objectivity, relationality—within a unifying description of reality. But now, it seemed as if there was an impassable yet self-evident gap between who we knew we were and what we knew of the body in and by which we sought to live in a world. (There is a further issue, which I cannot do more than advert to here: once the Cartesian meditations transformed the very nature of Western philosophy, a great deal of modern recovery of pre-modern thought on the self was structured in Cartesian terms.)

My starting point is the suggestion that, for all their sophistication, the Indian thinkers did not undergo anything like the Cartesian shock. All modern thought—which

[1] In comparison, the classical Chinese tradition appears not to have been troubled by this; see Ram-Prasad 2005: chapter 2.

[2] For the location of the concept of 'enworlding' in transcendental phenomenology, see Bruzina 1990: 177–8.

[3] The literature on this is vast, but for an example of careful and subtle exploration of what I have put very simplistically, see Rozemond 1998.

for several centuries was identified with Western thought—had to deal with the extraordinary impact of the Cartesian revolution, which developed epistemological inquiry around that divide between the human being as essentially an unquestionable, 'internal' thinking entity (the *cogito*), and its bodily extension in an 'external' world that only inquiry could establish.[4] Seen this way, much subsequent thinking about the human being is thoroughly post-Cartesian. The Anglo-American analytic philosophical paradigm is predominantly reductionist in its commitment to a naturalized study of human beings[5] (although by no means only reductionism; note the recent interest in panpsychism[6]). European phenomenology necessarily structured itself as a creative response to the dialectic of mind and body, especially from Merleau-Ponty onwards.[7] What we therefore find is a particular trajectory to the impulse and vocabulary of contemporary Western thought (and by hegemonic influence, global discourses) on the nature of the human being: it seems as if we must choose between dualism, physicalism, or some new healing of this divide.[8] Indian thought, almost entirely pre-modern in the period and circumstances of its flourishing, was innocent of this trajectory.

Yet, we should see that this post-Cartesian experience offers a productive motivation for comparative and intercultural philosophy. On the one side, it is precisely the Cartesian revolution that has led to a sharpened recognition of the fundamental challenge posed by the nature of subjective presence—that is to say, that intrinsic constitutive feature of subjectivity which is its presence to itself.[9] Such recognition has prompted sweeping investigative programmes in Anglo-American analytic and Continental Phenomenological traditions. The Western articulation of a thematic study of the human being in terms of subjectivity and its conditions has helped contemporary scholars of Indian philosophy to look afresh at the debates in their texts. But on the other, far less widely recognized side, the re-reading of Indian texts has been bringing out resources to think about the human being that are not restricted—even crippled—by the post-Cartesian assumption that the philosophical task is either reduction of one or the other of subject and object, or the ontological bridging of the gap between them. The Indian traditions worked their way through many possible approaches to the nature of the human being, and their standing outside the history of Western philosophical modernity makes them potential sources of new formulations of the human condition. In any case, they have not been shoehorned into the apparent necessities that post-Cartesian philosophy has placed on inquiry.

This book is not about the subjectivity of the human being in terms of the 'mind–body' relationship, or the 'hard problem' of consciousness, or the definition of the self, all

[4] For example, Hatfield 2014.

[5] Pereboom 2011 is a powerful recent example.

[6] Adams 2013, in his review of and response to Pereboom.

[7] Evans and Lawlor 2000.

[8] On the third option, for example, Andy Clark has been influential at the cognitive scientific end of the analytic philosophical spectrum, with its commitment to a largely scientistic naturalism; Clark 1997.

[9] See Ram-Prasad 2007: 51–99 on this intrinsic feature, which the classical Indian epistemologists called 'luminosity (*prakaśata*), and the many debates surrounding it.

of which have proved to be productive prompts for comparative/inter-traditional philosophy. Rather, it approaches the specific question of how the body as a conceptual category is imagined to be integral to the narrative of human experience. In that sense, the body is not confined to the West, although the cultural bases of a vast literature sound as if it were. It is of advantage for a comparativist to have the orientation and thematization of this literature when reading other cultures. In the case of India, Hinduism particularly, there has been a growth in the anthropological study of the body that utilizes Western theory.[10] Yet there has been virtually no attempt to think of the category of the body through the conceptual resources of pre-modern India; theory remains Western, applied to Indian materials.

Indian texts from the earliest period use concepts (in Sanskrit and Pali) that can be translated with good lexical justification as 'body', 'mind', 'consciousness', 'human being', and the like. Philological, literary-historical, and philosophical studies have long established that the classical Indian tradition used many concepts in a way directly comparable to their function in Western tradition; so I make no further argument for Indian philosophy as such. The specific case of the concept of 'body' is relatively clear; that is, these Indian texts certainly asked questions about its nature, constitution, functions, and relationship to subjectivity. However, there is relatively little textual work on conceptual themes on the body,[11] especially those that are explicitly comparative in their engagement with contemporary debates.[12]

The cultural context of philosophical investigation should never be underestimated, and it forms a powerful background to the task of this book, which is to look at Indian material in the light of Western debates only so as to make a contribution to an intercultural discussion. Stephen Burwood, for example, maintains that many phenomenologists, in arguing that the lived nature of 'strange' experiences—such out-of-body experiences, or forms of illness, or being forced to confront prejudice against bodily appearance (race, disability)—have supported the intuition of dualism, seems to suppose that 'the phenomenology...leads to the theory, which is that we may naïvely take a certain phenomenology and its description to be "natural". That is to say, we may think that the experience of lived embodiment is given to us raw and uncooked by the context in which it occurs.'[13] Burwood contrasts this with the thought that 'phenomenology stands in need of interpretation in the light of theory and culture and the practices that embody these. The phenomenology, or at any rate how we represent it (i.e. think about and report it), is not untainted by our historical, political and cultural perspectives. And this means, more particularly, it is not untainted by our philosophical perspectives. The relationship between phenomenology and philosophical theory is not clear-cut and is doubtless a complex one of the interplay of influences; but just as certain is that these flow in both directions. Thus, our phenomenological descriptions may be equally

[10] Alter 2004; Lamb 2000; Michaels and Wulf 2011.
[11] Flood 2006; White 1996; Wujastyk 2009.
[12] Böhler 2011. [13] Burwood 2008: 276.

theory-led... [W]e could plausibly claim that it has been historically true that our phenomenological descriptions have attained popularity and credibility only in so far as they have harmonized with our favoured philosophical doctrines.'[14] It seems to me that—although he does not specify the comparative dimensions of his consideration—this is clearly consistent with my thought that we are going to find phenomenological descriptions in the Indian materials that are inflected by native theoretical reflections, so that even such an idea as a distinction between subject and body—i.e., some notion of dualism—is articulated very differently.[15]

Many specific topics that I have not dealt with in this book need further exploration, including the relationship between body and world; the bodily expressiveness of emotions; the purposes, capacities, and modalities of bodiliness; the metaphorical and literal readings of the body; the ways in which bodily discipline is sought or imposed; and so on. Only close attention to the internal consistencies and expressive formulation of ideas in these texts will bring out their philosophical potential in a conversation with the Western tradition.

Body and the Intuition of Dualism: Cross-cultural Negotiations after Descartes and Phenomenology

Let me begin to lay out the conceptual framework of this book by taking a closer look at the way 'body' figures in the accounting of subjectivity in the Phenomenological tradition. In a searching examination of the history of how 'body' has come to be thematized in Phenomenology, Chris Nagel offers the following argument: 'First of all, the turn to the body presupposes that phenomenology should have to do with any sort of "body" in the first place—that is, the "body" as in some way the "objective" side of a "subject." Would phenomenologists, or any other modern philosophers, have confronted this particular "body," if Descartes had not come along? Otherwise, would it have occurred to Husserl, or anyone else, even to investigate consciousness in relation to lived body? That is to say (in agreement with Merleau-Ponty himself) that the phenomenology of the body, as a way into the ontological question of the origin of meaning, is guided in advance not by *die Sache selbst,* but by an inherited philosophical problem *in the presupposed terms of which* the phenomenology of the body has been carried out.'[16] Secondly, he notes, it is not fully clear why there would be a phenomenological investigation of the lived body (and certainly not clear why phenomenology would necessarily need to account for the body) without a presupposition of that Cartesian problematic. Otherwise, what, in phenomenologically "reduced" experience,

[14] Ibid.

[15] For example, while we consider the theistic Vedānta system of 'Dvaita' as 'dualist', it becomes quickly evident that dualism has a quite different metaphysical motivation there compared to Cartesianism and its Western successors. This is so even without any explicit comparison; e.g., see Sharma 1981: 1–6.

[16] Nagel 2012: 21 (emphasis in text).

under the bracketing of the natural attitude, would not only draw attention to the body, but make it the focus of so many phenomenological writers?[17] From this he concludes, 'After all, if a basic tenet of the discipline of phenomenology is presuppositionlessness, it is always possible that, following the bracketing and reduction, the phenomenologist finds that what had seemed to be a region of reality has been utterly destroyed. If we plan to adhere to that discipline and to take its rigor seriously, then the only way phenomenology of the body could begin is if, following the reduction, there appears this series, "the body," that can be described. In short, we would have no idea at all, in advance, not only what can be achieved by phenomenological investigation, but whether there would be "the body" to investigate.'[18]

On the one hand, I agree of course that Phenomenology comes in the post-Cartesian trajectory, and that therefore the very idea of making embodiedness the object of investigation in this particular way is a product of Western philosophical history. On the other hand, it strikes me that Nagel's own position itself smuggles in precisely that Cartesian thematization of the body that he says is indulged in by phenomenologists (especially the French existentialist ones): for why would it be the case that 'the body' is required to become an appearance in reduction for it to be studied, unless you already grant that it has some kind of occurrence in conception as a possible object of recognition in the process of reduction?

In answer, let me offer the following consideration. One possible way of talking about the body through Indian material would be to distinguish between (i) intuitions of dualism, and (ii) the specific Cartesian dualist metaphysics that seems to be the natural implication of such intuitions. In the West, these usually amount to the same thing. 'Our body does not always have meaning, and our thoughts . . . do not always find in it the plenitude of their vital expression. In the cases of disintegration, the soul and the body are apparently distinct; and this is the truth of dualism.'[19] The point is that 'the testimony of embodied experience, far from being unfavourable to dualism, may actually promote its central thesis that we are not, in some important sense, our bodies'.[20] But they are not the same from the perspective of Indian philosophy. It is of course true that in the classical Indian traditions—in particular, those that combine systematic epistemology with a gnoseological goal—there are expressions of a sense that one can be distanced from the body.[21] This distancing does not happen across a Cartesian divide between 'body' and 'mind' as such, but rather, within some unifying ontology of the real; in the case of Advaita Vedānta the distancing even extends to one between a reflexive luminosity of awareness and the very 'I'-thought by which a state is ascribed to that awareness.[22] So, we may say that there is a deep intuition about the objectifiability of body in different cultures, but the very next step, namely, the articulation of that

[17] Ibid., pp. 21–2. [18] Ibid., p. 22.

[19] Merleau-Ponty 1965: 209. [20] Burwood 2008: 264.

[21] E.g., the ancient and influential metaphysics of the Sāṃkhya system, see Burley 2007. Another case is the theological vision of Rāmānuja in the eleventh century, Ram-Prasad 2013: 105–11.

[22] See Ram-Prasad 2011 and Fasching 2011 on Advaita; Albahari 2011 on Buddhism.

intuition, immediately takes us into some sort of a philosophical presupposition that does not hold across philosophical cultures. In the classical Indian context, that articulation can take fundamentally different forms depending on the cultural context of specific religious-philosophical systems.[23]

Contemporary work on Indian thought—e.g., in the studies mentioned above of Flood or Michaels and Wulff—can trade on the conflation of the distinction made above, by delineating ways in which various Indian metaphysical systems deal with 'body', where that conceptual category is given as if it had the same role in culturally loaded intuition as in modern Western thought. I aim to adopt a different approach here. The Western Phenomenological tradition as a metaphysics of subjectivity has isolated the body as a theme in its inescapable response to Cartesianism. A fundamentally different approach is required when looking at a culture of intellectual self-awareness that did not encounter metaphysics in that very particular way. So I approach the matter of the body obliquely, through how explorations of subjectivity occur in different genres of classical Indian writing.[24]

At the same time, these texts are philosophically aware in a broad sense, so that they do seem to me to yield a rich harvest of insights for a philosophical project such as mine that is also cross-cultural.[25] Phenomenology is here only a necessary methodology for depicting the truths of being human, that is to say, depicted through attention to the endless, fine details of subjectivity. (On phenomenology as methodology, more below.) Here, I think that the texts and genres I look at offer the right place to act on a dictum of Merleau-Ponty's (although he himself does not adhere to it). Merleau-Ponty argues that philosophy must 'reject the instruments reflection and intuition had provided themselves, and install itself in a locus where they have not yet been distinguished, in experiences that have not yet been "worked over", that offer us all at once, pell-mell, both "subject" and "object".'[26]

[23] See the wide range of papers, centred on the role of the concept of self, in Kuznetsova et al. 2012.

[24] It is for this reason that I think Paul Hacker was looking in exactly the wrong place for a philosophical anthropology, in his essay, 'Śaṅkara's Conception of Man' (reprinted as chapter 8 in Hacker 1995). At the core of the classical Advaitic view, enunciated by Śaṅkara, is the interpretation of necessarily bodily experience as the fundamental mistake of self-consciousness. This does require a careful analysis of how a broad conception of body (including not just materiality and sensation but also mental activity and even the ascription of 'I') seems to individuate consciousness; but if the teleology of that analysis includes the dissolution of bodiliness, then it is positively perverse to use Śaṅkara to ask how the human being is conceived in classical Indian thought. There are answers to many questions in Śaṅkara, but not this. I thank Chris Minkowski for prompting me to note that it was extremely odd for Hacker to look to Śaṅkara for a philosophical anthropology.

[25] Might a study of Western genres reveal ways of looking at bodily being in a way that so thoroughly challenges dominant Western notions of body, so that I should abandon the comparative project altogether? Perhaps, although one will then have to embark on a quite different inquiry into the relationship between philosophy and literature in the West, and ask if they could have developed in such radically different ways that questions of body and mind in various genres were quite without mutual influence—the necessary condition for the comparisons that I embark upon in this book. I thank Laurie Patton for asking the question.

[26] Matthews 2002: 165–6, drawing on Merleau-Ponty 1968: 130.

In this book, I hope to develop a fruitful way of doing comparative and mutually illuminating philosophy. From the Western materials there comes the very formulation of the question of how the human being is to be understood through her bodiliness, together with the complex and reflexive theories that have given us contemporary philosophical discourse. It would have been perfectly possible to have had a *pas de deux* with the equally complex and reflexive materials of Indian metaphysics; indeed, on many questions—consciousness, selfhood, the divine, the world of experience—I have done exactly this in the past. Although few and far between, there have also been studies—especially focusing on Advaita Vedānta—on the phenomenological nature of a metaphysical self's relationship with body.[27] But in this book, I wanted the interaction to take the form of a more fundamental questioning of the nature of the comparative philosophical enterprise, because it seemed to me that, in the matter of the body, even comparativist language—the very use of English today—is soaked through and through with the Cartesian version of the intuition of dualism: the idea that we are fundamentally a mind and a body that must be either related ingeniously, or else reduced one to the other. Instead, by deliberately looking at genres that pertain to other aspects of being human, I seek to go deeper into texts that simply start elsewhere than with intuitions of dualism, even while being engrossed in the category of the experiential 'body' (in all its translational variety in Sanskrit and Pali). So, in as much as I come to these texts with the academic awareness of the Western philosophical programme regarding the body, I hope that the texts in return will open up other possibilities for thinking about how the human being is a bodily being.

To clarify, my primary concern is not with a conceptual analysis of 'body', but rather, how 'body' is used in the exploration of the nature of the human being; that is to say, in the intriguing way in which 'body' is the ineliminable presence in experience. Stephen Burwood concludes his essay with a reading of the well-established phenomenological insight 'that my body has a double aspect and is something that challenges a strict dichotomy of subject and object. What we have are not two wholly separate phenomena, my body as a set of capacities and an extension of my subjectivity and my body as a material object..., but rather a single reversible existence. It is at once both a set of capacities and an object in the world. The lived-body is also an object in the world.'[28] Of course, he is here echoing Maurice Merleau-Ponty's later philosophy of the chiasm, which talks of 'a single reversible existence'. As I describe now, Merleau-Ponty's is an ontological response to the Cartesian problem, reworked as the mystery of the phenomenologists—how body can be both the subject and the object of experience. By paying attention to how Merleau-Ponty was compelled to work out the bodiliness of experience through a radical revision of assumptions about body, we can begin to see how classical Indian texts open up the needlessness of such

[27] Sinha 1985; Gupta 1998 are notable examples, although only the former tackles the role of body in an Advaita phenomenology, which has generally been neglected by scholars of Advaita (including me).

[28] Burwood 2008: 277–8.

assumptions, simply because their treatment of bodiliness is not a response to the Cartesian problem. As such, Merelau-Ponty is a persistent, if often penumbral presence in this book.

Engaging with Merleau-Ponty

The Western phenomenological tradition helps with a re-envisioning of Indian traditions in a globalized world. Merleau-Ponty brought out within the phenomenological tradition a critical aspect of the 'lived body', that it constitutes one's perspective on the world and therefore cannot just be an object in that world.[29] He did this by way of the observation that one's own body cannot be, as a whole, an object of contemplation; for to do so, 'I would have to use a second body, which would itself be unobservable.'[30] Obviously, this is not just an artifact of the geometry of the eyes but a deeper point about the way bodily presence is the passage between subject and object. Anyone with passing acquaintance with the Upaniṣads will immediately be reminded of such passages as *Kena Upaniṣad* I.6, 'Which one cannot see with one's sight, by which one sees the sight itself...', that became significant in the development of later Vedāntic theories of self. Yet modern Indian philosophy has tended to confine its attention to the implication this has for a theory of consciousness and reflexivity, without considering that this ancient insight applies to bodily being—and precisely is expressed in the *Kena Upaniṣad* in terms of the senses (including the mind as inner sense).

Merleau-Ponty is the major Western influence on this book for two interrelated reasons. First, he stands out for his determination to work himself out of the post-Cartesian requirement of finding an account of how 'body' and 'mind/subject' are related, in the context of a world that must at once be grasped by the mind even while, through body, it finds itself in that world. Even in his earlier magnum opus, *The Phenomenology of Perception*, he had seen the need to think the bodily human presence into its world: 'The psycho-physical event can no longer be conceived after the model of Cartesian physiology and as the juxtaposition of a process in itself [the body] and a cogitatio [the mind]. The union of soul and body is not an amalgamation between two mutually external terms, subject and object, brought about by arbitrary degree. It is enacted at every instant in the movement of existence.'[31] 'Our own body is in the world as the heart is in the organism.'[32] This required seeing body in a way that did not punctuate an objective world but rather was continuous with it: 'My body is the texture common to all objects.'[33] This line of thought was eventually expressed in his last, incomplete work through a variety of evocative metaphors: 'The body and the world "crisscross", so that the body's parts, like the hands are such that their own movements are incorporated

[29] Carman 2008 is an excellent guide.

[30] Merleau-Ponty 1962: 104. This, of course, goes back to Husserl, 'The eye does not appear visually' (Husserl 1989: 147).

[31] Merleau-Ponty 1962: 88–9. [32] Ibid., p. 248. [33] Ibid., p. 273.

into the universe they interrogate, are recorded on the same map...'[34] Most famously, this is expressed through the idea of the 'chiasm': 'The chiasm is not only a me–other exchange... it is also an exchange between me and the world, between the phenomenal body and the "objective" body, between the perceiving and the perceived.'[35] This is also connected to the idea of 'flesh': 'Flesh is being as reversibility, being's capacity to fold in on itself, being's dual orientation inward and outward, being's openness, its reflexivity, the fundamental gap or dehiscence of being that Merleau-Ponty illustrates with a favorite example—the notion of "double sensation," the capacity of one hand to touch another that is itself touching an object.'[36] Such a search for an ontology at once whole and interactive, diversified and yet unified, was a dramatic response to the question of how to thematize the body in the analysis of experience.

It is certainly not the case that Indian philosophical traditions lacked an awareness of similar challenges about consciousness and world; but they were not articulated in the specific context of a sceptical challenge to the very possibility of knowledge. And for a variety of historical reasons, the use of concepts translatable as 'body', 'mind', 'world', etc., did not coalesce around the supposedly intuitive appeal of metaphysical dualism, so that we do not find there anything directly comparable to the pervasive use of mind–body language (whether in endorsement of dualism or in idealist or physicalist rejection) prevalent in contemporary, Westernized discourse. So, in a project aiming to explore how Indian texts offer views of the human being as bodily, enworlded being without operating with the supposed intuition of Cartesian dualism, it is more than worthwhile thinking comparatively through a Western philosopher who paid sustained attention to language about the human being that worked out of the history of early modern Western philosophy in order to be free from that supposed intuition. Second, Merleau-Ponty thought about the post-Cartesian subject through the reconceptualization of the very nature of body and (life-)world, and their relationship. For a book looking at how 'body' is expressed in the experiential world of the Indian imagination, yet again he offers useful comparative insights.

'Bodiliness'

The Phenomenological tradition has, of course, made 'body' an intense focus of analysis, and I will try to take my bearing now in relation to some aspects of that analysis, in order to indicate where I stand with regard to the texts studied in this book.

A critical observation that some phenomenologists have made concerns the misleading ease with which 'body' enters into philosophical discourse. It is as if concepts emerge directly from and in experience. Chris Nagel warns against this transition, tracing back to Husserl the sense that there is a deeper point of departure. He terms as 'embodiment', 'the 'residuum that would be there for there to be any... enjoyment, displeasure,

[34] Merleau-Ponty 1968: 133. [35] Ibid., p. 215. [36] Grosz 1993: 44.

objectification' for any given body.[37] This is roughly what is called 'Life' or '*Leib*' or especially for Husserl, 'passive synthesis'. Importantly, talking about this embodiment is not about saying what it is. 'Rather than a *what* that is present in experience, embodiment has to do with *how* experience appears.' This is pre-given, even 'pre-experience'. '[W]e can distinguish "self" as the passive synthesis which the embodied animal simply is, from the "self" as the ego *for which* and *to which* the passive synthesis "gives" objectlike formations. It is in this way that embodiment is the origin of the ego's "consciousness of... something," its worldliness, its *meaningful* lived experience. Not an ego-subject, but embodiment, which I suggest is best understood and investigated as our being subjected to the pre-given..., is the origin of both ego and body.'[38] I too do not wish to talk about 'body' as that which is constituted in consciousness, because that leads to the traditional phenomenological 'mystery' of how the body is both subject (as lived body) and object of consciousness.

Instead, I suggest the term 'bodiliness', to indicate the general human way of being present in experience, without unwittingly implying either an ontology of consciousness and materiality, or its overcoming. To some extent, 'bodiliness' overlaps conceptually with Nagel's 'embodiment': a way of talking about body as not what is unified in experience and becomes its object, but as the unity which permits of experience at all. But I am less sure that this is wholly a matter of passivity or merely the 'subjection' to givenness that Nagel assigns to embodiment. That claim seems to flout the impossibility of being able to say what it is that Nagel himself has adverted to. I want strictly to pursue the question of how experience appears (which, oddly enough, includes a sense that bodily presence is also constituted in experience). So it seems best to say that in this book I am interested in pursuing how experience is depicted through bodiliness, which is to say, subjectivity that makes no sense except with bodily pre-condition. If this places my endeavour orthogonally to a major concern of the Phenomenological tradition that explores the metaphysics of subject–body relationship (the 'mystery' of being in and of the world), it is nevertheless aligned to the perhaps minor Phenomenological tradition that treats phenomenology as the methodology for delineating in fine detail the aetiology and manifestation of experience.

In this version of the phenomenological undertaking, body is not a mystery to be solved but the starting point of the enjoyment of a different mystery. This is not the ontological mystery of how we experience the world through body while the body is part of that world; it is the poetic mystery of how we experience so much. In its oblique way, this approach suggests that we need not start with the presupposition that our existence is an ontological puzzle; for there is no such puzzle without that presupposition.

This book is about that point at which the 'absent body'—as Drew Leder terms what renders experience possible but is itself not recognized as an object in the content of such experience[39]—comes to presence. It is present as that which occupies the creation

[37] Nagel 2012: 29. [38] Ibid., p. 30. [39] Leder 1990.

of phenomenology (in the four chapters of this book, as medical practice, as the locus of gendered spiritual discipline, as the focus of contemplative practice, as the expression of erotic-romantic love) but absent as the thematic of phenomenology. My hope is that, by shifting between phenomenological contexts, we see how the bodiliness of the phenomenological subject shifts too in constitutivity, range, ambience, capacity, and teleology. We can see the uses of the category of 'body', but must also become sensitive to the irreducible multivalence of its nature, even if on occasion it runs counter to what seem robust intuitions about body.

Case by case, we will see that it is not that we start with the self-evidence of the body in experience, and subsequently go on to study experience in terms of its manifestation. Instead, by considering carefully the descriptions of manifestation in their respective contexts, we begin to see in each case how 'body' functions in each narrative of the experiential human being. To play on Leder's term, we see that in each case the absent body is not only absent in different ways but that when it comes to presence it is construed differently. We learn not to talk of 'body' as a self-evident term stable across contexts and genres.

This openness to the modes by which body occurs as and in experience suggests that we can only work through its occurrence in various narrations of experience, with the illimitable boundaries drawn in each narration. Here I concur with Bruno Latour's argument that the body is 'an interface that becomes more and more describable as it learns to be affected by more and more elements.'[40] The virtue of this definition is that 'there is no sense in defining the body directly, but only in rendering the body sensitive to what these other elements are. By focusing on the body, one is immediately—or rather, mediately—directed to what the body has become aware of.'[41] This connects with my resistance to Nagel's insistence that his 'embodiment'—what I call 'bodiliness'—be strictly defined through 'passive synthesis'. Not only does that seem to flout the requirement that we ought not to treat body as a transcendental object of inquiry (because that would involve making just the sort of claims that have been disavowed) but also because there is an active, reactive, constructive dimension to bodiliness—the learning that is critical to phenomenology. Latour gives the example of the training of 'noses' for the perfume industry as an example of learning to be affected. The connection across the chapters of this book is given by just such phenomenological 'learning' (where, to complete the analogy, the scholar is the nose in training)—about illness and wellbeing, about gender, about contemplative practice, about the love that strengthens in lovemaking, what is learnt by the protagonists (the physician, the king who loses a debate with a woman renouncer, by the monk-practitioner, by the lovers), by the writers, and by us.

Yet again, Merleau-Ponty is a useful foil for these considerations. As Lewis and Staehler see it, Merleau-Ponty strives to talk about the limit between body and world without making assumptions about subjects and objects, and does this by way of 'the

[40] Latour 2004: 205–6. [41] Ibid., p. 206.

idea of the lived body as a sensible for itself', the 'enigma that there is a seeing and touching which is embedded in the world and, at the same time, sees and touches it, thus folding the world onto itself'.[42] Merleau-Ponty says that the world that is seen and touched becomes 'inhabited' by touch and vision.[43] Through thought or reflection, the question arises of 'how there is a centre', the centre being the unity of consciousness.[44] Crucially, this unity, argues Merleau-Ponty, is based on the 'prereflective and preobjective unity of my body',[45] and it is this unity of lived body that presents itself as the limit between itself and world, albeit one without a clear boundary, and more like a thickening, a node, within the tissue of the world. I wonder, however, if this does not then raise the question of what it is to say at one and the same time that the body is pre-reflective, and yet thematize it as body; surely this ungrounded starting point is subject to varying intuitions about its givenness, as is amply evident in our consideration of different thinkers, genres, and texts, in the West and in India. What we need to take away from the insight about the fungible constitution of the lived body is that something is indeed given, but also that it is given only through context-inflected intuitions (intuitions that come to be interrogated, directly or implicitly, didactically or gently, as we will see in our studies). It is this that prompts my exploration of the bodily human in different genres: not as a way of settling on a determinate ontology beyond dualism, but for opening up ways of talking about matters of lasting human import through attention to the inescapably originary nature of body in any phenomenological depiction.

As a matter of fact, this methodological openness is implicit in Merleau-Ponty's later writing on 'flesh', although he generally strives to provide through that concept a way of working out an ontology beyond dualism, even when he is painfully conscious of the limitations imposed by the relationship of Phenomenology to the tradition it was challenging: 'the problems posed [in Phenomenology] are insoluble because I start from the 'consciousness'–'object' distinction', he ruefully acknowledges.[46] His unfinished ontology concerns a 'synthesis' of two aspects of an 'ultimate truth',[47] and the crisscrossing between those aspects is 'irreducible and cannot be synthesized', they can 'only be described again and again',[48] as Lewis and Staehler point out. I adopt this way of carrying out the phenomenological task, but without the same telos.

Phenomenology in Minor Key

I have implied that, while I share a certain methodological approach with the Phenomenological tradition, I am not concerned to develop a unifying ontology of human subjectivity (or more precisely, the conditions for the possibility of subjectivity). Undoubtedly transcendental phenomenology is the major theme of the tradition, the motivation for so many different accounts. At the same time, phenomenologists can sometimes also talk about their undertaking as a methodology. 'I assert that the core

[42] Lewis and Staehler 2010: 205–6. [43] Merleau-Ponty 1968: 135. [44] Ibid., p. 145.
[45] Ibid., p. 141. [46] Ibid., p 200. [47] Ibid., p. 155. [48] Ibid., p. 208.

meaning of *phenomenology* is best understood as a *discipline* of thought rather than a *theory* of experience, knowledge, or consciousness—or, for that matter, "the body".'[49] A particularly clear articulation in terms of the distinction between these two ways of looking at phenomenology is given by David Carr (although I would not wish to be drawn into supporting his claim about Heidegger): 'Contrary to the widely accepted interpretation of Heidegger, transcendental philosophy is not a metaphysical doctrine or theory, but a critique of metaphysics, of science, and of the experience that underlies them. A critique is not a theory but a research program or method, a way of looking at and interrogating experience so as to bring to the surface its deepest-lying, uncritically accepted assumptions.'[50] That is how I intend to let the studies in this book function, with the cross-cultural claim, made earlier, that their historical and conceptual context permit me to probe in particular the assumptions that are so pervasive in post-Cartesian discourse, both lay and academic. So my approach is methodological and non-ontological. Again, this is something that some contemporary Western thinkers have taken to be the requisite attitude towards philosophical treatment of body. Latour puts in this way: 'I want to try to approach it by theorizing not the body directly but rather "body talk", that is, the many ways in which the body is engaged in accounts about what it does. Under what conditions can we mobilize the body in our speech in such a way that we are not immediately led to the usual discussions about dualism and holism?'[51]

Although I do not systematically engage with the classics of the Phenomenological tradition (apart from a recurrent recognition of Merleau-Ponty), one technical point must be made to clarify what I mean by phenomenology in minor key—that is to say, phenomenology as methodology, which is of course a necessary accompaniment to the Phenomenological tradition's transcendental project to determine the conditions of the possibility of the subject. I want to emphasize that I do not think of this methodological phenomenology as merely and only a part of the transcendental project. It can operate on its own. As Eric Matthews has pointed out, Merleau-Ponty was troubled by the Husserlian framework in which phenomenological examination was only the activity done within the famous period of 'bracketing'. 'The framework in question was of philosophy as a "transcendental" activity, in which a "transcendental subject" "suspended the existence of the world". This was the *epoche*... in which the subject was supposed to "put the world in brackets", to treat it as if it did not exist, or at least not to raise the question of its existence. The objectionable thing about this [as Merleau-Ponty saw it] was that it implied a distinction between the subject, or consciousness, and its object...'[52]

[49] Nagel 2012: 23. [50] Carr 2003: 181.

[51] Latour 2004: 206. Although his understanding of this programme takes him in a very different direction (to a 'political epistemology' in a time of 'bio-power'), his basic approach to the phenomenology of body is part of that 'minor tradition' of phenomenology to which my project is akin. I take his mention of 'holism' to mean any project for 'bridging' the ontological divide of dualism, which is to say, a post-Cartesian metaphysics.

[52] Matthews 2002: 161.

The fine-grained descriptions considered in this book therefore should not be equated with Husserlian 'bracketing', i.e., a suspension of questions about the existence of the world. Such a suspension, as Merleau-Ponty argued later, itself starts with the highly charged metaphysical assumption that there is a world (including body) which is separable from the subject considering its subjectivity. By contrast, it is precisely because the texts I am considering here do not make that distinction as a metaphysical given (although in the first two chapters we certainly find metaphysical frameworks of some sort or another) that their exploration of subjective states is not articulated as the establishment of a subject's relationship with body and world; the details of experience are already just the whole of human existence (howsoever ruptured particular experiences may be, those ruptures are emotional, ethical, or narratological, but not metaphysical).

To return to the idea of phenomenology as methodology, and its lesser but significant place in the tradition, Merleau-Ponty's own later work in particular, and contemporary interpretations of it, tack between a still-persistent commitment to transcendental ontology (the accounting of the subject through the delineation of the conditions of its possibility) and analytic methodology (as the disciplined interrogation of the details of experiences in their contexts). In rejecting the very notion that he was doing 'phenomenology', Merleau-Ponty meant that he had abandoned the project of accounting for a (presumed, unquestioning, pre-defined) subject's relationship with its object, and instead adopted what he called 'ontology', by which he appears to have meant, as Matthews says, 'the attempt to set out the nature of subjectivity and objectivity, the manner of being of subjects and objects, the aim of doing so being to put these same characteristic doctrines on a sounder footing in a better account of our situation in the world'.[53] (This seems to me to be only the familiar claim, made by so many modern Western philosophers (yea, unto Derrida and Deleuze) to do something completely different while in fact only trying to do the same thing better—for surely, earlier phenomenologists would have recognized Merleau-Ponty's new task as exactly theirs.) As I have made clear, my objective in this book is not to develop such a transcendental account, to 'set out the nature of subjectivity and objectivity', still less to put our account of the world on 'a sounder footing'.

Yet Merleau-Ponty also presents what he is doing in a very different way; and this is not the same as the search for a total ontology. 'It is a "bad dialectic" that works in the manner of the textbook descriptions of Hegel's philosophy, proceeding through "thesis" and "antithesis", which are then reconciled in the form of a "synthesis". A "good" dialectic, indeed a good philosophy, will not attempt in this way to offer *solutions,* to resolve the contradictions. Philosophy will be one of the "artefacts [Merleau-Ponty uses the English word here] of culture", involving a creative use of language... [I]t is part of the very nature of human existence that we are perpetually interrogating ourselves about that existence, taking our bearings in our situation in the world, but not aiming

[53] Ibid., p. 170.

at *knowledge* of any new facts or *answers* to any cognitive problems. Philosophy is that self-questioning at its most fundamental level. Our situation in the world is not purely cognitive; we are not what Merleau-Ponty sometimes calls by the Greek word "*kosmotheoros*" ("world-spectator"). Our situation is one of active involvement with things and so with other human beings, and "taking our bearings" is therefore not simply a matter of formulating propositions.'[54] This is phenomenology in the minor key, as methodology, as the 'creative use of language', not for giving new 'answers' but for 'taking our bearings'. It is in this way that Merleau-Ponty is a cultural companion for the explorations undertaken in this book.

Of course, a significant aspect of the Phenomenological tradition's response to the Cartesian notion of interiority is the contrasting notion of a situated subject, a being-*in*-the world. But this response is fundamentally ontological, going on then to seek a singular account of what being is such that the subject is in the world and the world is for the subject. As I will argue, the tradition in minor key (perhaps even a minor tradition) sees this situatedness not as the prompt to a coherent ontology but a guide to an exploratory methodology that looks at the manifestations and existential implications of such subjectivity.[55]

Ecological Phenomenology: Engagement with Contemporary Issues

Let us summarize the upshot of these considerations.

First, the background: no doubt there is an intuition shared by Western and Indian philosophical traditions that there is a manifest subjectivity which appears to have a puzzling relationship with all that it is a subject of. When the nature of that subjectivity is delineated, there are persistent questions both about how it occurs at all, which is to say, how its presence is reflexive; and what its objects are and how they come to be its objects. These are the questions of traditional philosophy, Indian and Western. But the critical development that marks modern Western philosophy's relationship to these questions is Descartes' meditative inquiry, which offers a clarified account of that subjective presence, at the price of bringing its objects into question. The responses to this restructuring of the subject represent the many, ramifying developments where the bipolarity of subject and object is worked out as a necessary response to the metaphysical gap that he had opened up. In the meantime, we notice that the variety of views about subjectivity in the Indian traditions did not lead to anything like the Cartesian crisis of a fundamental epistemological and ontological polarization of subject and object—for better or for worse.

[54] Ibid., p. 168.

[55] For a slightly different sketch of the idea of phenomenology as methodology, see Heim and Ram-Prasad 2017 [Early Release]/2019.

Second, the Western tradition of Phenomenology, amongst other features of its post-Cartesian investigation, notices the peculiarity of body in the subject–object relationship: it appears to be both object of subjectivity and, as 'lived body', the means by which there is a relationship between subject and its objects. Consequently, there is a recognition that body needs to become the bridge across the divide that Descartes had opened up between subject and object. This is an intrinsic feature of the transcendental project of phenomenology, wherein a final account—an ontology—is sought by which the rupture may be healed.

Third, however, working through the role and nature of body in the investigation of experience (that is, the dynamics of the subject–object relationship) some contemporary phenomenologists, especially following Merleau-Ponty's insights, have argued that the phenomenological discipline of such investigation does not result in a decisive ontology. Those who are drawn to this insight tend to focus on the discipline itself, and suggest that interrogating assumptions about experience is itself the objective of phenomenological investigation.

Finally, bringing these points together, we can make the following case. If Western phenomenology is historically tied to being a response to Cartesian dualism and the Indian traditions are not similarly conditioned, then whatever mutual illumination is cast by phenomenological investigation between the two cultures of thought, the utilization of phenomenology for an ontological purpose (determined by the post-Cartesian puzzle as it is) raises the comparativist question of what phenomenology and Indian philosophy contribute to the other. Although relatively little has been done in comparative phenomenology—focusing especially on such specific philosophical traditions as Advaita Vedānta—since the pioneering work of J.N. Mohanty[56] (compared to the analytic comparisons most influentially associated with B.K. Matilal), this is a field awaiting more productive work.

In this book, I do something very different, and adapt the practice of phenomenology as a methodology for the interrogation of experience. This has a cross-cultural benefit: on one side, the reading of Indian texts on experience in varied genres is helped by articulating their treatment specifically as a phenomenological undertaking. On the other, the restrictions that Cartesian conceptual terms place upon Western phenomenology being absent in the Indian materials, they in turn can offer a fresh and perhaps wider approach to the interrogation of experience and the assumptions that inform it. What I offer is not an ontology, nor a totalizing theory of body; far from it. Instead, I offer a deliberate acceptance that the interrogation of experience throws up an irreducible plurality of ways in which bodiliness can be articulated. Maria Heim and I have dubbed this approach to bodiliness 'ecological phenomenology'.[57]

[56] Mohanty 1992 is perhaps the most well known of his many books in this respect. Bina Gupta is one of the few systematic exponents of a phenomenological approach to Indian philosophy: e.g., Gupta 1998; Gupta 2003.

[57] In a forthcoming work, Maria Heim explores ecological phenomenology in a study of emotion in classical Indian texts, and to that extent her analysis will complement my focus on bodiliness.

Our considerations so far should lead to the conclusion that it is necessary to not assume any self-evident definition of body in the study of subjectivity, because such an assumption smuggles into the proceedings ideas about subjectivity that are itself meant to be investigated. But if we are sensitive to how body occurs in the examination of our being self-present subjects of experience, then we see that its nature and boundaries are not already fixed. Again, Merleau-Ponty was aware of this. As Chris Matthews says, our relationship with the world and other subjects, according to Merleau-Ponty, is best described as dialectical;[58] not sharply dichotomous but in a constant movement in which, according to Merleau-Ponty, 'each term is itself only by proceeding toward the opposite term, becomes what it is through the movement'.[59] Becoming sensitive to this stops us from falling back into a non-dialectical notion of our subjectivity as something we withdraw into, thereupon throwing into question our relationship with the world and other subjects.

It is therefore necessary to resist the temptation to start with certainties about the way we are bodily subjects in the world, and then seek to explain how the world becomes our object. This is because, if we did so, we would be in danger of presupposing the nature of our bodiliness in terms of its objective presence in the world—when it is the nature of our relationship to objects that is supposed to be determined subsequently. Instead, we should begin to see that what permits us to feel ourselves to be enworlded bodily subjects is also what renders body what it is. An important element of Merleau-Ponty's radical thought is his readiness to make this switch, and make understanding of bodily subjectivity (the lived body) subsequent upon our experience of the world. Françoise Dastur puts it well: 'It is therefore necessary to reverse the "natural" order of explanation: "it is through the flesh of the world that in the last analysis one can understand the lived body."[60] Likewise, the solution to the "regional" problem of the relations of the soul and the body is not to be found in a new definition of their union but in "the unicity of the visible world and, by encroachment, the invisible world".[61] It is not by a generalizing induction and by a projection that one passes from the being of the subject to the being of the world. On the contrary, it is rather the being of the subject that appears as a variant of the being of the world.'[62]

It could be said that ecological phenomenology takes its metaphor in the opposite direction to Merleau-Ponty's 'flesh', and perhaps more in keeping with the 'unicity' that he talks about. For whereas 'flesh' is taken from the initial understanding of the human body and its order of application 'reversed' so that he can begin with the 'flesh' of the world and then proceed to the lived body, ecological phenomenology decentres the lived body in its phenomenology, for the very notion of the ecological begins with the world.

My own task here does not rest on an abstract theoretical claim for the special advantages of 'ecological phenomenology' over Merleau-Ponty's later philosophy of

[58] Matthews 2002: 167. [59] Merleau-Ponty 1968: 91.
[60] Ibid., p. 304. [61] Ibid, p. 286. [62] Dastur 2000: 34.

flesh and the chiasm. There are as many comparable features as contrasting ones between the two. Ecological phenomenology is to be best thought of as a suggestive framework for the deep and occasionally implicit perspectives towards bodiliness in the texts I study here; its features and functions will emerge gradually in the specific contexts of each text and topic. There are, therefore, points at which I emphasize a contrast with Merleau-Ponty, while there are other places in the book where comparison is more natural.

Turning to contemporary philosophers, there are resonances to ecological phenomenology in Alva Noë's work, although his concerns and motivations are very different from what those explored in this book. A part of his larger project certainly involves drawing attention to the ecology of the human being. In an evocative passage, he says, '[W]e are involved—that is to say, tangled up—with the places we find ourselves. We are of them. A person is not like the berry that can easily be plucked, but rather like the plant itself, rooted in the earth and enmeshed in the brambles.'[63] Of course, he uses this ecological paradigm to argue specifically for an expanded understanding of mind that is biologically explanatory and yet not narrowly brain-based. So, 'To do biology, we need the resources to take up a nonmechanistic attitude to the organism as an environmentally embedded unity.'[64] Or, 'To study mind, as with life itself, we need to keep the whole organism in its natural environmental setting in focus.'[65] Nevertheless, I would want to follow this through not as an ontology (howsoever subtle) but as a phenomenological method—the objective is to explore how we can be both like a berry and like the plant, that our bodily being can find expression, depending on context, as alone, untangled, separate; but also as located, tangled, integrated. Unicity consists in being the locus of an intersection of various experiential vectors, that is to say, in the way a phenomenology is found to itself—in an ungrounded but nevertheless creatively useful way—through factors of its environment.

To sum up, the concerns of ecological phenomenology are consistent with but oriented differently from Noë's position. In this book, I work broadly within the framework of understanding the whole human being through an ecology consisting of dynamic and interactive elements of a life-world. But just as he is looking to displace too dominant a notion of us as 'minds' limited to brains (that might as well be in vats) with one in which we are shaped by enactive relations formed in the complex environment of brain, body, others, and world, I am pointing out that we need to challenge the notion of the body as some sort of self-evident material given and instead see it as emerging in different ways out of different genres of experiential analysis. For example, Noë asks, 'Where do you stop, and where does the rest of the world begin? There is no reason to suppose that the critical boundary is found in our brains or our skin.'[66] He focuses on this issue with regard to our brains, while I do so, albeit through a completely different approach, with regard to our skin (whether in the contemplative practice of

[63] Noë 2009: 69. [64] Ibid., p. 41. [65] Ibid., p. 45. [66] Ibid., p. 68.

Buddhaghosa's *abhidhamma* analysis or in the lyrical depiction of subject-making and lovemaking in Śrī Harṣa's poetry).

The enactive case for an ecological theory of consciousness is a literal claim about the fact of the 'life process' sculpting the 'natural world' within which it occurs, a claim about the 'interplay of organism and environment'.[67] I am sympathetic to such a view but this book is not about such issues as such. Rather, I am suggesting that ecology functions as a metaphor (or perhaps a metonym) for the phenomenological method followed in this book: the way to use our intuitions about the analytic features of experience is constantly and consistently to locate them within the contextual terms of what 'shows up' (in Noë's phrase) in a particular exploration of such experience.

While such considerations as well as more general post-Cartesian ones prompt recent, ambitious theories like that of the 'extended mind', my motivation in this book is rather more modest than laying the conceptual foundations upon which a new science of mind could be built.[68] I only want to point out that it may in fact be the case that certain neuroscientific projects find it appropriate to function within a Cartesian restriction of mental activity to the brain-in-the-body, while others find a more adaptive and extended conception of mind appropriate. These are not to be seen as competitors but as complementary, and context- and motivation-dependent. Less contentiously, it can easily be granted that further away from combative philosophical paradigms, poetic motivations matter too, as too edificatory or spiritual-contemplative ones. As such, ecological phenomenology does not call for a radical revision of the content of theory or practice in any particular case. Its significance lies in calling for a change in attitude to the diversity of theory and practice, together with a reflexive questioning of ontological presuppositions lying hidden within apparent intuitions about the human being that in fact derive from specific historical developments in the philosophical culture of the West.

Ecological Phenomenology II: General Features

The notion of ecological phenomenology is consistent with the need to not presume that body is explanatorily self-evident, and instead to think of it as whatever is yielded contingently within the parameters of any particular account of experience. An ecology is a continuous and dynamic system of interrelationships between elements, in which the salience accorded to some type of relationship clarifies how the elements it relates are to be identified. The spatial version of this is a natural and compelling metaphor (by which we live), but emotions are ecological without being spatial, as are other ways of being, such as illness. This should be remembered so as to not let the structure of metaphor get in the way of the deeper methodological point that ecological phenomenology seeks to articulate.

[67] Ibid., p. 121.

[68] See Rowlands 2010 for a lively and wide-ranging defence of such an enterprise.

In an ecology, the 'same' thing' looks 'different' depending upon the context within which one frames inquiry: that is where the ecological model gets its bite, as when in the Blue Mountains of Oregon, there is both a delicate, upstanding little mushroom (to be plucked and used in a fine dish) and the world's largest organism, a honey fungus colony of clones (to be written about in popular science columns). Obviously, it would be misleading to think that this is some sort of an ontological puzzle of the 'one and the many' variety. The salience of our motivation determines the structuration of the elements of the ecological system. Similarly, the paradigm of ecological phenomenology obviates the need to choose between what might hitherto have seemed to be polar or at least incompatible perspectives on the locus of subjectivity and the identity of the bearer's phenomenal states. The perspective and the role it plays in the figuration of subjectivity are as much a part of a phenomenology as the particular understanding of that subjectivity.

It is quite obvious that ecological phenomenology's programme will not satisfy the ontologist in search of a determinate theory of subjectivity (and reality as a whole). At no point do I want to claim that there can be no ontological enterprise, let alone that metaphysics as a whole is illegitimate; after all, the most famous and celebrated systems of philosophical thought in classical India are metaphysical through and through. My aim is two-fold. First, to broaden the scope of phenomenological analysis; and correspondingly, the sources from which we may glean philosophical insights, which range far beyond the systematic metaphysical texts that are normally counted as Indian philosophy. Second, to ask, critically, whether philosophers too quickly make the study of subjectivity an ontological quest; and demonstrate the productivity of reading subjectivity (specifically bodiliness) through a non-ontological methodology of fine-grained, analytic phenomenological description.

When I talk about 'ecological phenomenology' in this book, I refer to its two inseparable sides. One is of it as the method of analytically describing experience, in which the context always matters and determines the way we can absorb a text's particular set of descriptions. 'Context' in this methodological sense includes: the genre with its literary conventions and lexical registers, the stated purposes of the text, and the narrative or other locating devices by which the significance of the textual passages in question is foregrounded. Ecology here is hermeneutic, and permits shifts of scope and constitution. By seeing the thematization of bodiliness in this hermeneutic, that is to say, as always emerging into our attention in terms of the generic contexts of the text in which it occurs, we are not bound to think of each account as a fundamentally incompatible theory of reality.

The other side of ecological phenomenology is as a philosophy of the nature of experience. In this book, it is specifically about experience as intrinsically bodily in nature. (Ecological phenomenology could be about other things, e.g., like the aetiology, identification, and naming, and the functions of emotions, which Heim and I are developing in forthcoming work.) Here, ecological phenomenology argues that the analysis of the bodily manifestation of subjectivity is always dependent on context. 'Context' in this philosophical sense includes: material constituents of the objective body whose boundaries and features vary, ambient features of the sensory range, affective artefacts in the environment, norms of conduct, and the dynamics of social identity.

What I hope to show in the chapters is that what is taken to be the category of body, and consequently its relationship to the subject, can shift and reconfigure according to what aspect of context becomes salient. What constitutes phenomenology is therefore not an abstract process of introspection, but a context-dependent manifestation of subjective presence. Some phenomenal states are analytically describable without reference to material aspects of bodily constitution if that is not what one is concerned with, but at other times such aspects are ineleminable. For example, it is pointless to list chemical activity in the brain when offering a poetic truth about grief, but quite relevant when studying neurological data. The careful description of some states may range over extended material entities: e.g., after catastrophic injury, rehabilitative attention would include prostheses within its reflexive scope. In the profound matter of living with disabling illness, assumptions of bodily functionality are destabilized, while various formations in the environment become aspects of bodily subjectivity.[69] And so on.

Now, this book is not a direct engagement with the phenomenology of people; it would be a different, fascinating task to draw out people's own context-dependent phenomenologies, thereby probing a certain traditional philosophical confidence in the presence of a formal context-independent subjectivity. What we have, instead, is a reading of texts whose genre and stated concerns already indicate what aspects of the ecology of experience they treat as salient. It is their imaginative achievement that then comes to be studied analytically by the philosophical phenomenologist.

The relationship between the methodological and philosophical aspects of ecological phenomenology should be evident. By starting with the premise that the hermeneutic context indicates what features of experience are the concern of these texts, we are able to proceed to pay attention to the phenomenological context that is then presented within them.

The examples studied in this book therefore abstract away from the continuity of life in which experience is the pell-mell undergoing of change; the constraints of phenomenological study that helps with theorization no doubt is at an artificial remove from the fluidity of the unexamined life. This book is, certainly, limited by the nature of philosophical analysis to the examination of life, and thus a life examined.

In our cases, we can see context determining a particular narrative of bodiliness, and that context yields too clues about the ecology within which that bodiliness is located.

These rather general thoughts will, of course, be grounded in the specific concerns of each chapter. While the chapters are self-contained, I think that the implications of

[69] For a deft and creative reading across Merleau-Ponty and the changed parameters of bodily function in disabling conditions (immediately recognizable to that class of people who are philosophers with rheumatoid arthritis) see Salamon 2012.

ecological phenomenology emerge gradually across the whole of the book. It will also be clear that the claims for its theoretical application are constantly hedged by acknowledgement of scholarship in both Western philosophy and literary Indology. I would not wish to overstate the originality of any particular move or argument, while also claiming that ecological phenomenology as a whole does make a novel contribution to thinking cross-culturally about the philosophical understanding of human experience.

With these quite wide-ranging reflections, we can now turn to the case studies of bodiliness and ecological phenomenology.

1

The Body in Illness and Health

The *Caraka Saṃhitā*

Situating the Text: Medicine, Body, History

The conceptualization of the human being as bodily being—especially for our purposes, the indication of a phenomenology that takes the organic self-presence of the human being as implicated in a rich environment—is clearly evident in the *Caraka Saṃhitā*.[1] We call it a medical compendium; on its own terms, it is a book of *āyurveda*, that is, a sacred text of knowledge (a *veda*) of health (*ārogya*—freedom from disease); or vigour (*āyus*), which is synonymous with living long (*dīrghamjīvitīyam*).[2] 'That is called *āyurveda* in which beneficial and detrimental and contented and sorrowful life, and what is beneficial and detrimental to it, and its assessment, and [life] itself, are described.'[3]

From the beginning, the *Caraka Saṃhitā* strives to balance its apparent focus on physiological functions with a more complex understanding of what makes the human being. 'The unified combination (*saṃyoga*) of body, senses, mind and self is called "longevity", and is synonymous with "bearing up", "living", "perpetuation" and "mutual attachment" [of the combinatory factors].'[4] The healthy life, whose attainment and sustenance is the purpose of this practice of knowledge, therefore concerns the whole person—a concept which we will explore in more detail in terms of the text's own theorization of the 'person' as the total human subject. A person may be analysed—for reasons of treatment and regimen—into several constituent factors; but this does not undermine the holistic view of the human being in the text.[5] What we have to remember is that the assignment of the most lexically reasonable English word to a Sanskrit

[1] *Caraka Saṃhitā. Text with English Translation and Critical Exposition Based on Cakrapāṇi Datta's Āyurveda Dīpikā* 1976–2001. 6 Volumes. Ram Karan Sharma and Vaidya Bhagwan Dash. Varanasi: Chowkhamba Sanskrit Series. All translation is author's own.

[2] For the definitive outline and annotated bibliography of pre-modern *āyurveda*, see Meulenbeld's *magnum opus*: Meulenbeld 1999–2001.

[3] *hitāhitaṃ sukhaṃ duḥkhamāyustasya hitāhitam /*
mānaṃ ca tacca yatroktam āyurvedaḥ sa ucyate // Sū,1.41.

[4] *śarīrendriyasattvātmasaṃyogo dhāri jīvitam /*
nityagaścānubandhaśca paryāyairāyurucyate // Sū,1.42.

[5] For a subtle and far-reaching study of Caraka and the later āyurvedic tradition, on their conception of the human being as presented through medical narrative, see Cerulli 2012.

term does not exhaust the conceptual weight of either; the text's use of what we translate as 'mind', 'self', 'body', and the rest must be very carefully followed, so that we are able to read back into English the ideas expressed through the Sanskrit terms. Although there is something apparently, even intuitively, obvious in thinking that we ought to start by looking at a medical text in order to see what it says about the body, the task here is really to permit the ideas in the text to destabilize and then open up the presumed conceptual content of the meaning of the English word 'body' itself.

Throughout, I want to see how our very usage of 'body' can be informed (perhaps altered, or broadened) if we think through the *Caraka Saṃhitā* (and in their different ways, the texts dealt with in the subsequent chapters). With this thought, we can return to the text's articulation of its subject matter:

> Mind, self and body—these three are like a disciplining triple staff (*tridaṇḍa*).[6] Through their unified combination the world is fixed, they are the point of fixity for all things. This [unified combination] is the human being; it is sentient, it is the subject of this sacred text…[7]

The way I read the text is that it functions with an analytic understanding of different components of the human subject according to the functions it assigns to them: hence the enumeration of mind, self, and body. But it treats the 'human being' (*pumān*) holistically, as we will see, as the bodily subject (the 'mind' being an organ, and 'self' being the transcendental horizon of subjectivity). It can be said that the *Caraka Saṃhitā* equivocates creatively between talking of 'body' (*śarīra*) as (i) the material composition that is the object of the physician's attention, and as (ii) the qualification for being a subject (*puruṣa*); and I try to capture this by talking of the 'bodily subject'. Depending on context, the text's attention and language switches between the different aspects of the human whole. (This is evident in its discussion of psychiatric illness and its relationship to 'mind', but that requires a separate study.)

While chapter after chapter of the *Caraka Saṃhitā* is about the practicalities of diagnosis and the treatment of particular medical conditions, the text also steps back at certain points to delineate its ideas about who and what the bodily being is that is the subject-matter of the sacred knowledge of health and longevity. Thus, in the Section on Body (*Śārīrasthāna*), before devoting chapters to procreation, embryology, and organs of the body, the text seeks to explain systematically what it means by the 'ordinary person' (*katidhāpuruśa*); and it is here, in its theorization of the human being as bodily being, that—if we are attentive—we see how it treats body thematically.

The fact that the text is framed as being concerned with longevity—and not immortality or ultimate freedom—immediately orients us to the bodily nature of its human subject, for by longevity is meant the flourishing of the living body (one could say, the

[6] The term '*tridaṇda*', which literally meaning a triple staff, also means metaphorically the triple control of thought, word, and deed that is signified when a renunciate carries such a staff. So the implication is that the world is one disciplined or controlled by thought, word, and deed; and it is because of this that the world is the world **of** the human being.

[7] *sattvamātmā śarīraṃ ca trayametattridaṇḍavat/lokastiṣṭhati saṃyogāttatra sarvaṃ pratiṣṭhitam//sa pumāṃścetanaṃ tacca taccādhikaraṇaṃ smṛtam*/Sū, I.46–47a.

biological body). I will begin my study by noting that, while the text speaks primarily in the voice of the physician attending to a patient, it also frequently shifts register to see the world in terms of a subjectivity common to persons on either side of medical practice. As such, it is helpful for our purposes to begin with an awareness of the weight it gives to human agency. It takes the aims of life as being shared by all human subjects, practitioners, patients, and healthy people. The *Caraka Saṃhitā* does not place the physician outside the world of medical subjects and give him (for he is male) a God's eye view of the human condition, despite the fact that its dominant concern is the physician's procedures on patients.

I will then go on to look at the most sustained philosophical passage in the text, the first chapter of the Section on Body, which is on the 'ordinary person', in the context of the *Caraka Saṃhitā*—that is to say, keeping in mind that this chapter is not part of a text whose main aim is to develop an account of ultimate reality, or argue for a particular epistemology against others, or teach the truths of existence. We should look at this particular chapter as being a reasoned statement on the subject who is the subject-matter of the physician's empirical investigation, interaction, treatment, and guidance. It is about what the text takes to be the nature of the human being, such that medical activity towards that being can follow. The *Caraka Saṃhitā* does not, therefore, base its description upon what is found through medical investigation itself, but upon a coherent set of claims that it thinks explains why humans are the way they are. It is only because they are that way that humans become the subject-matter of medical investigation. As such, this chapter offers us the text's philosophical anthropology, the conceptual background to its immediate medical interests. Here, the *Caraka Saṃhitā*'s usage of 'body'-terms emerges in multiple registers.

Having seen how the text treats 'body' in different ways, I will then turn to how this bodily being is constantly reconfigured to himself or herself in the experience of illness and the search for wellness. We see this primarily in the surprisingly bilateral diagnostic relationship between physician and patient with regard to the phenomenology of illness (illness being what someone experiences of disease that threatens longevity); and in the discipline of social integration that the text expounds as the means to regain and retain health. Finally, having seen how the body is conceptualized according to context, i.e., according to how it is experienced by the subject, by the physician and his team, by involved fellow humans (like family and servants), and by society, we will see emerging what was called in the Introduction an 'ecological phenomenology'. The methodological hypothesis of an ecological phenomenology is that inconsistent or even conflicting intuitions about bodily subjectivity can be seen through a pluralistic yet integrated approach to the way human experience is attended to by both the subject(s) and the student(s) of such experience. Rather than seeing particular framings of our experience as in tension with each other, we should see each such framing as playing its own role within a larger, interdependent, and mutually implicated set of contexts. The analytic focus called for—in introspection, conversation, diagnosis, relationships, contemplation, etc.—determines which element is attended to, or else recedes as the phenomenological focus shifts. For example, the inner–outer distinction thickens or thins depending on whether we are examining a patient's pain (cut off from anything the physician might feel in a comparable neural description) or her mood in response to it (where the physician and ambient norms are critical to the constitution of the phenomenology of illness). To reiterate, the aim of this book is to offer not another ontology of body, but a methodology for understanding any human reality at hand; this chapter focuses on understanding such a framework around classical Indian medicine.

Before we set out on that journey, here is a quick summary of the text and its historical context. As a contemporary authority on *āyurveda* says, 'When, in... this book, I refer blithely to Caraka's *Compendium*, it is well to remember that this expression hides a great deal of poorly understood literary history'.[8] Very roughly, this text is presented by itself as a system taught by Agniveśa, who learnt it by being taught by the sage Ātreya. Caraka is mentioned at the end of each chapter as only having 'edited' (*pratisaṃskṛta*) the text. Circumstantial evidence leads contemporary scholarship to think that the earliest layers of the text were composed by the third or second century BCE. But around the fourth or fifth century CE, someone called Dṛḍhabala not only seemed to have organized or reorganized it, but also added large sections, his name mentioned in various chapter endings. The *Caraka Saṃhitā*, as it comes down from that time, has 120 chapters, divided into eight sections.[9]

1. *Sūtra* (rules)—thirty chapters on drugs and their uses, food, diet, the duties of a physician, and other topics including some philosophical discussions.
2. *Nidāna* (primary causes)—eight chapters on eight major diseases.
3. *Vimāna* (arrangements)—eight chapters on topics like pathology, tools of diagnostics, and medical studies.
4. *Śārīra* (relating to the body)—eight chapters on philosophy, embroyology, procreation, and anatomy.
5. *Indriya* (the senses)—twelve chapters on using the senses for diagnosis and prognosis.
6. *Cikitsā* (therapies)—thirty chapters on therapy.
7. *Kalpa* (pharmancy)—twelve chapters on the preparation of medicines.
8. *Siddhi* (completion)—twelve chapters on further general therapy.

The *Sūtra-sthāna* and *Śārīra-sthāna* will dominate our philosophical exploration.

Human Agency as the Frame for Medicine

A striking feature of the *Caraka Saṃhitā* as medical compendium is that its detached attitude to not only disease, but also illness—which renders the human condition the object of the physician's gaze—is nonetheless located within a broader understanding

[8] Wujastyk 2003: 5.
[9] See Wujastyk 2003 for a good bibliography and pointers to further readings.

of that human condition. It offers a general justification for what humans are thought to want normatively, something that must of course apply as much to the physician as the patient. In the typical manner of pre-contemporary traditions, the human condition is directed towards 'mankind'—pertaining to men and women when it comes down to it (in the sense that principles, requirements, and medical states of affair do not fail to apply to women), but addressed to men (of particular social classes).

Almost at the very beginning of the text, there is an invocation of the famous ancient formula for the four-fold 'goals of man' (the *puruṣārthas*):

Health ('without disease') stands as the very foundation of the virtuous life, material prosperity, pleasure and spiritual freedom. Illness destroys it as well as a propitious life.[10]

As is well understood, these four goals or ends narrow and widen semantically, and should not be read in any one single way;[11] what is clear is that the *Caraka Saṃhitā* is acknowledging the influential and prestigious conception of the quadruple (*caturvarga*) of goals: a conception at once descriptive of the activities that humans are supposed to engage in naturally, and also prescriptive of the ends towards which the properly lived life must tend.[12] It is bold, and yet perfectly reasonable for the text to point out that these goals—including the highest goal, freedom, that might (in most teachings) even entail freedom from bodily conditions—depend on health. It can therefore plausibly be argued that, 'while religious knowledge may help in the world to come, medical knowledge helps in that world and also in this. It is twice as useful.'[13] Since health is most evidently a biological quality, the text self-servingly brings a fresh perspective to bear on the normative conception of human life. The task of the physician—which is to preserve health—is deftly placed at the very core of the most influential hermeneutic of human life then available.[14]

The *Caraka Saṃhitā*, however, has a more individual way of justifying itself within a general account of the facts and norms of human striving; one, moreover, that makes evident the centrality of its conception of the human being as a bodily being. In a later chapter of the Section on Rules (*Sūtrasthāna*), it articulates its view through the concept of the three *eṣaṇās* or 'pursuits'.[15]

[10] *dharmārthakāmamokṣāṇāmārogyaṃ mūlamuttamam//rogāstasyāpahartāraḥ śreyaso jīvitasya ca*/Sū, 1.15b–16a.

[11] Malmoud 1981: 44–6.

[12] See Davis 2005 for a thorough study of the scholarship on the combined factual and normative nature of these goals in classical Indic thought. For a philosophical reading of the implications of the four-fold goals, see Ram-Prasad 1995.

[13] Wujastyk 2004: 837.

[14] 'The physicians of pre-modern India, then, recognised a healthy life as being of fundamental, even primary importance, since without it no other goal of life would be possible. In various ways and with different arguments, they subordinated the quest for dharma to the quest for health'; Wujastyk 2004: 838.

[15] Seeking to give the reader a sense of the constellation of ideas contained in *eṣaṇā*, Wujasktyk translates it as 'ambition', 'will', 'drive', and 'aspiration'; Wujastyk 2003: 22ff.

A man of unimpaired mind, intelligence, virility, courage, who wants to discover what is beneficial in this world and in the next world, should strive to develop three pursuits.[16] These are: pursuit of life-breath, pursuit of wealth, and pursuit of the world beyond.[17]

This is a quite general idea about the ground conditions for being human, in terms of what humans want and towards what they direct their will. On its own terms, the *Caraka Saṃhitā* here sounds less obviously like an echo of the hegemonic formula of the four-fold goals, and more like an appeal to ordinary intuitions about what we want in life. The terminology at just this point (although not elsewhere) subtly by-passes the weighty and evocative language of virtuous conduct and social order (in two important senses of *dharma*) altogether. Here, it comes across as being concerned primarily to argue for the existence of medicine: human agency is the very motivation for why medicine should exist. It is what the patient wants that makes for the very idea of well-being, and this is why the techniques of the physician are adumbrated.[18]

We accord priority (*pūrvatara*) to the 'pursuit of life-breath'. It is in consequence of this that the tasks of medicine emerge in the first place.

When the life-breath is lost, everything is lost. So it can be safeguarded by a healthy person continuing a healthy regimen, the sick one by carefully attending to relieving the disorder.[19]

Then the justification for the pursuit of wealth is laid out bluntly, as a corollary to the first pursuit. 'There is no worse misfortune than a long life without means.'[20] Various proper means of livelihood, like farming, animal husbandry and trade are then suggested. Although this is laid out briefly, the various means of employment it lists are notably tied to physical effort, again foregrounding the somatic stresses of the pursuit of prosperity—and the consequent importance of health.

[16] On *eṣanā*, Filliozat 1993. He argues that, although the root here could be √*iṣ* in the sense of 'to desire' (pres. *icchati*), the context as well as Cakrapāṇi's gloss shows that the root here is √*iṣ* in the sense of 'to go' (pres. *iṣyati*), implying 'going to the goal'; pp 94–5.

[17] *iha khalu puruṣeṇānupahatasattvabuddhipauruṣaparākrameṇa hitamiha cāmuṣmiṃśca lokesamanupaśyatā tisra eṣaṇāḥ paryeṣṭavyā bhavanti. tadyathā: prāṇaiṣaṇā, dhanaiṣaṇā, paralokaiṣaṇeti.* Sū,11.3.

[18] I am reading the text philosophically, in terms of its conceptual purposes. So what I say is not inconsistent with the text-historical consideration that the writers and redactors of the text were concerned to articulate a justification for their medical profession through invoking the terminology and values of the brahmanical culture in order to benefit from its high status. Preisendanz draws attention to the possibility that this three-fold version may be an adaptation of the Upaniṣadic conception of pursuing a male off-spring, property, and this world; Preisendanz 2015: 138. Later in the very same chapter, when defining 'reasoning' (*yukti*), the text says it helps with the three-fold ends (*trivarga*); Sū 11.25. This could be a reference to the standard three 'worldly' ends, excluding here the final one of liberation; there is a hoary debate in Indological scholarship on the relationship between the three-fold and four-fold classification. It is, however, puzzling why the text should cut out liberation after having included it at the start of the first chapter of the *Sūtrasthāna*. Or it could be that it is referring to its own three-fold classification, and rather cheekily claiming the term 'three-fold' for itself. Or it may be that, despite the differences in detail, it takes the three *eṣanā*s to in fact be mappable on to the three-fold *puruṣārtha*s.

[19] *prāṇaparityāge hi sarvatyāgaḥ. tasyānupālanaṃ svasthasya svasthavṛttānuvṛttirāturasya vikārapraśamane'pramādaḥ*; Sū 11.4.

[20] *na hyataḥ pāpāt pāpīyo'sti yadanupakaraṇasya dīrghamāyuḥ*; Sū 11.5.

The third pursuit is for the 'world beyond' or 'another world' (*paraloka*) (Sū,11.6). It should be pointed out that what is mentioned here is not necessarily the idea of a succession of states (*saṃsāra*), that is, the idea of repeated lives (*punarjanma*) which is widely associated with ancient Indian religious traditions. Just at this juncture, the *Caraka Saṃhitā* seems to confine itself strictly to—even possibly one—rebirth (*punarbhāva*). This means that what we have is 'the pursuit of the so-called other world, that is, purposeful activity in view of a renewed existence after death in another setting, especially and foremost, a heavenly existence'.[21] Even more pointedly, this is very different from liberation (*mokṣa*), which the various traditions that offer competing doctrinal accounts all agree is freedom from repeated rebirth. The absence of *mokṣa* terminology should incline us to think that, at least at this point, the *Caraka Saṃhitā* is primarily seeking to be descriptive of the human tendency towards certain ends, rather than offering a normative framework for the ideal life per se. The text then acknowledges frankly that there is some doubt (*saṃśaya*) about the viability of this desire, for there is dissension within sacred texts (*śrutibheda*) themselves. It then articulates its own formula for the various means of knowledge (the *pramāṇas*), before claiming that they indeed establish that there is rebirth (Sū.11.33).

We saw that the first two pursuits imply how humans should behave if they are to attain their ends: for life-breath, an absence of illness is required, while for prosperity, it is gainful (and active) employment. The third pursuit too—once it has been established as epistemologically well-grounded—brings its own requisite conduct. The *Caraka Saṃhitā*'s recommendations illustrate powerfully its overall conception of the good life, a dynamic interplay of factors at whose nexus is found the bodily person of the elite male, who possesses the relevant resources to lead such a healthy life. The means to that life consist in:

> attending to the teacher, study, practising vows, taking a wife, having children, caring for servants, showing reverence to guests, giving donation, being without greed, being sparing, not being spiteful, having unwearied body, speech and mind, scrutinising body, senses, mind, intellect and self, and having a settled mind.[22]

Such a life offers both a good living in this world and leads to a celestial realm (*svarga*) beyond. Human agency leads to the aspiration for a good life beyond this life, and for that aspiration to be fulfilled a range of existential tasks must be mastered.

As we will see in the course of the chapter, the *Caraka Saṃhitā* repeatedly returns to many of these requirements on the path to health. The desiderata for being human are many; and in the complex of those requirements lies the Carakan conception of the human being. The human being as social being is expressed naturally by the text in bodily terms. Some of the requirements for what it is to be human are tied to

[21] Preisendanz 2015; 138.

[22] *guruśuśrūṣāyāmadhyayane vṛtacaryāyāṃ dārakriyāyāmapatyotpādane bhṛtyabharaṇe'tithipūjāyāṃ dāne'nabhidhyāyāṃ tapasyanasūyāyāṃ dehavāṅmānase karmaṇyakliṣṭe dehendriyamanorthabuddhyātmap arīkṣāyāṃ manaḥsamādhāviti*; Sū, 11.33.

intuitions (prevalent across different cultures, one might hazard) about the body, because they call upon the material aspects of bodiliness—the sexual and the procreative, as well as the activity involved in the conduct of service, welcoming guests, undertaking economic responsibility, and even charity (in the actual rituals of giving away goods). But as we will see soon, even the more abstract moral and cognitive disciplines are in fact functions of a bodily existence that ranges beyond the purely material elements of the body.

The Subject as the Complex of Natural Elements

The first chapter of the Section on Body steps back from direct medical concerns, to present its understanding of the ordinary subject (*katidhāpuruṣa*) who is to be the patient of the physician's knowledge and skills. In many ways, it is a difficult passage to interpret. First, the text clearly draws on the conceptual vocabulary of systems that were developing at the same time, but adapts them to its own purposes, making our knowledge of those systems more often a hindrance than a help in our reading of the philosophical stance of the *Caraka Saṃhitā*. Second, even if we try and read the text on its own terms, its battle to explicate its conception of the human being results in semantic shifts that are hard to spot. These shifts mostly concern the use of two terms, '*puruṣa*' and '*ātman*' (and occasionally and even more confusingly, '*paramātman*'): at times they are contrasted, and at others used synonymously.

The guiding heuristic in my reading of this chapter is that the text is seeking to get at the human subject. The subject is that which undergoes experience. It is that which has feeling (*vedanā*), understood in its intensified sense as pain or misery. The difficulty is that, on the one hand, there are reasons to think that these feelings—whose occurrence leads to medical intervention—are bodily states, but that on the other hand, the possibility for such states to occur at all seems to require something which is not just reducible to a bodily component. To get to the position of talking about the subject as the bodily being—not as occupying a body and not reducible to the body, but as being a subject that is bodily, Caraka has to say what is it to be a subject in a way that makes it neither something that is wholly body nor something that has nothing to do with the body. I take the text to be doing this through two moves. (i) One is to talk about 'self' as that which renders the bodily being subjective, which is to say, what makes it something like to be that body. The other is to talk about what else than the material limits of the compositional body makes for subjectivity, to which the answer is two-fold: (ii.a) the physician's intersubjective relationality with the patient-who-is-subject, and (ii.b) the social environment that gives meaning to subjectivity.

So the scene is set with a sequence of questions. What is the division of constituent elements (*dhātubheda*) of the ordinary subject; but at the same time, in what way is that subject (*puruṣa*) the motive principle (*kāraṇa*) of those elements (Śā.1.3)? What is the sign (*liṅga*) of this *puruṣa* (4)? But then the pondering shifts to the other term with which the text must wrestle, the self (*ātman*):

Those cognisant of the self say that the self is without activity, independent, autonomous, omnipotent, all-pervasive, cogniser of the body-field and witness. But how is it, lord, that there is activity to that without action? How is that which is independent born into this unfortunate species? If autonomous, how overwhelmed by the strength of sorrow? If omnipresent, why is he not aware of all misery?[23]

There are, then, two overlapping aspects to the text's approach towards subjectivity: The first concerns the compositional nature of the human being, which implies that the compositional elements together entirely constitute the phenomenal subject. Somehow, the elements together seem required to explain why there is a being that feels; in particular, that feels pain which must be alleviated. The second looks at the horizon of subjectivity itself, the posit of a self (asserted by sources the text takes as authoritative) that is not contained in the natural elements of the human being but which—the text assumes—must be invoked to explain how that being can be a phenomenal subject at all (and not simply a lump of natural materials). The crucial tactic the text adopts is to see the *puruṣa* as both an elemental part of the bodily human being and yet also as somehow implying the self that makes that human being capable of agency and illness. The body as material object made up of constituent parts is not the main concern of the physician (except in a forensic sense that is not obvious in the *Caraka Saṃhitā*); it is the alleviation of suffering. In other words, the physician's training in knowledge of diseases and medical procedures is ultimately motivated by observation of the subject as subject of illness. But whence that subjectivity? What is the nature of the human that explains its presentation as patient to the physician? Hence the text's essay into philosophical anthropology, which I understand as the attempt to make sense of the nature of the bodily human in terms that would explain the very possibility of phenomenology (and therefore specifically of suffering that can be alleviated through treatment).

We can detect in the *Caraka Saṃhitā* a certain fluidity over the conception of the bodily nature of the ordinary human subject. Depending on objective and context, it can be the material body that yields the text's physiology; but at other times, it concerns various aspects of the phenomenological body that justifies the need for a physiological understanding in the first place. (Quite simply, it is because people feel ill that the study and treatment of illness becomes a task.) The phenomenological body—the living subject with its agency and goals, and its illnesses and suffering—is itself determined in different ways, depending on the concerns of the text. We are also made to confront the question of what the body is such that it is the locus of subjectivity,

[23] *niṣkriyaṃ ca svatantraṃ ca vaśinaṃ sarvagaṃ vibhum/vadantyātmānamātmajñāḥ kṣetrajñaṃ sākṣiṇaṃ tathā//niṣkriyasya kriyā tasya bhagavan vidyate katham/svatantraścedaniṣṭāsu kataṃ yoniṣu jāyate/vaśī yadyasukhaiḥ kasmādbhāvairākramyate balāt/sarvāḥ sarvagatvācca vedanāḥ kiṃ na vetti saḥ*//Śā.1.5–7.

a situation that is not made any easier by the fact that the text is not always clear about how the self is meant to be the source of subjectivity.

As has been well established, the *Caraka Saṃhitā* uses terminology and conceptual organization that is found in systems contemporary to it, although the exact chronology and consequent likelihood of the direction of influence remain contested.[24] There is a variety of lists of constituent parts of a human being, spread across the text, drawing on concepts available to the authors at that time.[25] I want to concentrate on the most sustained exploration of this issue, which is in the first chapter of the Section on Body. *Śārīrasthāna* 1.16 says that the *puruṣa*—let us already commit ourselves to calling this the 'subject'—is by tradition (*smṛti*) said to be constituted by the five material elements (*mahābhūtas*) and consciousness (*cetanā*); together, these six are the constitutive elements (*dhātus*). (In its more physiological sections, the text uses '*dhātu*' specifically in the sense of 'body tissue', i.e., the constitutive material of the different organs and structures of the body.) But the very next verse tries out an alternative schema:

> Or yet again, it is said to consist of twenty-four constitutive elements: the mind, the ten [sensory and motor] organs, the five objects [of the senses] and the functional entities made up of the eight constitutive elements (the five forms of matter, the 'I'-sense, the faculty of judgement, and the primordial base of these).[26]

This frank acknowledgement of alternative accounts is in itself interesting: to the physician, neither of them is within his diagnostic ken while either will suffice as an explanation for how a person presents himself or herself to the physician: feeling ill and having something wrong explains that feeling. In a sense, the text here exemplifies its naturalistic attitude: that is to say, as a medical compendium, its primary concern is to take the human being as another object in the natural world. This is evident in its usage of ontological classifications in order to describe its subject-matter through elements that are of a piece with the world (for the world is made of the five forms of matter). Also, by offering competing classifications, it implies that it is willing to accept different ontologies so long as they are consistent with its primary concern, which is the ill human subject.

Of course, its naturalism is a rather vague and certainly not methodologically explicit attitude; and we should not expect anything more. In twentieth-century analytic philosophy, Peter Strawson influentially argued that there can be both a hard naturalism that only deals with humans as specific types of objects reducible to parts of nature, and a soft naturalism that accommodates the subjective aspects of human beings as part of their 'nature' and therefore part of nature in a more 'catholic' or 'liberal'

[24] On Sāṃkhya terminology, Ramakrishna Rao 1962, and Larson 1987. On classificatory terminology—and even verses directly—shared with Vaiśeṣika, see Comba 1987.

[25] Maas 2008.

[26] *punaśca dhātubhedena caturviṃśatikaḥ smṛtaḥ /*
mano daśendriyāṇyarthāḥ prakṛtiścāṣṭadhātukī // Śā.I.17.

sense.[27] Whichever way we look at it, the *Caraka Saṃhitā*'s naturalism is certainly soft, since it includes aspects of subjective human nature in its classification at verse 17: the 'I'-sense (*ahaṃkāra*) that reflexively structures the ascription of experience from a particular perspective; and the intellect or the faculty of judgement (*mahān* or *buddhi*). Judgement is a constituent element of the subject for the *Caraka Saṃhitā*.

Thought, investigation, consideration, imaginative meditation and determination, and whatever else can be known by means of the mind, all those are its objects of understanding. Mental action is the control of sense organs, self-regulation, examination, and investigation; after that is the operation of intellect (i.e., judgement).'[28]

It should be noted that the inclusion of 'mind' (*manas*) here is not particularly 'soft': although it is not physically evident like the five sensory organs for the perception of various environmental states, it is still conceived as a further sensing organ whose contact with the other senses is required before there can be cognition (*jñāna*):

The characteristic of mind is that: there can be right cognition or not but it is not there even when there is contact between self, senses and their objects [but without contact with mind], while right cognition is accomplished only when the mind is in conjunction with them. It is said that the two features of mind are its subtlety and its unity [i.e., one per subject].[29]

The text can also occasionally sound like it is using 'mind' and 'intellect/judgement' interchangeably: 'It is said that because of varied actions, senses and objects, there are many judgements, each born of the contact of self, and the senses and their objects.'[30] But usually, it also makes a distinction between mind and intellectual judgement, judgement being the eventual discharge of the mind's work as reasoning. This is the

[27] Strawson 1985. On the general idea of hard and soft naturalisms with regard to scepticism about external bodies, see chapter 1: 'Skepticism, Naturalism and Transcendental Arguments'; on its application to persons, in the specific context of morality (where hard naturalism is explained as stripping the objective world of moral dimensions), see chapter 2: 'Morality and Perception'. Strawson's anti-sceptical argument for soft naturalism is primarily that it is natural—and therefore unavoidable—that humans have moral beliefs. In chapter 3: 'The Mental and the Physical', he goes back to his famous theory from an earlier book, *Individuals*, that persons are unitary beings that have both mental and physical predicates, and while there may be a general dependence of the former (seen as states of consciousness) on the latter, the two cannot be conflated. There is a thriving literature on this issue, which we cannot go into. But I think two comments are germane. Firstly, if there is to be any line of causal dependency for the *Caraka Saṃhitā*, then it is of the physical on the non-physical, and if it is claimed that that suffices to destroy its naturalism, howsoever soft, then so it has to be. Secondly, as we will see, we have to pay attention to the *Caraka Saṃhitā*'s unease over where exactly to draw the line on the entitative natural world.

[28] *cintyaṃ vicāryam ūhyaṃ ca dhyeyaṃ saṃkalpyam eva ca /*
yat kiṃcin manaso jñeyaṃ tat sarvaṃ hyarthasaṃjñakam //
indriyābhigrahaḥ karma manasaḥ svasya nigrahaḥ /
ūho vicāraśca tataḥ paraṃ buddhiḥ pravartate // Śā.I.20–1.

[29] *lakṣaṇaṃ manaso jñānasyābhāvo bhāva eva ca /*
sati hy ātmendriyārthānāṃ sannikarṣe na vartate //
vaivṛttyānmanaso jñānaṃ sānnidhyāt tacca vartate /
aṇutvamatha caikatvaṃ dvau guṇau manasaḥ smṛtau // Śā.I.18–19.

[30] *bhedāt kāryendriyārthānāṃ bahvyo vai buddhyaḥ smṛtāḥ/*
ātmendriyamanorthānāmekaikā sannikarṣajā// Śā.I.33.

closest the text comes to specifying what judgement means; we should therefore be careful to not read it in some strict way, say, as propositional assertions, although the implication here—in that it seems to follow from a set of 'actions of mind' (*manasaḥ karma*)—seems to be that it is some manner of intentional action deriving from understanding (*saṃjñā*).

Thought, investigation, consideration, imaginative meditation and determination, and whatever else can be known by means of the mind, all those are its objects of understanding. Mental action is the control of sense organs, self-regulation, examination, and investigation; after that is the operation of intellect (i.e., judgement).[31]

Since the text takes intellectual judgement (*buddhi*) as the outcome of mental activity, it does not treat them separately; the term '*buddhi*' can therefore also be translated as 'mental faculty' (i.e., the faculty of judgement). 'The intellect of creatures functions on the basis of the appropriate sense organs.'[32]

From this outline of what is meant by 'mind', it is clear that the *Caraka Saṃhitā* is not making the distinction between 'mind' and 'body' with which we are familiar in our contemporary folk-language with its roots in the popular reception of Cartesian dualism.[33] Rather, 'mind' (*manas*) is a particular functional constituent of the entire bodily complex ('*rāsi*', an assemblage) of the human subject, a separate organ for cognition, that has unity (*ekatva*) specific to each bodily complex and, unlike the five senses, not directly observable (being 'subtle', 'fine' or 'minute' (*aṇu*)). There is no systematic exploration of a theory of *manas* here, in contrast to philosophical systems like Nyāya or the Buddhist Abdhidhamma that were developing at that time, although there is a fascinating suggestiveness to the terse statements on offer. If the earliest layers of both Vaiśeṣika and Nyāya systems do not conceptualize the *manas* as an inner sense organ, but the next extant layer of both—which is just after the last redaction of the *Caraka Saṃhitā*—do,[34] then this text is probably the earliest to talk this way about 'mind', even if it is not clear about what it is proposing. But for our purposes, it is sufficient to note that, when it talks of 'mind', it means an inner sense organ, which is therefore not on the other side of a putative divide from the body but is simply part of it.

31 *cintyaṃ vicāryam ūhyaṃ ca dhyeyaṃ saṃkalpyam eva ca /*
yat kiṃcin manaso jñeyaṃ tat sarvaṃ hyarthasaṃjñakam //
indriyābhigrahaḥ karma manasaḥ svasya nigrahaḥ /
ūho vicāraśca tataḥ paraṃ buddhiḥ pravartate // Śā.I.20–1.

32 *yā yadindriyamāśritya jantorbuddhiḥ pravartate*/Śā.1.32a. I realize that it requires a whole other undertaking to argue precisely why we ought to think of 'function' as the crucial English word for the concept suggested by *pra-√vṛt*, given that functional theories of mind do not stretch back in the West beyond Kant and are systematized only in the late twentieth century; see Meerbote 1989. But different traditions alight on ideas at different times and various forms, without implying any particular notion of progression.

33 It is not that easy to offer a genealogy for the contemporary language of dualism in medicine (and other subjects) that goes directly back to Descartes, because it is not that clear exactly what Descartes meant when he talked in medical contexts about the objective body (the 'body-machine' as distinct from the *cogito*). See, e.g., Zaner 1981.

34 Comba 1987: 44–5.

We should therefore read the text's concept of the subject as bodily complex loosely as a naturalistic stance. What we are in effect saying is that it considers the bodily human being to be made of material constituents, or strictly speaking, the same constituents as make up the rest of the world.[35] Soft naturalism about body then means the inclusion of constituents that are not of a piece with the rest of the world: the experiential aspects of the human being, namely, thought, feeling, and judgement. However, the *Caraka Saṃhitā* is unclear over precisely how to situate its understanding of subjectivity within its account of bodily being. Verse 1.16 itself, having said that the *puruṣa* is comprised of the six constitutive elements—the five material ones and consciousness—then equivocates: 'Tradition holds that the element of consciousness by itself constitutes the subject.'[36] Since it then offers another concept in the next verse, in which the subject is said to comprise of the twenty-four constitutive elements with nothing left over, we get the indication that the text prefers not to postulate a dualism of subject and body (which might have been the view of 'the tradition' that it was quoting in the previous verse).

Even if the *Caraka Saṃhitā* would prefer to somehow locate the subjectivity of the ordinary person entirely within the natural complex of the constituent elements, it is reluctant to assert that there is nothing else to the subject than those elements. It is not given to a straightforward reductive naturalism, and does not want to confine its account entirely to the elements.[37] Instead, it calls upon the 'self' (*ātman*). But I want to argue that its treatment of *puruṣa* in terms of *ātman* is a methodological departure from the classificatory attitude with which it approaches the *puruṣa* in terms of the constitutive elements (the *dhātus*). Instead, it permits the notion of the subject (*puruṣa*) to be used more flexibly than as just the totality of the constitutive elements (as verse 17 states). Instead it reaches for a principle of subjectivity that can explain the phenomenological life of the human: what makes a human **be** human. For this, even the enriched (soft naturalistic) account of bodiliness will not do. There is a philosophical sense in which 'beyond' the body is self, but we have to be careful about what that might mean.

Here we have what can metaphorically be called the 'vertical question' about the boundaries of the bodily subject: what renders body capable of being subjective, **above** and **beyond** the elements that constitute it? The *Caraka Saṃhitā*'s answer is *ātman*; but not, I suggest, as another, albeit supernatural, element of the human being, but as the

[35] For simplicity's sake, we set aside the issue of animal subjectivity: the commentarial tradition agrees that it applies to animals, but here it specifically concerns human beings who exemplify the subject. See Sharma and Dash: 314, drawing on Cakrapāṇidatta's commentary.

[36] *cetanādhāturapyekaḥ smṛtaḥ puruṣasaṃjñakaḥ*//Śā.1.16b.

[37] Doctrinally, this is because it would not want to be a 'nay-saying' (*nāstika*), that is to say, dissenting, unbelieving system: from a wider brahmanical perspective, this usually includes Buddhists and Jains, but since in its arguments for the reality of another life it calls those who deny it '*nāstika*', and Buddhists and Jains do not deny it, it must have a narrower set of more radically anti-spiritual and 'materialist' opponents in mind: presumably such as the Ajīvikas and Cārvākas, although historically their identity and doctrinal commitmets are not entirely clear; see Schermerhorn 1930.

explanatory limit to what renders life possible. After that examination, we will turn to look at the complementary, 'horizontal question' about bodiliness: what **else** contributes to the subjectivity, **other** than the elements that constitute that body? For that we will consider the affective relationships the patient-subject has with the physician and with society.

The Bodily Subject and the Transcendental Self

The *Caraka Saṃhitā*'s philosophical anthropology seeks to account for what would explain how human subjects are such that they can become ill or well. It is evidently unsure, as we have been through all of history, about how to locate consciousness as an occurrence in the natural world. But even though it falls short of providing an explanation that will magically solve the 'hard problem', we can see its physician's-eye view of the phenomenological truth of our subjectivity. Our being human consists in our being such entities as undergo existence (and do not merely exist). For it to be—to use Thomas Nagel's famous phrase anachronistically—'something like it is to be' human, our existence has to be bodily; it is neither just a set of physiological functions that mysteriously generates phenomenality, nor is it a bringing together of two metaphysical principles, one the physical locus (the body as physical) and the other the non-physical mind. Of course, the text also tries to close in on what the nature of that subjectivity is, because it realizes that that cannot lie in those things that can continue to exist without subjectivity. But I want to argue that the *Caraka Saṃhitā*'s philosophical anthropology requires a sort of 'transcendental' understanding of subjectivity, as what we need to believe must be the case for there to be bodily human being, but only so as to then turn to what can become legitimate objects of (the physician's) study.

The *Caraka Saṃhitā* generally points to the relationship between the bodily subject and its 'self' through the simple yet enigmatic term '*para*', which can be translated by anything from 'beyond', 'farther than' and 'remote', to 'other than' and 'different from', or 'superior', 'highest' and 'ultimate'. As I want to make a particular claim about how its conception of self is different from, yet complementary to, the treatment of the bodily subject we have seen above, I deliberately choose to stay with the uninflected translation, 'beyond'.

Even early on, in the Section on Rules, the text gestures to self as something that cannot be dealt with in the same way as the natural factors of the human being:

> Unaltered is the self beyond; through mind, elemental entities, qualities and senses, it is the principle of consciousness. It is eternal, the observer that sees all activity.[38]

In the medical context, being unaltered has the specific meaning of being free of the changes brought about by illnesses, but the more general, metaphysical meaning also

[38] *nirvikāraḥ parastvātmā sattvabhūtaguṇendriyaiḥ/caitanye kāraṇaṃ nityo dṛṣṭvā paśyatihi kriyāḥ//* Sū.1.56.

holds. Caraka uses the same features ascribed to self from the earliest layers of the Upaniṣads onwards: being eternal, and being the core witnessing awareness present across all cognitive changes.[39] A basic distinction is therefore set up in our understanding between self and the complex bodily subject. This idea is returned to in the discussion in the first chapter of the Section on Body, in relation to the subject (*puruṣa*).

What is beyond holds the conjunction of intellect, sense organs, mind and sense objects. That complex of twenty-four entities [already discussed] is understood as the subject.[40]

In some sense then, what is beyond is that which bears or holds (√*dhṛ*) the subject that is constituted by the twenty-four elemental entities. No direct explanation of the meaning of bearing/holding is given; but a series of verses refines the text's distinction between this self 'beyond' and the natural subject.

As the self beyond has no beginning, no origin can be ascribed to it; the subject, being a complex [of the twenty-four entities], is to be understood as born of the consequences of delusion, desire and aversion.[41]

The beginningless subject is eternal, the opposite of that is what is born of a cause. What is causeless is eternal, but otherwise is that which is born of a cause.[42]

That [eternal self] cannot be grasped by any being, because the eternal cannot be [grasped] by anything. That is why that is said to be unmanifest and unthinkable; while the manifest is otherwise.[43]

The manifest, the sensate, is that which is grasped by the sense organs. What is other to it is the unmanifest, beyond the senses, which is grasped only by its sign.[44]

The distinction between self and the bodily subject is first made through the conventional classical Indian idea that birth is caused by the accretion of negative consequences from epistemic and emotional vices from previous births. (Here at least, the text is committed not just to this life and another, but to the notion of an ongoing stream of lives, although it does not say more about the disputed matter of exactly what goes through the succession of lives.) Given this idea of action that consequentially structures the next life, the subject at hand is that which is born, lives and dies; it is what

[39] As it is not clear whether the *Caraka Saṃhitā* treats self and consciousness as synonymous or consciousness as a quality flowing from the self—theoretical alternatives that were hotly debated in subsequent centuries—it seems sensible to think of its use of '*kāraṇa*' in a neutral way—as 'principle'—that links self and consciousness without asserting anything further. It will do for our present purposes.

[40] *buddhindriyamanorthānāṃ vidyādyogadharaṃ param/*
caturviṃśatiko hyeṣa rāśiḥ puruṣasaṃjñakaḥ// Śā.I.35.

[41] *prabhavo na hyanāditvādvidyate paramātmanaḥ/*
puruṣo rāśisaṃjñastu mohecchādveṣakarmajaḥ// Śā.I.53.

[42] *anādiḥ puruṣo nityo viparītastu hetujaḥ/*
sadakāraṇavannityaṃ dṛṣṭaṃ hetujamanyathā// Śā.I.59.

[43] *tadeva bhāvādagrāhyaṃ nityatvaṃ na kutaścana/*
bhāvājjñeyaṃ tadavyaktamacintyaṃ vyaktamanyathā// Śā.I.60.

[44] *vyaktamaindriyaka caiva gṛhyate tadyadindriyaiḥ/*
ato'nyat punaravyaktaṃ liṅgagrāhyamatīndriyam// Śā.I.62.

undergoes various cognitive, agentive, and deliberative states; it is what experiences illness and health. All of this happens to that complex that is bodily being.

Here too is found the text's attempt to see the notion of 'subject' in two ways: there is a way of speaking about the subject in terms of the bodily being with birth and death, but there is also the 'beginingless' subject, which is synonymous with self. We can now turn to think about the significance of begininglessness.

The main contrast is between the temporally limited bodily being ('the subject') and its self (the 'beginningless subject'), which latter has none of the natural features of the former.[45] Self is eternal, has no origin, no cause. But what does it mean to talk of the self in this way? The critical meaning of this description of the self then emerges: the description is purely formal, that is, there is no empirical content to the description. What is manifest in experience must be caused, and what is caused cannot be eternal. It is just a way of saying that the self is not what is manifest in the investigative procedures of the physician (here, as we will see in more detail later, the physician is also the epistemologist). It is beyond the physician's ken. In this—a text about what can be investigated and understood—there is a central mystery, the self that cannot be 'grasped'. Self in this sense lies outside the realm of the science of health, i.e., the symptoms that the physician handles, and whose aetiology he traces back to causes. It cannot be an object of knowledge. It is even asserted as being unthinkable (*acintyam*). It cannot be unthinkable in a literal sense, because the text precisely is attempting to think of how the self can be thought of. So it must be unthinkable in the way the natural elements (of which the human subject is constituted) are in fact thinkable. An indication of what unthinkability means here comes from the other term applied to the self, that it is 'unmanifest' (*avyakta*). The world of human beings is manifest in that it occurs in the phenomenology of those beings. Not just the material elements of the world but the feelings, judgements, emotions, and other subject-states too are manifest subjectively and (there is no suggestion of solipsism here) intersubjectively. But the self is not in the content of experience.

Then why posit it? Why try to think of that which is declared as unthinkable? We must try to answer that by starting with a different question: what is the manner in which the text seeks to grasp the self after having argued for its ungraspability? Here the *Caraka Saṃhitā* re-uses the Vaiśeṣika list of the 'signs of self' (the *ātmaliṅgas*).[46] The *Caraka Saṃhitā* lists the following signs of life (*liṅgāni jīvitaḥ*)—breathing (*prāṇāpāna*), the blinking of the eye (*nimeṣa*), the shifting of perceptual attention (*manaso gati*), movement [of attention] between the senses (*indriyāntarasaṃcāra*), mental motility (*preraṇa*) and stability (*dhāraṇa*), 'travel to another land in dreams'

[45] Reading Caraka through Cakrapāṇi, Cerulli and Brahmadathan also spot the way the text makes a distinction between the 'bodied self' and what is not, and rightly note that the physician's concern is with what is bodied: Cerulli and Brahmadathan 2009. However, they locate the dual-use in *ātman* rather than *puruṣa*. Moreover, they do not see the non-bodily subject through the terms that I argue for here.

[46] See Comba 1987: 49–50; I set aside here the controversy over whether Caraka precedes or succeeds the *Yājñavalkyasmṛti*, which lists some of these signs.

(*deśāntaragatiḥ svapne*), comprehension of [impending] death (*pañcatvagrahaṇa*), what is seen by the left eye registering (*avagama*) in the right as well,[47] desire (*icchā*), aversion (*dveṣa*), effort (*prayatna*), happiness (*sukha*), sorrow (*duḥkha*), resolution (*dhṛti*), judgement (*buddhi*), memory (*smṛti*), and the sense of 'I' (*ahaṃkāra*). These signs are not found in a dead body, which latter is just the state of the five material elements (the *mahābhūtas*). These signs of life (*liṅgāni jīvitaḥ*) are the very signs of the self that is beyond (*liṅgāni paramātmanaḥ*)(Śā.I.70–4). The question for us is how to read the text's usage of these signs, and what it means to call the self that is adverted to here as 'beyond' (*para*), and translate that as 'transcendental'.

The 'signs of self' are used in Vaiśeṣika to establish its theory of the nature of self.[48] Primarily, this is meant as a response to the Buddhist denial of an *ātman*, challenging the non-self theorist to explain these features of life without resorting to a self. The *Caraka Saṃhitā* does not have this polemical concern, so it is not putting down this list for the purpose of arguing against someone who denies commitment to self. Presumably, these philosophical passages were redacted in this form so as to mark a commitment to a larger view of human nature on the part of the physicians who were the transmitters of this text. Despite the difference in motivation, however—anti-sceptical on the part of the Vaiśeṣikas, merely expository on the part of the *Caraka Saṃhitā*—the structure of the argument appears the same. Previously, the text has already talked of a mode of investigation (*parīkṣā*) called *anumāna* (i.e., inference) (Sū.11.21–2), which it does not define as such but exemplifies. This mode relates to past, present, and future. Regarding the present and the future, the inference that there will be a tree in future from seeing seeds now is determined by having seen trees grow from seeds before. The example pertaining to the present is inferring fire from smoke, while that pertaining to the past is intercourse from pregnancy. The text is innocent of the subsequent development of the analysis of the various forms of inference in other systems. But just from the examples, we can already say that it understands inference as follows: given Y, the case is made that it is invariably correlated with X. If all concerned agreed on Y, that leads to the conclusion that X.[49] Crucially, it is granted that this correlation is possible because the correlations have been perceived before. (This leads various subsequent thinkers, with different motivations, to argue that inference reduces to perception.)

But the text recognizes that the case with the signs of the self is not the same, and so it does not invoke inference at all here. This is because the whole point is that the X (self), which it is said correlates with Y (signs of life), precisely is never perceived in the way Y is. Perception does not underpin this reasoning in the way it does inference in the strict sense of *anumāna* (regardless of whether *anumāna* is a separate 'means of knowledge' (*pramāṇa*)). As such, the resort to the signs of life bears a resemblance to

[47] This sounds like a basic grasp of binocular vision, and is a characteristically medical addition that is not found in other lists.

[48] E.g., Frauwallner 1984.

[49] Gokhale 1992: chapter 1.

the modern Western notion of a 'transcendental argument', whose strong form is that if Y is the case then it is a necessary condition that there is X; this is meant to defeat a sceptic who denies X but cannot deny Y.[50] The discussion of the difficulties with transcendental arguments has been long and complex, and usually centres on the grounds for claiming that any form of necessity links X and Y.[51] Since there is no display of such modal reasoning in *Caraka Saṃhitā*, the parallel cannot be so precise. But formulations of more 'modest' transcendental arguments do bear a resemblance to what the *Caraka Saṃhitā* is doing here. One way of looking at it is that, in keeping with its naturalistic stance, the text is saying simply that, when confronted with our experience of the living, bodily human being, it is only natural for us to believe that that human being is a self in a way that distinguishes it from the dead body.[52] It is not deliberately developing the idea of a transcendental argument by any means; but if we see what it is doing in such terms, then we can better understand its intention to find a way of delineating its medical interests through the philosophical concept of *ātman* (that was already dominant by then) without actually offering any substantive theory by itself.

Seen this way, the text's term '*paramātman*' may reasonably be translated as 'transcendental self', in the sense that it is the self that is posited as beyond experience in order to explain what we in fact experience. It is not really an issue for the physician, who is only concerned with the subject encountered in treatment. The transcendental self is the boundary of our understanding of the human being, because it is under its sign that the human being lives. The *ātman*, then, cannot be located in any direct way in relation to our bodiliness. So the *Caraka Saṃhitā* is not espousing a dualism in which it says the physician is concerned with the body but not the self. Nor, despite its naturalism, is it reductivist about the body. The self simply is not the physician's concern at all, as far as the text is concerned. But it is given as the limit of what can be said by the physician about the living body.

We will see soon how central is the text's concern for the patient's experience and self-understanding, as well as the physician's own experience of learning medicine and applying it. The *Caraka Saṃhitā* is deeply engaged in the phenomenology of illness and health. But we will have noticed that its arrival at the posit of the transcendental self is not phenomenological at all. Unlike, say, Advaita Vedānta—and as it has struck many in this regard, the phenomenological tradition following Husserl[53]—the *Caraka Saṃhitā* does not think of the transcendental self as that which is to be approached through a phenomenological reduction of experience. As we have seen, its concept is formal, and totally based on an effort to demarcate the diagnostic capacity of the

[50] Articulated in Strawson 1959: 31–58; and in his reading of Kant in Strawson 1966.

[51] Most influentially in Stroud 1968, and the huge literature thereafter.

[52] This response follows the later Strawson in Strawson 1985. See also Callanan 2011. Transcendental arguments in this 'modest' sense are therefore held to be about what we must believe and not about how things have to be.

[53] Sinha 1955; Chattopadhyaya et al. 1992. It is quite another matter as to what Husserl himself (mis) thought about Indian philosophy.

physician to observe the living human being, and point to what falls outside his purview. For Caraka, this conception of the transcendental self is wholly at the service of the bodily human being that is the focus of the medical relationship.

For this reason, the text also clarifies that this understanding of the self applies to each and every bodily being. The transcendental self is not some common stratum of all subjects; it is not the core intersubjectivity of all human beings. Inasmuch as the formal reasoning about the distinction between 'dead' and 'alive' applies to all human beings, the same posit of a self applies to each of them.

> Although self can be anywhere present, it is restricted to each its own body by sensory contact. That is why a self cannot have all sensations of all bodies.[54]
>
> It is permanently bound with the mind in accordance with bodily action. In the state of every born body, it should yet be known as limited to one born body.[55]

With this we complete our examination of how Caraka answers the 'vertical' question of what is 'beyond' the body. The body is bounded by self in the sense that its transcendental presence marks the limit of our understanding of what we can know about the human subject in relation to itself, that is, the unique perspective from which it is a subject. But while the bodily subject is made explicable by the transcendental self, bodily subjectivity is not fixed simply by the constituent elements of the material body. The body in experience is more fluid than that, and the boundaries of bodily being are fixed according to context in the *Caraka Saṃhitā*.

In order to see how the human being is understood contextually by the text, we should turn to the 'horizontal' question of its philosophical anthropology: what does the phenomenology of human health and illness say about the subjectivity of the human being in relation to its bodiliness? One answer is that that subjectivity is constituted between physician and patient, bodiliness being the field of that constitution. Another answer is that the social world of other subjects also helps form the bodily nature of that subjectivity. We shall look at these in turn.

Diagnosis: Phenomenology in-between Physician and Patient

For some decades now, scholars have been critical of the abstract model of diagnosis that approaches the patient as a biological object, while also pondering on what that critique implies.[56] But the epistemological advantages of this objective study of the

[54] *dehī sarvagato'pyātmā sve sve saṃsparśanendriye/*
sarvāḥ sarvāśrayasthāstu nātmā'to vetti vedanāḥ// Śā.I.79.

[55] *nityānubandhaṃ manasā dehakarmānupātinā/*
sarvayonigataṃ vidyādekayonāvapi sthitam// Śā.I.81.

[56] For one of the most widely cited early essays on this theme, see Engel 1977.

body can hardly be gainsaid.[57] In this critical narrative that calls for a recognition of the 'lived body'[58] in medicine, a cultural contrast is often made between traditions 'where the body is viewed as the centre of self-actualization' with its care being in the hands of 'the shaman or healer', and the modern approach to the body as a machine where, when it breaks down, it is put in the care of the doctor as 'scientist-technician', working with an objective epistemology.[59] The striking thing is that the *Caraka Saṃhitā*, as we have seen, certainly frames its undertaking in terms of human 'self-actualization', the 'pursuits' (*eṣaṇās*). At the same time, it also has a technical discourse on diagnosis that clearly includes the treatment of the patient as an epistemological object. As scholars of the *Caraka Saṃhitā* have long noted, it offers perhaps the earliest systematic taxonomy of the means of knowledge (the *pramāṇas*) that in the subsequent millennium became the common ground of epistemological debate in India.[60]

Under the discussion of the grounds for the pursuit of rebirth into the next world (which we have looked at already), four types of investigation (*caturvidhā parīkṣā*) are listed and described through how they function (rather than how they are structured):[61] the teachings of the authoritative (*āptopadeśa*), perception (*pratyakṣa*), inference (*anumāna*—which, again, we have already encountered), and reasoning (*yukti*), this last defined as 'judgement that sees things as outcomes of a synthesis of multiple causes'.[62] A slightly different version occurs in the long description of teaching, studying, and debate (*sambhāṣa*), the last extolled as the means to become a good physician, in chapter eight of the Section on Arrangements (*Vimānasthāna*). This contains types of debate and debating procedures, rhetoric, exegesis, and syntactical analysis. Included here are the causes of the obtainment (*upalabdhi*) of truth (*tattva*): perception, inference, traditional instruction, and analogy (Vi.8.33). These are brought to bear upon the patient (*ātura*), who is the 'site of practice' (*kāryadeśa*) of the physician (Vi.8.94).

The physician is the protagonist of the text, as befitting a medical compendium.

As already said, the doer is the physician. His examination [is thus]—The physician is he who heals, is expert in applying the ideas of the core teachings, and understands life in all its aspects.

[57] A phenomenological critique, which asks for a focus on the lived- rather than the machine-body, nevertheless grants to begin with that, 'Viewed as a machine, the body can be tested experimentally and blueprinted in detailed anatomical study. Furthermore, the body is revealed as susceptible to mechanical interventions. The scope of clinical possibilities thus widens commensurate with that of expanding research and technologies. As machine-like, the body can be divided into organ systems and parts to be repaired, surgically removed or technologically supplemented in relative isolation. As subject to mathematical analysis, the body reveals its true condition through laboratory values adjustable by drugs and diet'; Leder 1984: 30.

[58] I use this term in a theoretically minimalistic way, simply as the body as experienced, rather than the body as a material object. But of course, this notion, as 'Leib', has its origins in Husserl and is elaborated in a particularly influential way by Merleau-Ponty; Smith 2007.

[59] Ibid., p. 35.

[60] On approaches to the comparison and contrast, as well as the possible historical connections, between the epistemological system in the *Caraka Saṃhitā* and in the *Nyāya Sūtra*, which latter is usually seen as first systematically having propounding a common system of debate and inquiry in classical India, see Preisendanz 2009. Also, Prets 2000.

[61] Sū.11.17. [62] *buddhiḥ paśyati yā bhāvān bahukāraṇayogajān*; 25.

He should first of all be self-reflective, desirous of balancing all the constitutive elements (*dhātus*)... The following are the qualities of a physician, having which he is capable of bringing about the balance of the constitutive elements: accomplishment in the authoritative texts, experience of practice, skill, cleanliness, dexterity, possession of equipment, correctly functional sense organs, knowledge of the human constitution, and knowledge of procedures.[63]

It is clear, then, that the *Caraka Saṃhitā* is not lacking in an understanding of the systematic and objective study of the body; diagnosis is first epistemology. The interesting thing, then, is how this very epistemological framework in fact treats as intrinsic to it an intersubjective phenomenology in which the affect of illness is constituted between physician and patient. This worldview offers a contrast to what contemporary writers are concerned is the fraught relationship between the biomedical objectification of the material body and the phenomenological subjectivity of the lived body.[64] This emerges in particular in Caraka's location of the physician within a complex medical relationship.

The physician, the medication, the attendant and the patient are the fourfold matter [of the text]. They are responsible for the curing of illness, if they have the right qualities' (Sū.9.3). The activity of all four is required for 'therapeutics' or 'medical science' (*cikitsā*) (Sū.9.5).

Within this complex, the physician and the patient should have the requisite properties for a therapy to work. The four qualities of a physician are: accomplishment in medical texts (*śrute paryavadātatvaṃ*), extensive practical experience (*bahuśo dṛṣṭakarmatā*), dexterity (*dākṣyaṃ*), and purity (*śaucaṃ*) (6). The four qualities of the patient are: good memory (*smṛti*), following instructions (*nirdeśakāritvaṃ*), courage (*abhīrutvaṃ*), and being informative (*jñāpakatvaṃ*) (9).[65] The patient's role in a sense is symmetrical to the physician's when it comes to the emergence of the therapy as a whole, which is striking given the recognizable imbalance of epistemic and institutional power inherent in the very concept of a medical science.

In short, the patient's capacities as a living presence are inherently part of the practices with which Caraka is concerned. Although the presentation of diagnostic epistemology appears to treat the patient as an object, the *Caraka Saṃhitā*'s description of what happens in diagnosis reveals instead a much more complex situation: the patient's whole, bodily, living presence structures the physician's practice, which in turn shapes that bodily self-presence by interpreting its meaning in terms of health

[63] *kāraṇaṃ bhiṣagityuktamagre. tasya parīkṣā—bhiṣaṅmām yo bhiṣajyati yaḥ sūtrārthaprayogakuśalaḥ yasya cāyuḥ sarvatā viditaṃ yathāvat. sa ca sarvadhātusāmyaṃ cikīrṣannātmānamevāditaḥ... tatreme bhiṣagguṇā yairupapanno bhiṣagdhātusāmyābhinirvartane samartho bhavatiḥ tadyathā paryavadātaśrutatā paridṛṣṭakarmatā, dākṣyaṃ śaucaṃ jitahastatopakaraṇavattā sarvendriyopapannatā prakṛtijñatā pratipattijñatā ceti.* Vi.8.86.

[64] For an exemplary recent expression of the problem, see Vogt et al. 2014. Their conclusion is that systems medicine, despite being patient-centred, still cannot account for value and interaction between humans, and the search must continue.

[65] For a vivid account of the continued significance attached to the patient's description of the experience of illness into the early twentieth century, see Zimmermann 2006: 'The physician listened "quietly and attentively" to what the patient had to say' (no page numbering).

and illness. We can see this in an extended passage in the chapter on the understanding of the specific characteristics of diseases (*rogaviśeṣavijñāna*), chapter four of the Section on Arrangements, on what is to be known by inference (*anumānajñeya*) in the specific (*bhūyas*) sense of the patient's contribution to the inquiry. Of course, observation is required on the part of the physician, for that is the core of diagnosis. But we also find that the efficacy of diagnostic observation itself depends on agentive presentation by the patient of his own nature.

The factors that are listed as inferable, and the bases on which they are inferred range across different dimensions of the patient's subjectivity (which is bodily in the extend naturalistic sense of the term we have already explored). This rich and suggestive list includes the following (Vi.4.8): strength can be inferred from the capacity to exercise (*balaṃ vyāyāmaśaktyā*); hearing, etc. from the grasping the relevant object, like sound (*śrotrādīni śabdārthagrahaṇena*); mind from fidelity to its objects (*mano'rthāvyabhicaraṇena*); understanding from intentional performance (*vijñānaṃ vyavasāyena*); passion from sexual intercourse (*rajaḥ saṅgena*); perplexity from lack of understanding (*mohamavijñānena*); anger from vengefulness (*krodhamabhidroheṇa*); sadness from depression (*śokaṃ dainyena*); excitement from gladness (*harṣamāmodena*); pleasure from satisfaction (*prītiṃ toṣeṇa*); fear from unease/anxiety (*bhayaṃ viṣādena*); courage from ease/composure (*dhairyamaviṣādena*); vigour from initiative (*vīryamutthānena*); confidence from intention (*śraddhābhiprāyeṇa*); recognition from recollection of name (*saṃjñāṃ nāmagraheṇa*); shame from embarrassment (*hriyamapatraṇena*); diseases with latent symptoms (literally, concealed signs) from [what turn out to be] suitable and unsuitable therapies (*gūḍaliṅgaṃ vyādhimupaśayānupaśayābhyāṃ*).

It is important to note that these and other inferential correlations are made in the same list. It is not as if the *Caraka Saṃhitā* lacks the analytic capacity to isolate different aspects of the patient in front of the physician: we have seen that its philosophical anthropology already has a detailed understanding of material constituents of bodily being.[66] But it is striking that what might seem, in a different conceptual scheme, very different areas of being human and of medical inquiry present themselves within the same framework. That framework, I have already argued, is that of the human subject conceived as bodily being, liberally conceived. This is a diagnostic epistemology that brings together observation, inference, judgement, and learning, but it can itself function only through the engagement of the patient with the physician.[67] There is no metaphysical language to pull apart what makes the subject and what makes the subject's body; instead, Caraka sees the subject just as bodily being.[68]

[66] I should make clear that I am not saying that the text displays a grasp of anatomy and physiology that would be recognized in any simple way by 'modern' medicine. But it clearly has a grasp of the conceptual need to think of the patient in broadly naturalistic terms, as consisting of systematically explicable parts.

[67] It has been argued by medical philosophers that the epistemology of modern medicine, which combines description and normative judgement, is insufficient to address the doctor–patient relationship; Kushf 2013.

[68] How to talk about the patient as the bodily being continues to vex contemporary medical philosophy. For a marshalling of various arguments that medical thought continues to be inescapably dualistic,

The organic connections between different aspects of human subjectivity evident in this list show how the patient's living presence is the locus of the physician's examination. What we therefore have is not a way of combining two different epistemic approaches, namely, knowledge of the disease and of the sick person.[69] Instead, we have a worldview in which there cannot be knowledge of the disease **without** the knowledge of the person—or to be more precise, the self-disclosure of the person. If the patient tells the physician how he or she lives, the latter can enrich the diagnostic process with that knowledge, since there is an intimate connection between how one lives and one's afflictions. The very nature of what is required for diagnosis demonstrates that it happens in the phenomenological giving, taking, and mutual making between physician and patient. The presence of the patient is not that of a strictly physical object whose malfunctioning becomes the focus of medical attention. Instead, there is a subjective presence whose bodiliness is a matter of muscular exertion but also of cognitive focus, imbalances in the three bases of maladies (*doṣas*—wind, bile, and phlegm) but also display of character, acknowledgement of private facts together with sensitivity to social conduct and epistemic capacity, as well as physiological response to medication.

By the very nature of what it is to be a patient, then, the subject is brought into intersubjectivity. What it is to be a patient is both communicated by the patient to the physician and, through diagnosis, made meaningful to himself and the patient by the physician. In the context of therapy, the *Caraka Saṃhitā* demonstrates that it thinks of the human subject as a bodily presence that is constantly negotiated by the offering, reception, and reworking of its phenomenology. As I have said before, this is not some radical revisionary error-theory, which holds that our normal theory of human subjectivity is wrong, and that we ought to strive to reach some deeper truth. It is just that Caraka's worldview brings to our attention a different way of looking at the human being in the medical encounter. It does not involve what critics argue characterizes the dominant contemporary discourse, where the physician's need to treat the patient as objective body in diagnosis conflicts with the patient's call to be treated as a phenomenological subject of feelings, fears, and hopes.

An influential study of contemporary medicine[70] argues that it is structured by the dichotomy of a physician's world and a patient's world, the former that of 'theoretical disease constructs'[71] and the latter that of 'immediacy in the context of the world of

in thinking of a body with a mind in it, see Mehta 2011. For an equally vigorous argument that the reason modern medicine is unable to address the doctor–patient relationship (rather than just the patient's disease) is physicalism, Whatley 2014.

[69] For an eloquent plea for this combination, within the development of modern medicine and its focus on 'disease' and 'body' rather than 'person'—' [T]the four tasks of the clinician—diagnosing, seeking cause, treating, and prognosticating—cannot be accomplished in the absence of knowledge about both the disease and the sick person'—see Cassell 2004.

[70] Toombs 1987. (These ideas amongst others are developed in greater detail in Toombs 1992.)

[71] Toombs 1987, p. 229.

everyday life'.[72] Toombs suggests that the focus should be on the 'eiditic' characteristics of illness, that is, 'those that are essential to the thing-itself', which 'transcend the peculiarities and particularities of different disease states and constitute the meaning of illness-as-lived'. This alone can make for a shared world of meaning between physician and patient: so there will be 'not only an understanding of illness in terms of clinically definable disease states, but also an understanding in terms of the existential predicament of the patient'.[73] Our exploration of Caraka has shown precisely that diagnosis, treatment, and the discipline required for health (and the experience of wellness) are always and already a shared world of meaning. Diagnosis itself involves defining disease (in howsoever inadequate or mistaken a manner in the light of contemporary knowledge) through not only (what we can justifiably call) clinical data but also the 'existential predicament' of the patient. The *Caraka Saṃhitā* does not take recourse in anything like an eiditic approach, but then it does not need to since it conceptualizes the medical encounter in a way that precludes the problem.

It is reasonable to think that a philosophical approach to the patient as human subject ought to preserve the autonomy of the patient and the training of the physician, and Caraka nowhere suggests that there are fewer than two subjects involved in the therapeutic encounter. So to that extent there must be a 'fusion of horizons', as Frederik Svenaeus suggests, invoking Gadamer.[74] This should be seen as an overlap of understanding between the two distinct presences of patient and physician. But because the *Caraka Saṃhitā* does not have the particular history of modernity—and modern medicine—against which to situate itself, it does not see that fusion as an agonistic one, in which the clinical objectivity of disease classification is the contribution of the physician, while the existential predicament of illness is the contribution of the patient, the two somehow needing to be brought together through a radical change of perspective on the part of the former. What we see in Caraka is that while there are indeed distinct subjects involved, the therapeutic encounter is constitutively intersubjective. Diagnosis is always already the constitution of meaning in-between physician and patient.

If the bodily subject (the patient) is not to be understood just as a conglomerate of material entities but as a phenomenology-possessing being, with that phenomenology hermeneutically constituted between subjects (the patient and the physician), then we can see why the *Caraka Saṃhitā* worldview implies that bodiliness is fluid, and the subject is not limited to some self-evident material ambit.

The Well Body: The Subject and Virtuous Life

We have now looked at one of the two answers in the *Caraka Saṃhitā* to the 'horizontal' question of what other than the material body makes for the bodiliness of the human being, namely, the diagnostic intersubjectivity between patient and physician. The text also gives another answer: the wider world of subjects, specifically through

72 Ibid., p. 228. 73 Ibid., pp. 234–5. 74 Svenaeus 2000.

the practices of social discipline. Now, the text talks mainly of what it is to live well, so that the subject can avoid being a patient. We should remember that it does not make the contemporary distinction between the 'essentially psycho-social' dichotomy of wellness/illness as how the human being feels, and healthy/diseased, which 'has to do with physical and psychological dysfunction and function' and concerns how the human being is.[75] But we have already seen that Caraka cares about both sickness and illness, that is, about both disease and how it is experienced by the patient. The obverse of this care is that it prescribes what is required for both health and wellness. This is obvious in the fact that it talks about how to avoid diseases as well as how to live well. With this point in mind, we can invoke a widely quoted dictum of Gadamer's as a good contemporary approximation of the *Caraka Saṃhitā*'s formulae for health and wellness: 'Health is not a condition that one introspectively feels in oneself. Rather, it is a condition of being involved, of being in the world, of being together with one's fellow human beings, of active and rewarding engagement in one's everyday tasks.'[76]

The argument that the *Caraka Saṃhitā* conceives of the human being's bodiliness as also determined through the social world of others is most evident in the chapter ostensibly on the sense organs. In this chapter, first there is a relatively brief and schematic outline of the sensory system—five senses, their material constituents (*indriyadravya*), the five organs—and the mind (as the operative base element (*ceṣṭāpratyayabhūta*)) in *Sūtrasthāna* 8.3–14. The senses as well as the mind can have malfunction (*vikṛti*) through overuse (*atiyoga*), underuse (*ayoga*) or misuse (*mithyāyoga*), and damage (*upaghāta*) happens to the mental faculty (*buddhi*); whereas, if there is suitable use (*sāmarthyayoga*), then normal or original function (*prakṛti*) is regained and 'mental faculty becomes full' (*buddhimāpyāyati*) again (15–16). Someone who seeks wellness, that is, his own benefit (*ātmahita*), can achieve health (*āryogya*) and control of the senses (*indriyavijaya*) simultaneously through following certain practices (17–18). For Caraka, wellness is the function of the organic body and the agentive subject, manifested in an elaborate discipline of normative conduct.

The most important articulation of this ecological conception of the human being is through the ritualized life by which a skein of relationships is woven between what it is to be to one self and what it is to be with others: one should honour (*arcana*) the deities, cows, Brahmins, teachers, the elderly, and the sages; perform the daily rituals of the twice-born; wash one's feet; cut hair, shave and cut nails three times a week; offer oblations. But this ritualization of daily life takes on a more general sense of bodily propriety: one should take care to smell good (by wearing perfume) and auspicious (by carrying the right herbs), and oil and comb one's hair. This then extends to social obligation: the elite male must offer the ritual ball of food (*piṇḍa*) to the ancestors, and be charitable. Bodily deportment too is an important aspect of this social discipline—he must be well-dressed, cover the head with turbaned cloth, carry an umbrella (*catra*) and cane (*daṇḍa*), and look modestly only six feet ahead. But social enworldment is

[75] Baker 1997: 398. Baker states that this is a 'common distinction'. [76] Gadamer 1996.

also shown to include an emotionally literate engagement with others: one should be kindly to all creatures, pacify the angry (*kruddhānāmanunetā*), calm the frightened (*bhītānāmāśvāsayitā*), and protect the needy (*dīnānāmabhyupapattā*) (18). Repeatedly, this proper life is defined through a code of comportment that has elements of both virtuous sensitivity and social normativity: for example, one should not lie, or disclose either ones own defects or the secrets of others; but also, to pick some from a long list, one should not ride dangerously, sit on a high seat, walk on uneven mountain slopes, or bathe in a turbulent river. And then again, politesse is vital: amongst relatively less arcane strictures, there should be no yawning, sneezing, or laughing without covering one's mouth; one should not go out without touching the feet of elders or teachers (19).

The relevant philosophical point is not the historically narrow and elaborate focus on the life of the elite male whose social and gendered identity at once qualifies him for such strictures and which is reciprocally maintained only through adherence to them. (We need but think of Caraka's contemporaries in imperial Rome and its turbulent province of Judea, in Parthian Persia and in Han China, to resist the temptation to make a special case of classical India.) Rather, it is the more generalizable point that what we now call 'life-style'—and not just impeccable moral guidelines—is folded into the conception of wellness, so that continual attention to the whole of our subjectivity is espoused as the model of the well life by Caraka.[77] It would, then, not be so puzzling to Carakan physicians that being able to resist sensory immersion in computer games or pornographic websites, and wearing sensible shoes, showering regularly, donating to charities, and taking time to talk to the elderly all seem to matter to the constitution of our sense of ourselves as being well. It should also be noted that the text's motivation for laying down these strictures is medical: it is health that is at the heart of the matter. As Dominik Wujastik has pointed out, where there is a need for therapy that might flout social discipline—most notably, eating particular meats as part of a treatment—Caraka (and the subsequent āyurvedic tradition) firmly, and often without any self-justifying explanation, opts for the requirements of health.[78]

[77] It has been pointed out by Foucault, regarding the very different context of ancient Greece, that in Plato's *Alcibiades*, there is the first Western expression of the thought that one should 'take care of oneself' (*epimelesthai sautou*). In Plato, the discussion of how one should take care of oneself tends to centre on the famous principle, 'Know yourself' (*gnothi sauton*), which in modern Western thought, Foucault argues, has eclipsed the former idea. But long before modernity, half a millennium after Plato in the Rome of Seneca, Plutarch, Epicetus, and the like, he says, Plato's 'pedagogical model' for preparation for political life was replaced by a 'medical model'; so care for the self was not learning as a student but a constant tending of oneself throughout life; Foucault 1998: 16–49. Of course, there were many changes in these different stages and texts (not to mention the distinctive directions in which early Christian thought took these ideas), concerning the understanding of 'self', as reflexivity ('auto' or 'the same', cognate with the use of '*ātman*' as reflexive pronoun), as body, and as soul. But this quick comparative look helps us see that the *Caraka Saṃhitā* too has its own distinctive 'medical' approach, literally and metaphorically: to have ultimate goals requires one to know oneself, and to know oneself is to care for oneself throughout life. We look more closely and critically at this issue in chapter 3, when studying Buddhaghosa's contemplative practices in the *Visuddhimagga*.

[78] Wujastyk 2004: 833–6.

I will conclude this section with a striking illustration of Caraka's holism: the case of 'urges' (*vegāḥ*) and their multidimensionality. Physiological urges are folded into the discipline of deportment, and then urges are also interpreted as the factors that need to be controlled in virtuous conduct. The Chapter on Non-suppression of Urges starts with a list of urges that should not be suppressed, and goes on to look at the illnesses caused if they are, and the treatment for those illnesses. One should not suppress the natural urges related to urine or faeces, semen, wind, nausea, or sneezing, clearing the throat, or yawning; nor the urgings of hunger, thirst, tears, sleep, or panting induced by exertion (Sū 7.3–4). An example where the absence of control leads to a medical problem, and where the treatment for it is an unexpected prescription of a civilized environment, concerns the urge to shed tears.

Suppression of tears leads to rhinitis, eye disease, ailments in the chest, loss of appetite, and dizziness. In such cases, sleep, wine and pleasant conversation are helpful.[79]

So the response to physiological problems involves interventions that are not themselves directed at the physical state that is the sickness.

Urges also include different aspects of behaviour by which the subject is located in the social environment. This is clear when the *Caraka Saṃhitā* talks about urges that should in fact be suppressed, as these mostly pertain to the requisites for a virtuous life.

Someone who desires what is good for him both here and in the hereafter should suppress the urges towards impetuous and dishonourable deeds of mind, speech and body. The intelligent person suppresses the urges of greed, grief, fear, fury, pride, shamelessness, envy, and excessive passion, as well as covetousness. One should suppress any urge that might arise to speak extremely harshly, critically, falsely, or inappropriately. One should suppress urges which involve causing bodily harm to another person, such as rape, robbery or injury.[80]

Caraka can clearly make an analytic distinction between 'mind' and 'body', provided we remember what is meant by them in the text, especially 'body' (here, *kāya*, often used to indicate the assemblage or compositional nature of the body). But the important point to note is the ecological perspective of the patient that is evident in the way the concept of the 'urges' structures subjectivity across what—on a different set of metaphysical intuitions—might seem to be the inner/outer, physical/mental, personal/social divides. The urge, in its expression and its suppression, its impact and consequences, is a phenomenological reflex; and while it is possible to say on a specific reading of 'body' as material locus that some urges are to do with the body and others are not, the salience of the 'urge' in a wider sense is that it opens up bodily subjectivity beyond the boundaries of that material locus. In offering a prescription for health,

[79] *pratiśyāyo'kṣirogaśca hṛdrogaścārucirbhramaḥ/vāṣpanigrahaṇāttatra svapno madyaṃ priyāḥ kathā*//Sū 7.22.

[80] *imāṃstu dhārayedvegān hitārthī pretya ceha ca/sāhasānāmaśastānāṃ manovākkāyakarmaṇām// lobhaśokabhayakrodhamānavegān vidhārayet/nairlajjyerṣyātirāgāṇāmabhidhyāyāśca buddhimān// puruṣasyātimātrasya sūcakasyānṛtasya ca/vākyasyākālayuktasya dhārayedvegamutthitam//dehapravṛttiryā kācidvidyate parapīḍayā/strībhogasteyarhisādyā tasyāvegānvidhārayet*//Sū.7.26–9.

Caraka provides us with a reading of the human subject as one whose bodily presence, even while having objective states available to the physician's gaze, is yet continually inflected by engagement with and reciprocal responses from the world of other living subjects. Wellness consists in a meaningful situatedness in that world.

The Body in a Medical Version of Ecological Phenomenology

We find, then, these elements to the *Caraka Saṃhitā*'s thematization of the human being. What motivates medicine is the depiction of the human condition as one characterized by suffering and an agentive direction towards overarching goals; the physician strives to treat that suffering, and to establish such wellbeing as permits those goals to be sought productively. The human being who is thus the subject of the ideal of wellbeing is objectively understood through a compositional account in which mind, intellect, and the subjective dimensions of being are approached functionally through constituents of a bodily individual. A self is acknowledged, but only as the horizon of the physician's understanding, a transcendental presence that permits what is observable about life but not itself established within the philosophical anthropology that motivates medicine. The text wants to deal with subjectivity—phenomenological being—through the extended bodily functions of sensations, thought, judgement, etc., even while acknowledging that such functions require more than the various natural elements of the person, namely, the self that is postulated as present but beyond the purview of medical attention. While the text routinely talks about 'body' also in a narrower, physiological sense in contrast to 'mind', its philosophical understanding of the patient as the 'ordinary person' consists in a liberal view of bodiliness, one that vertically integrates the material aspects of physiology with the subjective dimensions—evident in the experience of illness—given through the functions of mind and intellect.

This compositional, 'soft' naturalism of the patient as bodily being is then implicitly extended out, horizontally as it were, from the material limits of body into a dynamic, interactive phenomenological environment with the physician and others. This is brought out in its expression of a range of medical practices, from diagnosis to treatment of illness, as well as in regimes of health.

Altogether, this view of the bodily human being is searchingly analytic yet deeply holistic; it is this synthetic vision that can be called an ecological phenomenology. Indeed, only by adopting the methodological stance of ecological phenomenology can we not only resist the temptation to see the different aspects of Caraka's text as contradictory, but can also conclude that it provides a radical alternative to many contemporary efforts to suture the dehiscence of dualisms in modern Western philosophy of medicine.

Anthony Cerulli calls our attention to Francis Zimmermann's highly original work[81] on 'ayurvedic thinking about the body as but one fluid part of a universal stream of

[81] In particular: Zimmerman 1979, Zimmermann 1987, Zimmermann 2004.

being'.[82] But Cerulli also cautions us that we should not move 'too quickly away from the specifics of internal somatic associations and organization'. Āyurveda has homologues between body and cosmos, and these 'speak to the potential effects of people's environments on their diet and routines, maintenance of bodily integrity, and abilities to achieve health'. But Cerulli argues that we should respond to Zimmermann's famous dictum that in *āyurveda* there is no 'real anatomy'[83] as opposed to fluid physiological signs—'only an economy'[84]—by noting that this does not 'mean that Āyurveda lacks focus on somatic substance or anatomy'. His interpretation of Zimmermann leads him to argue that we have to 'understand the tradition's own method for explaining the human body, in theory and in practice, as a "closed" and autonomous physiologic unit as well as a system of health and disease "open" to the influences of the environment'.[85] He characterizes the classical Indian medical authors' thinking of the body as 'a flow between body and context—season, diet, land, society, religion—that signals a physiology larger than an individual's bodily functioning'.[86] Although Cerulli's method (an elegant investigation of the role of narrative in āyurvedic explanation) has a very different orientation, his general plea nevertheless resonates with Thomas Fuchs' appeal (in the specific context of contemporary psychiatry) for an ecological view that regards 'mind and world, as well as body and environment, as mutually overlapping, or as poles of unity'.[87] Clearly, there is much worth to this broad ecological view of the human being as existing in a web of interconnections, and one that is emerging cross-culturally as a paradigm for medicine.

To conclude, we can go back to the paradigm of an ecological phenomenology that was outlined in the Introduction, and suggest how this text is read in accordance with it. To begin with, we must keep in mind that contemporary articulations of an ecological paradigm respond either explicitly or implicitly to a dominant biomedical discourse, which is largely reductionist in its conception of the human being as an individuated object with specific biological functions, but which also continues to talk of a ghostly 'mind' that is held over from problematic dualist intuition. This discourse also tends to be insensitive to the systemic nature of affect, and the consequent importance of the environment for the patient. The notion of an ecological approach then has to be laid out in order to argue that there are in fact more complex interconnections than granted in the folk metaphysics of biomedicine.

But as we have seen, the *Caraka Saṃhitā* occupies a very different place in the cultural history of ideas of humanity. It demonstrates a sharply analytic capacity to parse human nature and the human situation, and therefore has the conceptual resources to talk about constituent aspects of the human subject, unlike many shamanistic cultures of practice (including in India itself). At the same time, it did not have to grapple with

[82] Cerulli 2012: 45.

[83] 'In saying there is no "real anatomy" in Āyerveda, Zimmermann refers specifically to the biomedical view that anatomy is a science of representing the shape and structure of an organism and its parts'; ibid., p. 43.

[84] Zimmermann 1979: 15.

[85] Cerulli 2012: 47.

[86] Ibid., p. 42.

[87] Fuchs 2005.

the specific and sustained challenge of the Cartesian question of human nature faced in modernity, which I explored in more detail in the Introduction. So the text does not start with facing the task of reworking the language of distinct and separate mind, body, and world into a theory of how they are in fact mutually implicated; and in consequence, it already and always works with an ecological view of the human subject. It is comparable to contemporary calls to an ecological view, but with an alternative aetiology. I hope that the textual material we have read offers a compelling enough case for this claim.

This way of looking at the *Caraka Saṃhitā*'s treatment of its bodily subject offers us an alternative to the terminology of 'embodiment', with its uneasy dependence on a dualist vocabulary of a human subject and its body, without letting its naturalistic treatment of the human subject becoming reductive. What we have is a different approach to our intuitions about ourselves, permitting movement between different saliences in our complex sense of ourselves as autonomous beings who are yet co-constituted with others, as material entities who also have permeable surfaces of experience, as unique sufferers whose suffering is nevertheless shared with and mitigated by others. It is far from the case that the *Caraka Saṃhitā* offers a radical revision of our ordinary experience; in fact it is wholly concerned with what we are in our daily lives. But because it has a conceptual vocabulary so very removed from the dominant language of our times, it helps us to ponder the question of whether and how we can reconsider ways to talk about ourselves as healthy or ill, given the jumble of intuitions we have about our bodiliness.

In the *Caraka Saṃhitā* we see a striking way to handle the relationship between the fluid generality of bodily being and the specificity of that being's undergoing of illness and wellness. To slightly rework Cerulli's formulation in terms of my exegesis, we should see Caraka's multiple articulations of subjectivity not as a mediation between two explanatory poles whose polarity (or duality) must be overcome, but as part of an ecology in which the very specific subjectivity that each of us experiences within a materially located bodily limit ('idiopathically')—the 'closed' human being—is also an element of the way that bodiliness and its subjectivity is constituted generally in a shared—'open'—phenomenological world.

Caraka could have collapsed the idea of body to material constituents either by holding to a strict, i.e., materialist, naturalism, or by taking *ātman* to be a separate entity that resides in the body (thus being 'embodied'). In either case, the conception of body would have been determined by what was contained under the surface of the skin (although, perhaps, with relevant prosthetic extensions). But I have argued that, firstly, the text's naturalism is liberal in including various phenomenal and other subjective states within bodiliness and that, secondly, the concept of self is transcendental, strictly just the explanatory limit of subjectivity. As such, the body is the locus of subjectivity, and therefore not just materially constituted, but formed through its phenomenological states. Thirdly, phenomenology itself is intersubjective in the sense that its content is constantly mediated and constituted through the shared world of subjects—patient, physician, society.

This is where the specific notion of an ecological phenomenology comes in. As it will have been noticed, my reading of the *Caraka Saṃhitā* does not find a master narrative of subjectivity, a specific metaphysics of the human subject and phenomenological content. Instead, at different points and for different purposes, the text articulates ways of dealing with the question of the bodily subject, in what its phenomenology consists, and how it is constituted. But this does not mean that there is just a collection of incompatible quasi-theories spread across the text; each such account does relate to the others, the whole permitting a view of the Carakan understanding of the human being to emerge. My reading is that not only must we see the *Caraka Saṃhitā* as talking about the human subject ecologically, but also that it exemplifies a particular way of considering the subject, which we have called an ecological phenomenology. It is possible to focus on the access a human subject has to pain or an emotion or motive, and consider in that context an inner/outer distinction to apply to the delineation of that subjective state; we can talk of what is transparent to oneself but not to others. It is also possible to look at that subject, and still use the inner/outer distinction but in the opposite way: states can be opaque to a patient who has them, but not to the physician (say, a psychiatrist). But if we look back at the emergence of diagnostic meaning in the physician's inferences from the patient's self-disclosure, we can think of the relevant phenomenological states as mutually constituted, in-between subjects in a way that makes the inner–outer distinction harder to make sense of. And yet again, when considering the social construction of a life of wellbeing, the experience of virtuous conduct is radically dispersed across subjects, so that only through social cognition and emotion can we make sense of how a particular subject may experience the well life.

A tenacious pragmatism sees the *Caraka Saṃhitā* work with shifting conceptions of the bodily subject so long as the teleology of health and wellness is always clear, so that each conception adverts to another aspect of the interactive whole that is the ecology of the bodily human being. The method must be suitable to what is studied, and the study of subjectivity in this text therefore follows different accounts of that subjectivity. In future chapters, we will see other ways and contexts in which classical Indian traditions destabilize the nature, constitution, and boundaries of the human as bodily being.

> Here is grounded action and its fruit, and right cognition. Here too, delusion, happiness, sorrow, life, death and ownership. One who knows this in truth knows the end and the beginning, continuity, therapy, and whatever else is worth knowing.[88]

[88] *atra karma phalaṃ cātra jñānaṃ cātra pratiṣṭhitam/atra mohaḥ sukhaṃ duḥkhaṃ jīvitaṃ maraṇaṃ svatā// evaṃ yo veda tattvena sa veda pralayodayau/pāraṃparyaṃ cikitsāṃ ca jñātavyaṃ yacca kiṃcana//*Śā.I.37–8.

2

The Gendered Body

The Dialogue of Sulabhā and Janaka, *Mahābhārata*, *Śāntiparvan* chapter 308

A Narrative on Gendered Phenomenology

This chapter draws attention to the relationship between (i) a narrative that demonstrates how gender is always already constructed in phenomenology; and therefore structures the bodily self-presence of the woman (ascetic), and (ii) the content of that woman ascetic's speech that deliberately develops an account of her situation in which gender is put within an emancipatory phenomenological project. At the intersection of these trajectories is the bodily presence of Sulabhā, the woman ascetic (who has renounced all ties with the social world).[1] In this didactic episode within the great Sanskrit composition, the *Mahābhārata*, we see a subtle and sympathetic rendition of the condition under which the human being who is a woman responds radically to finding her bodiliness already determined for her. I do not try to undertake the unwise task of delineating a theory of gender from these materials, both because of the historically complex nature of the text and the precarious hermeneutic position I am in as its male reader.

I should also make clear that the teachings of Sulabhā are not in themselves proto-feminist, if for feminist thought we require there to be an explicit engagement with the condition of women, and an explicit critique of the masculinist bias of existing philosophical positions articulated by men (that is to say, the bias by which the human condition is delineated by a man, marking him out as the normative human being). However, I do want to think through some of the ideas in play in both the narrative frame and the philosophical content of this episode, which offers as much subtlety over gender as one could possibly expect in texts produced in the masculinist paradigms of the classical world (Indian or Chinese or Western).

I will first outline the episode in its larger context, and then introduce the way I am going to read it through the person of Sulabhā. Thereafter, the chapter will follow the narrative sequence of the episode, starting with the circumstances and nature of Sulabhā's engagement with King Janaka; Janaka's justification for his own spiritual claims,

[1] My thanks to Jessica Frazier for first discussing the Sulabhā episode with me in the early stages of my thinking about gender and bodiliness.

and his criticism of Sulabhā; and then Sulabhā's response, consisting broadly of four 'movements', each a different consideration of the intersection of bodily being, gender, and the content and expression of freedom. Together, these arguments form a coherent whole, certainly in the minimal sense that they are not inconsistent with each other, although each might be relevant in somewhat different areas of contemporary interest. But, while my intention is certainly to orient these arguments to those relevant contemporary discussions, the coherence of the arguments consists precisely in the unique way in which they are held together. As I said in the Introduction, this is the methodological outlook of ecological phenomenology: depending on aspect and salience, the condition of being human is read in a particular way. There are then many ways of reading what it is to undergo being human, and their different depictions of being human should not be thought of as a single incoherent ontology but rather as a set of possible phenomenologies.

Furthermore, ecological phenomenology as a perspective on human experience is intrinsically consonant with the insights that have emerged from feminist thought: on how the whole, dynamic environment of physical functions and their interpretation, social norms and their negotiation, self-perception and its consequences for agency, all shape how women are to themselves. In her astute, groundbreaking deflection of Merleau-Ponty's phenomenology into the study of women in sexist society, Iris Young wrote, 'The modalities of feminine bodily comportment, motility, and spatiality which I have described here are, I claim, common to the existence of women in contemporary society to one degree or another. They have their source, however, in neither anatomy nor physiology, and certainly not in a mysterious feminine "essence." Rather, they have their source in the particular *situation* of women as conditioned by their sexist oppression in contemporary society.'[2] The distinctions between body and subjectivity that she drew were tied to Merleau-Ponty's earlier formulation of phenomenology in *Phenomenology of Perception*,[3] and I argue in this book that this necessarily post-Cartesian distinction is never articulated in the quite different intellectual circumstances of classical India. Nevertheless, Young's development of Merleau-Ponty led her to specify the situating of experience and activity within a set of environmental affects, and hers is a striking example of feminist phenomenology that is ecological in all but name.

In general, feminist thought has been marked by the awareness that there is a constant interplay between three vectors of affect. One is the set of normative forces that determine, from before any self-consciousness arises, what it is for a person to be woman (or it could be said, marked in some gender-specific way as female; I do not seek here to defend any particular vocabulary). Another is the intentional drive and

[2] Young 1980: 152.

[3] Thus, she says, '[O]nce we take the locus of subjectivity and transcendence to be the lived body rather than pure consciousness, all transcendence is ambiguous because the body as natural and material is immanence' (Young 1980: 145). That instinctive, intrinsic distinction between consciousness and materiality—even when it is sought to be overcome—is exactly what I will argue is irrelevant in the text studied here.

expression of agency by which these norms are met (negotiated, resisted, reworked). And between these two is the modality of self-consciousness—in bodily awareness, introspection, comportment, interpretation of emotion, etc. In Sulabhā we will see all this: how she is taken as a woman and a renouncer, how she shows her agency, and her/the text's presentation of the nature of experience in between normative restriction and agentive freedom. Ecological phenomenology names this whole situation: what is undergone, decided, acted out, received, and interpreted (by the person, by her interlocutor, by the narrator, and by the reader).

The Story and Its Possibilities

As is explained crisply by James Fitzgerald in his introduction to his classic translation of this episode, upon which I rely,[4] the outer frame is the teachings given by Bhīṣma to Yudhiṣṭhira. Bhīṣma was the prince who long ago took the vow—terrible for a warrior—of chastity, in order to reassure his father's new wife that he would not contest the line of succession going to her son. It is the grandsons of Bhīṣma's step-brother who are on opposite sides of the great war. Bhīṣma, the great-uncle of the warring cousins, fights on the side of the Kaurava brothers because their father is the reigning king and therefore his legitimate ruler; but his fondness is for the Pāṇḍava brothers (whose dead father had a prior claim to the throne). At the time of taking his extraordinary vow, he was given the boon of being able to die at a time of his own choosing, making him invulnerable. He kept his vow even in the morally dubious circumstance in which, after he had abducted three sisters to marry his step-brother but one was left (for complex reasons) unmarried and therefore bereft, he refused to marry her in order to save her honour. She killed herself after vowing to avenge herself in her next life.[5] Reborn a woman (Śikhaṇḍinī), she nevertheless performed penances and exchanged her sex with a forest spirit, so that as a man s/he could bring about Bhīṣma's death. In the great war, the warrior who had been a woman (although apparently not remembering the previous birth which motivated subsequent events) attacked Bhiṣma; but Bhīṣma (who knew Śikhaṇḍin was born a woman, and somehow knew too that he had been a woman in the previous birth as well) would not retaliate because he considered his attacker to still be a woman. Using the now-male warrior (Śikhaṇḍin) as a shield, the greatest of the Pāṇḍava brothers, Arjuna, overwhelmed Bhīṣma with his arrows. Resting on a bed of the arrows which had been shot into him, he prepared for death. In the period after the war, which the Pāṇḍava brothers won at immeasurable cost, Bhīṣma instructed the eldest brother and now king, Yudhiṣṭhira on a wide variety of issues.

[4] I have almost entirely adhered to Fitzgerald's probing and careful translation: Fitzgerald 2003. However, especially on specific philosophical terminology, I have on occasion made my own adaptation. For text: *Mahābhārata, Śāntiparvan*. 1999 Electronic text, Bhandarkar Oriental Research Institute, Pune, India. Text entered by Muneo Tokunaga et al., revised by John Smith. http://gretil.sub.uni-goettingen.de/gretil/1_sanskr/2_epic/mbh/mbh_12_u.htm (last accessed 22 January 2018).

[5] See also Chakravarti, n.d.

This story—the inner narrative frame—that he tells Yudhiṣṭhira is part of a response to the latter's question as to whether it is possible to gain transcendence—formally, the metaphysical freedom from the immanence of the human condition—while remaining a king, or more generally, while remaining a householder who performs ritual, domestic, and social actions. This idea, called the discipline of action (*karmayoga*), contests the view that such ultimate freedom can only be attained once all engaged activity has been renounced and the renouncer steps outside the social domain.

More study is required to develop on previous analyses of the androgyny of Śikhaṇḍin,[6] but I outline the context of the outer narrative frame simply to draw attention to—albeit without being able to develop further here—the complexity surrounding Bhīṣma: both his extraordinary withdrawal from sexual life and his deliberate courting of death through a particular interpretation of the aetiology of gender. It does not seem an accident that it is this strange warrior in whose mouth is put the most strikingly supportive and unambiguous narrative of a woman's autonomy in the *Mahābhārata*.

The inner narrative frame is given by Bhīṣma's story of the encounter between King Janaka and a woman ascetic, Sulabhā. She, a renouncer herself, hears of his fame as a king who has attained absolute freedom amidst the trappings of rulership, and goes to see if it is true. His reception of her, and the mode of their dialogue are striking and pointed. He asserts his attainment and his continued life as a king, and then questions her about her identity, honour, integrity, and knowledge. She responds with both didactic and critical arguments, so that her peroration leaves the king silent, the loser in this debate with her. King Janaka occurs often in the *Mahābhārata*. In particular, in the Book within which our episode is located—the Śānti Parvan, which contains Bhīṣma's final teachings to Yudhiṣṭhira—Janaka appears in a sequence of dialogues; Fitzgerald points out that the connection between the various Janakas is that they are all taught by (different) sages.[7] King Janaka is an honoured name in much older textual layers, known for knowledge and generosity.[8] In our narrative, he comes out badly.[9] As we will see, throughout, the narrative makes clear its lack of sympathy for him. If we look at it in traditional terms, then the story is a way for Bhīṣma to convey a negative answer to Yudhiṣṭhira: here is Janaka, who claims to have achieved just that absolute freedom from immanence, even while continuing to act in the social world of rituals, power, and sex. His reception of the almswoman (*bhikṣukī*) (who, having renounced the world, has no means of livelihood and has to depend upon alms to live) is presented in ambiguous light, his claims to knowledge are made to sound boastful, and his questioning of her is explicitly characterized as inappropriate. By contrast, her arguments are described as even more beautiful than her appearance, and develop in a coherent set of moves that culminate in a demolition of the king's position.

[6] E.g., see Dasgupta 2000; Doniger 2002. [7] Fitzgerald 2003: 648.

[8] Black 2007: 105–11. Janaka is also, in later and contemporary Hindu culture, held in affection as the rather hapless father of the foundling Sītā (who is won by Prince Rāma) in the *Rāmāyaṇa*.

[9] Piantelli 2002.

Almost all debates in the *Mahābhārata* have enigmatic conclusions, the opposing sides are often left in a delicate balance, and even if one side appears to win, subsequent events problematize the previous debate and leave the eventual outcome open-ended again. In this episode, Sulabhā is clearly declared the winner, leaving Janaka with nothing to say. If we think of the dialogues of the *Mahābhārata* schematically as being only about the major doctrinal questions within some single overarching but hidden metanarrative on the intellectual hegemony of brahmin composers and redactors, then we can read this dialogue as simply about the debate between householders and renouncers over the style of life appropriate for spiritual transcendence. But the *Mahābhārata* is full of counter-narratives, subversions, and so many exceptions that exceptions do not so much prove a rule as prove to be the rule. This episode is one of many in which a strong, articulate, and characterful woman challenges the masculinist order. The subtlety of this episode comes through its not being presented directly as a dialogue on gender between a man and a woman, as is the case in many famous dialogues between husbands and wives.[10] The doctrinal debate is given as one between householder and renouncer but the composers of the text choose the renouncer to be a woman. This immediately makes the debate one over gender, all the more powerful for emerging from within the elaborately constructed social site in which it occurs rather than as the explicit focus of discussion. We see this powerful woman in the context of an abstract debate, and my attempt in this chapter is to treat the episode as being particularly important precisely because the renouncer (who turns out to have been born into a kingly family too) is a woman of such ability. It is worth noting too that in one of the earlier chapters of this Book (12.18), which comes under the sequence concerned with the Instructions on Kingly Dharma (as opposed to the much larger number of chapters devoted to the Dharma of Freedom), a King Janaka has one other engagement with an articulate woman: in this short chapter, his (unnamed) wife and Queen, seeing him taking on the trappings of renunciation, castigates him for abandoning his duties as a king and householder!

It is peculiarly limiting (although, alas, typical of many readings of the *Mahābhārata* that would like to reduce its complexity to some simple ideological layout) to read the co-existence of narratives of 'fearsomely able women' and didactic assertions that women do not 'deserve independence' as nothing other than an 'almost accidental byproduct of . . . conflicting (male) religious goals'.[11] Looking at one example of Queen Draupadī's dialogue with her eldest husband, Yudhiṣṭhira, Angelika Malinar offers a fine structural analysis that suggests instead that there might in fact be creative ambiguities in gender relationships in the *Mahābhārata* that cannot be reduced to structural claims about doctrine: arguments between husbands and wives (in which the wife's

[10] Other episodes turn on motherhood rather than marriage, as when the distraught mother of the now-dead Kaurava brothers, in her lament, castigates Kṛṣṇa, cousin to both sets of cousins—and by this point of the narrative, in its settled form, revealed as the divine—for his role in their demise.

[11] Jamison 1996: 15–16.

status as a learned woman (*paṇḍitā*) is affirmed) have a vertical dimension construed according to the normative gender hierarchy, but at the same time also an horizontal one in which the social interdependence between husband and wife is shown.[12] Also warning against reductive readings, in the same volume, Laurie Patton dryly remarks, 'When we look for a single gender ideology in a tradition, we tend to find it.'[13] In line with this, Patton insightfully explores two of Draupadī's conversations with other women in which she talks about her husbands, and demonstrates how Draupadī alternates between different readings of gender roles and power within each conversation itself. The character of Draupadī draws the most attention for her presence in critical parts of the narrative.[14]

Sulabhā is not a character within the epic narrative, since she is found only within this didactic passage. Her character has both the advantage and the disadvantage of not existing through the narrative arc of epic events, and in being contained within a tight and specific framework. But she offers too the striking contrast of standing wholly outside the dynamic of marriage and of motherhood. As such, she cuts straight past questions concerning the import of both the biology of reproduction and motherhood, as well as the social institution of marriage. As we will see, her story and words do have a bearing on sexual difference, but in a radical alternative to both marriage and motherhood. In relation to Malinar's terminology, she offers a very different account of the horizontal relationship, and does so in a way that implies the rejection of the vertical one. (Whether this case for her particular situation is meant to have a more general bearing on women is another issue.) As Patton points out, there are many instances in the *Mahābhārata* (including the dialogue studied in this chapter) which help us think more broadly of the 'multi-layered' and 'polyphonic' rendition of gender in the epic's narrative.

We may also be tempted to distance the Dialogue from any possibility of being read as the voice of Sulabhā. Alf Hitlebeitel, for example, wants us to remember that Draupadī is 'a literary figure, not a woman': she may at best be a figure through whom male composers (whom he calls with elaborate, deliberate irony, Dead Indian Sanskritizing Males) present 'their sympathetic understanding of a woman's question.'[15] This observation helps block a temptation to draw concrete historical conclusions from literary material. Nonetheless, we should also note that this should not result in limiting what we can learn about the human condition from literature rather than history: such reasoning would remove the entirety of the Bible and the Qu'ran, and almost

[12] Malinar 2007: 90. [13] Patton 2007: 100.

[14] I find strange Mary Brockington's contention that Draupadī functions just to show the rightness of Yudhiṣṭhira's views, and is not a person in her own right; Brockington 2001: 256, 257—surely a facile claim for such a careful scholar of the text to make. Malinar is quite right to point out that in the dialogue with her senior husband in question, the dialogue is really a narrative feature to 'negotiate the relationship between the characters'; pp. 92–3.

[15] Hiltebeitel 2000: 116.

the whole of classical Greek literature, not to say Shakespeare, from saying anything about women other than as 'literary figures'. What this would do to contemporary feminist theology and philosophy boggles the mind. Hiltebeitel makes this observation in the context of the curious question of whether Draupadī is a feminist. Of course not; 'feminism' is so specifically thematized through particular formulations going back to the nineteenth century[16] that it is even contested whether figures from earlier in the modern period, like Mary Wollstonecraft and Mary Astell, are properly to be called 'feminist'. (Hiltebeitel modifies this claim in his conclusion, saying that Draupadī 'has thought up a good question, one that seems to have been good for feminists to think with'.[17]) What we face is not the empty task of deciding whether an ancient text is feminist, and if not, whether it then ceases to have all possibility of being read through today's feminist insights. Instead, we should take the proper role of historical context to be that it enables us to read text for our philosophical purposes today. So it is with the Dialogue of Sulabhā and Janaka, and with the figure of Sulabhā herself. We cannot prejudge what exactly it means to say men wrote about Sulabhā,[18] when we are engaged precisely in the task of exploring what a text does with gender, for that begs the question of what that text could possibly say about gender in the first place.[19]

Of course, this does not exactly help with my writing on Sulabhā, where I am a heterosexual male, amongst other things (in due course, I will perhaps be thought a minor Dead Indian Sanskritizing Male, howsoever doubtful from the perspective of my Dead Ancestors). Hiltebeitel gives an apposite quote from Gayatri Spivak about when 'men can theorize about feminism' or whites about racism: 'It is when *only* the former theorize that the situation is politically intolerable.'[20] I benefit, therefore, from colleagues who work on both the *Mahābhārata* and on feminism. To emphasize the limits of the task I am undertaking: it is an attempt to ask, from the perspective of my complex yet determinate situation (whatever my biography, it is obviously determinate), what I think could be learnt from the emplotment of this narrative, and the words of the character Sulabhā, that may constitute an intervention in some contemporary discussions about body and gender.

[16] On the complex history of defining feminism, especially in connection with nineteenth-century France, see Offen 2005.

[17] Hiltebeitel 2000: 121.

[18] Mary Brockington—rightly to my mind—expresses incredulity that so many scholars continue to think that no women were involved in the oral narratives that formed the *Mahābhārata*; comments at the symposium, Sanskrit Traditions in the Modern World, Manchester, 26 May 2017.

[19] A possibly fruitful line of comparison is with Luce Irigaray's exploration of how to read the role and presence of Diotima in her encounter with Socrates in Plato's Symposium. Substantively, Diotima's insistence on the spiritual rather than physical—i.e., reproductive—nature of immortality resonates with Sulabhā's arguments. In terms of feminist interpretation, Irigaray's treatment of the critical possibility that Diotima is a female figure used only to give legitimacy to a masculine view, together with her conclusion that much more is going on, is one that I find instructive. I thank Alison Stone for drawing my attention to this aspect of The Symposium. See Irigaray and Kuykendall 1988.

[20] Spivak 1988: 253.

Reading the Text through Sulabhā

We cannot come to easy conclusions about the extent to which the composers of this text meant to emphasize the gendered nature of Sulabhā's reception by Janaka. On the one hand, if we were to think of the conventional reading of this episode as just being about the doctrinal clash between householdership and renunciation, then presumably we would have to think too that their description of her reception as a woman was incidental and unthinking. On the other hand, if we start with asking why the renouncer in question is, unusually, a woman, then each time the text draws attention to Sulabhā's being a woman we will want to see that as a deliberate choice that permits us to think creatively with the text (and out of its context).

From this latter perspective, it is clear that the narrative has a series of devices through which we come to understand that Sulabhā is seen (internally by Janaka, outside the narrative by Yudhiṣṭhira, and finally by readers of the text), first as a woman; in the innumerable instances of male renouncers entering a scene, none starts with noticing his being a man as a critical element of the plot. We have, then, that particular asymmetry that Simone de Beauvoir drew attention to when inaugurating twentieth-century feminism. 'If her functioning as a female [*femelle*] is not enough to define woman, if we decline also to explain her through "the eternal feminine", and if nevertheless we admit, even if only provisionally, that women do exist, then we must face the question "what is a woman"? To state the question is, to me, to suggest at once, a first answer. The fact that I ask it is in itself significant. A man would never set out to write a book on the specific situation of the male of the human race. But if I wish to define myself, I must first of all declare: "I am a woman;" this truth is the background from which further claims will stand out. A man never begins by affirming that he is an individual of a certain sex; it goes without saying that he is a man.'[21] Toril Moi offers an analysis of this important passage: 'There are two facts: first, it is a fact that she is a woman, second, it is a fact that whenever she wants to define herself, she is obliged to draw attention to the first fact... If I am a woman, my claims are inevitably going to be taken to stand out from the background of my sex. This means that, however hard I try to define myself through what I am saying and doing... my interlocutors will try and reduce my assertions to my sex.'[22]

When Sulabhā decides to go investigate Janaka's claims, about which she is sceptical, she uses her yoga powers and puts on an 'incomparably beautiful' form (v. 10). As we will see, this is not at all to play the sexualized and conventional role of the attractive woman in relation to a powerful man, but rather to subvert that role by questioning the very basis of his power. Nevertheless, we can see this preparatory transformation as a statement that she is a woman and is obliged to draw attention to this fact—whatever her ultimate ends. Not only her speech but her bodily presence will be received as a

[21] Beauvoir 1949: xx–xxi. But I have stayed closer to Toril Moi's translation (Moi 1999: 191) than the standard Parshley version.

[22] Moi 1999: 193.

woman's; therefore, to even to begin to engage with that reception, she will have to start with the act of presenting herself as a woman, so she may as well do so in a manner that will later on suggest that it was a gambit in her critical engagement with Janaka. Now, it may well be that there is a larger background of how representations are made in the face of power: male courtiers will dress appropriately, and male renouncers may appear unkempt just to show that they have their own role in the negotiation of power between king and sage. But Sulabhā's egregious transformation is a supererogatory display of gender asymmetry: the man may have to choose how he will be present to the king, but the woman is without choice a woman. So she will choose how to be present as a woman.

This is why it is vital to not ignore the choice of the *Mahābhārata* to have a woman renouncer be the central figure of the dialogue. And while it is significant—as we will discuss at the end of the chapter—that Sulabhā as a whole remains mysterious (recall, she is not a character in the main *Mahābhārata* narrative), she does refer to her family line and her rigorous training, indicating that she is a specific woman, and not a generic figure. This renouncer is not only a woman, but a woman with a background in which gender intersects with other features to particularize her biography (even if in a sketchy way compared to many characters in the main narrative). And it is her being a woman that the narrative implies is central to the choices she makes in entering into her dialogue with Janaka. At the same time, her answer to Janaka's thoroughly masculinist reception of her is a lecture that, through different lines of thought, points to a conception of being human that seeks to transcend the conditions of a sexist society that she has necessarily had to negotiate.

In thinking of how to make sense of this episode, I was struck by the difficulty of deciding what exactly it implied about Sulabhā's teachings. That difficulty, it now seems, should be seen to lie at the heart of any effort to absorb the lessons of feminism as we look at the literatures of the world. In commenting on Beauvoir's declaration that she wants to talk, not about eternal truths but about the common background [*fond*] from which 'every particular female existence stands out', Toril Moi says: 'On the one hand, she may be taken to mean that in a sexist society... a woman's claims will always be heard with reference to her body, but that in a non-sexist society this will no longer be the case. On the other hand, however, she may be saying that although sexism insists on reading a woman's books against the background of her sex, in a non-sexist society the same thing will happen to men as well. Here, in a nutshell, we find encapsulated the feminist conflict between a certain understanding of equality and a certain understanding of difference.'[23] It would be foolish to pretend that, for all its rich implications and its subtle shifts, this episode resolves this conflict. Indeed, arguably, it is better that we think that the very existence of the conflict acts as a prompt to anyone today who wishes to figure their way through life in a feminist manner, whatever that might mean to them. My reading is that the episode expresses that tension in the locus of bodily being, for Sulabhā acts through a sense of difference over her being a woman renouncer,

[23] Ibid., p. 200.

but articulates too a sense of equality about the cognitive fruits of renunciatory pratice. I will argue that the sense of difference as a woman renouncer leads to the demonstration of an existential freedom and that her claim for cognitive equality shows her commitment to a metaphysical one. This doubleness is necessarily gendered in a social context in which she needs to start with her recognition that she is a woman but with which she seeks to teach us the possibility of being thoroughly human.

The Body as the Frame of Dialogue

The episode begins with Bhīṣma setting the scene, implying immediately a certain distaste for Janaka.

> [verse 4] Once there was a king of Mithilā, named Janaka, 'The flag-staff of Righteousness', who sought the fruits of renunciation.[24]

The word '*dhvaja*' meaning both banner or flag-staff as well as 'hypocrite', the translation of the endlessly polysemic term '*dharma*' as 'righteousness' nicely captures the ambivalence towards that virtue. So he is a 'righteous hyprocrite' too. But then Bhīṣma's description shifts to representing Janaka on his own terms.

> [5] He had studied the Veda, and the science of absolute freedom, as too his own science [of kingship]; reconciling his senses, he ruled the earth.[25]

The introduction of Sulabhā immediately introduces too an ambiguity over the normativity of social conditions.

> [7] Now, in that Age of Right, there was an almswoman named Sulabhā, who practiced the rule of *yoga* and wandered the earth alone.[26]

In the standard mythic chronology, each aeon has four ages, and the Age of Dharma is the first and greatest. By definition, a renouncer has no social ties and no fixed home. Sulabhā adheres to those norms because it is that Age. But what does that imply? Is it that it was permissible in that golden period but not now? Or is it that, because it was permissible and practised in the exemplary Age, it is normative and could be practised even now, in the strife-torn world of the *Mahābhārata*? And why was it permissible then? Perhaps because it was safe for a woman to wander alone? Does that mean that on prudential grounds, women cannot be renouncers unless society (in the extended conceptual sense that includes both habitations and wilderness) is such as to provide them the safety to wander? We have no answers, but already we know that the body and bodily norms matter for renunciation, that

[24] *saṃnyāsaphalikaḥ kaścid babhūva nṛpatiḥ purā/maithilo janako nāma dharma-dhvaja iti śrutaḥ//.*

[25] *sa vede mokṣaśāṣtre ca sve ca śāṣtre kṛtāgamaḥ/indriyāṇi samādhāya śaśāsa vasudhām imām//.*

[26] *atha dharmayuge tasmin yogadharmam anuṣṭhitā/mahīm anucacāraikā sulabhā nāma bhikṣukī//.*

sexual anxiety accompanies the formation of gender norms. That awareness would be elided in the discussion of renunciation as such, which is to say, renunciation just for men.

Sulabhā heard the mysterious (*susūkṣma*) talk of the King of Mithilā who also had absolute freedom (*mokṣa*), and doubting it, decided to see him. Now we have that enigmatic decision by her that I have already mentioned:

> [10–11] Casting off her previous form through her yogic power, she took on another bodily form, incomparably beautiful. Her eyes like lotuses below her lovely brows, she went to the capital city in Videha in the wink of an eye, traveling as swiftly as the lightest arrow.[27]

We must acknowledge the impact that this change initially has on the reader: such power, and it is for that most stereotypical of reasons, the male fantasy that all of a woman's capacity is for the purpose of displaying 'feminine wiles'? Sulabhā is in fact going to use her appearance to provoke in the king that befuddlement that she suspects lies beneath his claim to have 'reconciled his senses'. Yet it is not merely a strategem, for already it is highly suggestive that this bodily appearance—richly implied by the synecdochical reference to the eyes and eyebrows—in itself makes her a woman in the eyes of men, Sulabhā well knows. Hence my suggestion that we should look at the device of her yogic power to be a literary way of concretizing the awareness that, even to define herself and demonstrate her self-definition, Sulabhā must first acknowledge the background of her existence, which is that she is a woman.

She enacts this necessary starting point by transformation, not locution. She may have the capacity to work out her freedom, but it is a freedom that must be related to her being a woman—even though doing so requires that she must work herself **out** of the concrete situation of her being a woman. In a different context, Iris Young draws a contrast: 'Insofar as feminine existence lives the body as transcendence and intentionality, the feminine body actively constitutes space and is the original coordinate which unifies the spatial field and projects spatial relations and positions in accord with its intentions. But to the extent that feminine motility is laden with immanence and inhibited, the body's space is lived as constituted.'[28] I propose that we read the device of her yogic power to reconstitute her space radically as a way of imagining how Sulabhā is given as intentional through and through. As we will soon see, she resists being inhibited by Janaka's gaze; and furthermore, argues that it is he who is laden with immanence. Seen thus, this episode permits viewing as an enactment of the ecology of sexist containment and the intentional, agentive reconfiguration of gendered phenomenology as freedom.

[27] *tataḥ sā viprahāyātha pūrvarūpaṃ hi yogataḥ/abibhrad anavadyāṅgī rūpam anyad anuttamam// cakṣur nimeṣamātreṇa laghvastragatigāminī/videhānāṃ purīṃ subhrūr jagāma kamalekṣaṇā//.*

[28] Young 1980: 150–1.

That this assertion is for a semiotic purpose is clear when we consider that, although she has all these powers to present herself, she nonetheless also and at the same time, presents herself as a renouncer:

> [12] She reached the lovely capital Mithilā that was thronged with prosperous people, and she gained an audience with its lord on the pretext of begging alms from him.

And this has just the reaction she clearly intends to provoke. We immediately see how Sulabhā has merely caused the gendered nature of her reception to be heightened by her transformation.

> [13–15] When the king saw her extreme delicacy and her beauty he was overcome with amazement: 'Who is she? Whose is she? Where has she come from?' he said. He welcomed her, showed her the best seat, honoured her by having her feet washed, and had the best foods brought as refreshments.[29] Pleased by the food, the alms-seeking renouncer then, amidst men who knew all the learned commentaries on the learned teachings, challenged the king who was surrounded by his advisors.

Let us note that, at least due to its being the Age of Right, the fact of her being a renouncing ascetic is not immediately challenged by Janaka, and the protocols of receiving sages are preserved by him. But he is divided, as she had expected of a king who, as she will say later (v. 139), 'spends time in play with his women'. His amazement seems initially to be wholly a sexually charged aesthetic arousal to her beauty, but we should construe it as more complex than that. The critical understanding of how he receives her should not be reduced to a joyless disapproval of a man finding a woman beautiful! Rather, we should note specifically how, towards the conclusion of his criticism of her, at verse 54, he will clearly express what he sees as the antinomian nature of her presence—beautiful, youthful…and ascetic? But he has not yet absorbed fully the simultaneity of her appearing beautiful and her being an ascetic. Who she is and from where she is can only be tied together with the answer to whose she is.[30] It is then that events move forward.

The Mode of Conversation

If the first use of her yogic powers provoked us to see her as bringing to light the starting point that she is a woman and must refer to that fact, this next use is a riddle that provokes us to fruitful questioning.

[29] *rājā tasyāḥ paraṃ dṛṣṭvā saukumāryaṃ vapus tathā/keyaṃ kasya kuto veti babhūvāgatavismayaḥ//tato 'syāḥ svāgataṃ kṛtvā vyādiśya varāsanam/pūjitāṃ pādaśaucena varānnenāpyatarpayat//.*

[30] Steven Heim pointed out to me that this mode of query functions as the possibly formulaic aspect of the question as a general one about descent and lineage: the much later, popular *Hastāmalaka Stotra*, attributed to Śaṅkara echoes this by beginning with 'Child, who are you, whose are you, where are you going? (*kastvaṃ śiśo, kasya kuto'si gantā*)'. The young boy so asked turns out to be 'the form of true understanding' (*nijabodharūpa*). But whereas the question to the male pertains only to his father, to the woman it implies too a question about her (possible) husband. We will see how Sulabhā answers this in her own way.

> [16–19] Doubting whether he had really gained freedom in the midst of all his dharmic duties, Sulabhā used her knowledge of yoga and entered his essence with her essence. Just as he was about to address her, she fused the rays of his eyes to the rays of her own two eyes, and bound him with the bonds of her yoga power. Janaka, the highest of kings, merely smiled, and, keeping his being distinct from hers, he received her being with his being. Hear the conversation that took place in that one locus, a conversation between a man who had absolute freedom amidst the royal parasol and such things and a woman who had gained absolute freedom with the triple staff of renunciation.[31]

Decoding the puzzle of why Sulabhā does not simply sit and talk, but chooses this mysterious mode of communication helps us see not only the gendered nature of this dialogue but also how we may come to think of Sulabhā's position as a radical intervention in contemporary discussions. Our point of departure is the observation that Sulabhā has, until this point, been seen, and thus received within the terms of Janaka's gaze: that is, as—implausibly for him—both beautiful and a renunciant. Even if her powers permit her to look as she wishes, her choice of form demonstrates (one could say, to pursue the visual metaphor, reveals) that she will always be what Janaka sees her to be. In short, we must start with noting the significance of sight, if we are to elucidate the motivation for Sulabhā's peculiar use of her powers. We know that in classical Indian thought, visual evidence (*pratyakṣa*) is the foremost of the modes of knowledge (the *pramāṇas*).[32] Now, it is generally acknowledged too that the sense of sight is accorded primacy in Western philosophical tradition going back to Plato's claim for the pre-eminence of vision.[33] We also have, in critical vein, Luce Irigaray's elaborate and provocative identification of light—which renders primacy to vision—as the founding metaphor of Western metaphysics.[34] From this thought, Irigaray argues that the photo-logic of metaphysics upholds the fantasy of a self-reflexively present masculinity, which excludes any sense of the corporeality of the seer. With this exclusion, all sense of the material conditions of the body, which Irigaray sees as the maternal-feminine, is relegated from philosophy; philosophy is left as the imaginary male body. 'Irigaray sets out in "Plato's *Hystera*" to make apparent the isomorphic imaginary body which philosophy constructs for itself... In the course of this complicitous production, any form of feminine identity is effaced. Devoid of its own imaginary, the maternal-feminine is reduced to formless, mute, indeterminate, invisible bodiless matter which yields passively to the instruments of Man.'[35]

[31] *sulabhā tvasya dharmeṣu mukto neti sasaṃśayā/sattvaṃ sattvena yogajñā praviveśa mahīpate// netrābhyāṃ netrayorasya raśmīn saṃyojya raśmibhiḥ/sā sma saṃcodayiṣyantaṃ yogabandhair babandha ha//janako 'pyutsmayan rājā bhāvam asyā viśeṣayan/pratijagrāha bhāvena bhāvam asyā nṛpottamaḥ// tadekasminnadhiṣṭhāne saṃvādaḥ śrūyatāmayam/chatrādiṣu vimuktasya muktāyāśca tridaṇḍake//.*

[32] Matilal 1986: chapters 1–2 and 6. [33] For a recent analysis, see Herrmann 2013.

[34] Irigaray 1985: 234–364, 'Plato's *Hystera*', her reading of part of Book VII of Plato's *Republic*.

[35] Vasseleu 1998: 9.

No such quite general case has been made in connection with classical Indian thought. But if we keep in mind the role of vision as the dominant form of gaining knowledge in classical Indian thought, we can bring it to bear on the presence of the metaphysical terminology of the Sāṃkhya system in the *Mahābhārata* where a highly valorized attitude towards the female body in male renunciant discourse is manifest: 'This [Sāṃkhya] philosophy, as encountered in the *Mahābhārata*, proposes a set of dichotomies in which the masculine is identified with *puruṣa* [the term, at base, for "man"], the indwelling eternal self of an individual. This *puruṣa* is envisaged as being submerged in the playfully enticing, mutating femininity of *prakṛti* [primal matter]. Woman... is naturally identified with the senses and the seductive lure of the world... The link between woman and world in Sāṃkhya is so tenacious as to seem organic.'[36] Let us for the moment flag up the fact that Sulabhā's later use of Sāṃkhya terminology is conspicuously going to lack this male–female cosmogony. For the time being, let us note that if there is already a regime for male renouncers in which the sight of women becomes the threat of sexual loss of control (and therefore of the seminal potency that bespeaks of spiritual power), with Janaka we have an even more complicated situation. As Sulabhā's doubts indicate, he wants simultaneously to preserve the panoply of the king's masculinist gaze and to assert his freedom from the powers and desires that structure kingship. So he does not even seek to reject what he objectifies, as a male renouncer might.

But, in fact, no alteration to another perceptual mode would change the situation. She can and will be heard, but insofar as she is heard as the woman so seen by Janaka opposite him, she would still be performing under the sign of his objectification. Besides, in a world in which speech itself is objectified, albeit as a goddess (*vāc*), she will in any case be speaking on his terms. She will not escape her location in his hegemonic sensorium, so long as she speaks according to how she is seen. What she does is a radical response to that situation.

Of course, what she actually does is ambiguous, although richly so. As her own lecture on the composition of the bodily being mentions (v. 104), there is that called '*sattva*' which can vary in the strength of its presence in a person.[37] Although she does not explicitly name it as one of the three basic qualities (*guṇas*), the fact that its quantum of presence can vary indicates that this is what it is meant to be. It can, in many contexts (as we saw in the previous chapter), also be translated as 'mind' (*manas*—the inner sense-organ rather than some sentient entity comparable to the Cartesian 'mind'); but since in her exposition she distinguishes between the two, it seems sensible here to think of it as some essential quality whose variable presence marks the individual, a

[36] Dhand 2008: 79.

[37] In somewhat similar manner to the use of Sāṃkhya categories that we saw in the previous chapter on Caraka, Sulabhā uses them but with variations and additions suited to her purpose; and just as with Caraka, while there are interesting historical questions about the role of Sāṃkhya as an early model of ontology in texts at the start of the Common Era, it is unhelpful to constrain these imaginative uses to some one formal system of that name.

quality associated with calmness and—intriguingly in the context of the discussion about vision and light—illumination. We must therefore resist thinking of this as a 'mind-meld', in which we smuggle in a dualistic assumption that there are two bodies but that one mind 'possesses' the other. Sulabhā brings about a way of being-with Janaka that does not permit the play of the power of his gaze upon her but which allows for a proximity in which they communicate only with each other. I will shortly turn to Sulabhā's own use of vision.

We must recall that the invocation of yogic power, by which bodily form is re-formed, has already given us a narrative device through which assumptions of the nature of the physical body have been destabilized. It is that yogic power which further destabilizes the assumption of a fixed locus for her presence: for this conversation, the physical body of Janaka is the lived body of Janaka and Sulabhā, in that that is a shared phenomenological field, shared, of course, due to her assertion of agency. Here we can think of Merleau-Ponty's dictum: 'To "live" a thing is not to coincide with it, nor fully to embrace it in thought.'[38] Merleau-Ponty is talking of how the physical body and the lived body, as the merely spatio-temporal entity and its experienced character respectively, cannot be disambiguated without loss to the meaning of phenomenological being; in his analysis, we can neither coincide with our physical body nor can we have a complete and purely intellectual grasp of what it is to be a physical thing. But the narrative device of yogic power helps us push the lack of complete contiguity between the physical and the phenomenological to its formal limits.

Only in a story, so to say, can we imagine the formal possibility of ambiguity in relation to what, objectively, is given as 'another' body but whose phenomenological field is shared. Provided we do not already see this filtered through the idea of body–mind duality mentioned above, we can free ourselves to imagine how fluid and fungible is the nature of our bodily being in its relationship to another. Indeed, we should think of this formal narrative device as a means through which to ask ourselves what intuitions about our bodily phenomenology we have when we read of this event. What we have, then, is Sulabhā 'living' Janaka, neither easily distinguishable from him nor with a coincidence of their thoughts.

What does this gambit do (regardless of how we are tempted to interpret it metaphysically)? Jean-Paul Sartre thought that the issue is how to have 'the freedom to define oneself through one's own action and free choice... [from] an other's self-interested objectifying point of view';[39] feminist criticism has taught us that it is the masculinist gaze that so objectifies. So her entering his essence with hers removes from Sulabhā's encounter with Janaka that fixation of her as the object of his gaze which vitiates the agency of her presence. She will not be vulnerable to his judgement of her bodiliness (the beautiful bearer of the triple-staff of renunciation). This is how she responds to that existential situation. She dissolves the distance—socially normative between men and women—that hems in her freedom and makes her be on his terms. What is this

[38] Merleau-Ponty 1962: 325. [39] Vasseleu 1998: 55.

alternative, and how is it to be read? Would it be to replace the problematic of sight with the possibilities of touch, in anticipation of what some phenomenologists (especially feminist ones developing Merleau-Ponty's work) have suggested? The text offers the mechanism for the mysterious process: it is through the fusion of the light of their vision (drawing on the idea popular in the classical world, Greek and Indian, that vision is due to the light going from the eye to its object). It is not just that Sulabhā gazes back. It is also true she does that, of course; and that is already to discard the feminine trope of the downcast eye (although, yet again, the woman who gazes back will be re-read as hussy). But to gaze back is already to have conceded the precedence of the male gaze, and it represents at most the taking up for herself the already available tool of her objectification, so that she can be a woman on the man's terms.

Sulabhā does something much more striking. She transforms vision into some supra-sensory version of touch (i.e., it cannot be simply a change from one ordinary sense to another, but rather, the best phenomenological description of a radical way of being proximate). This enables her to speak as she chooses. She collapses the modes of perception, and she opens up his sensorium into one he must share with her. She reverses the perceptual process to get to the original and formal state of a phenomenological field from which spring the modes of perception, with their imbrication in the masculinist epistemic order. In a literal sense, we do not actually have the power to go back into the way of being which contains the modes of perception in their undifferentiated forms. That is why the field is formal, not contentful in our experience. But once more, the imaginative truth is given to us through this device of yogic power by which Sulabhā shares her 'essence' with Janaka. What would it be like to use the very perceptual process by which gender is read into the situation, and reverse it back to an originary phenomenological field? That is what is given to us, in this necessarily mysterious act.

As we will see, Janaka and Sulabhā have very different interpretations of the nature of this intra-corporeity, this folding together of two subjectivities across conventional presumptions about the unitary body.

The King's Speech: Being a Man, Being a Woman, in a Man's World

Social Order and Masculinist Narrative

Janaka then addresses her in three parts. (The mysteriousness of the yogic fusion is further heightened by the fact that Sulabhā's act might appear to suggest that their conversation will be conducted in their shared field alone; yet in his remarks, by asking that she answers to this assembly (*samāgama*), he seems to suggest that the conversation is audible to all.) First of all, he admits his discomfort with her subversion of his epistemic grasp of her:

> [20–1] 'Where have your homeless wanderings taken you, blessed woman? And where will you go? Whose are you? And where are you from?' asked the king. 'I cannot

> quite grasp the real state of affairs concerning your learning, or your age, or of the social group you were born in, so first please give answers to these matters in this assembly of the good.'[40]

Then, claiming that he has 'distinguished knowledge' (*jñānaṃ vaiśeṣikaṃ*) taught by 'the aged Pañcaśikha, the highly exalted mendicant of the *gotra* of Parāśara', he attempts to set forth the subject of absolute freedom. He claims of his teacher that [27b] 'he taught me the threefold absolute freedom and yet he did not make me move away from my kingdom.'[41]

He then defines this freedom in terms that Sulabhā will not dispute; it is important to keep in mind that they are not talking at cross-purposes over the content of transcendence: First [29a], 'Now, dispassion (*vairāgyam*) is the highest formula for absolute freedom.' Then, this dispassion is defined [30b]: 'The great principle is freedom from the pairs of opposites; this passes beyond all stages, and is fulfillment.'[42] It is on this basis, he claims [31b] 'I now act in this world with my errors removed, set free of all distraction (*moha*).' Acting thus, he accrues no consequences (*karma*), his actions are seedless (*abīja*). His detachment from immanence he describes in a vividly virile manner (what else can we call it but 'macho'):

> [36] 'He who smears sandal paste on my right arm and he who hacks off my left with an ax are both the same to me.'[43]

Now he moves on to a general argument against (male) ascetic renunciates, so that the contrast is with him, the king as male householder.

> [41] 'In regard to general ethical restraints, special ascetic restraints, aversions, desires, having belongings, respect, hypocrisy, and affections, these [ascetics] are just like those who have families... [47] Wearing the ochre-colored robe, shaving the head, the triple staff, the water pot—in my judgment these emblems are beside the point, they do not lead to freedom... [50a] Freedom is not in just having nothing, and bondage not in just having things... '

He claims dispassion as a stance that he can have even with all the power he has:

> [52] 'With the sword of "Giving Things Up" sharpened on the whetstone of freedom I have cut the noose that is the governing of a kingdom, that noose that binds one to the various points of affection.'[44]

What is striking about Janaka's position is that he makes clear how the relationship between immanence and transcendence—between living within a structuring reality

[40] *bhagavatyāḥ kva caryeyaṃ kṛtā kva ca gamiṣyasi/kasya ca tvaṃ kuto veti papracchainām mahīpatiḥ// śrute vayasi jātau ca sadbhāvo nādhigamyate/eṣv artheṣūttaraṃ tasmāt pravedaṃ satsamāgame//.*

[41] *śrāvitas trividhaṃ mokṣaṃ na ca rājyād vicālitaḥ.*

[42] *mahad dvaṃdvapramokṣāya sā siddhir yā vayotigā.*

[43] *yaśca me dakṣiṇaṃ bāhuṃ candanena samukṣayet/savyaṃ vāsyā ca yastakṣetsamāvetāvubhau mama//.*

[44] *rājyaiśvaryamayaḥ pāśaḥ snehāyatanabandhanaḥ/mokṣāśmaniśiteneha chinnastyāgāsinā mayā//.*

and gaining the capacity to be detached from that structuration—is essentially a masculinist narrative, supremely so in the person of the king.

The Subalterning of the Woman/Renouncer

Finally, he turns to denigrating her, as renouncer but also as woman. Whereas so far his denial that renouncers have any special gnostic status is directed at male renouncers (note the 'shaven heads' in v 47), his criticism of her shifts to issues of gender.

> [53b–54] 'There is something wrong with your appearance. I will speak. Listen to me on this. Your delicacy and your form, your preeminent beauty and your youth—you have all of these and asceticism too? I wonder.'[45]

His interpretation of her daring to bring their beings into contact (*bhāvasparśa*) is that it is a violation, whose sexual nature is eventually brought out:

> [57] 'Hear now from my side of it what transgression (*vyatikrama*) you commit by taking residence in my first enclosure (*pūrvaparigraha*) with your being (*svabhāva*) . . . [58b] By courtesy of whom did you enter into my heart? (*kasya vā saṃnisargāttvaṃ praviṣṭā hṛdayaṃ mama*).'

He accuses her [59–61] of mixing both class (*varṇa*) and pattern of life (*āśrama*); and making clear his sexualized understanding of their communication, he also accuses her of risking violation of the rules of exogamy.

His next set of accusations brings out an important point about the gendered nature of Sulabhā's renunciation, in that Janaka cannot countenance her ascetic autonomy without contrasting it with an assumed background of marital dependence. If her husband was still alive, she was making him, Janaka, flout the prescription, 'One should not go unto another's wife (*agamyā parabhāryeti*).' Maybe she is independent (*svatantra*)? (Ironically, of course, by this independence he does not mean autonomy, but being 'free' of a husband.) Then [64] it must be through some fault of her own, rendering her supposed learning useless. All this culminates in the most obvious accusation of all, made even more potent by sanctimonious euphemism:

> [65b] 'You give every sign of being a wicked woman. There! What needed to be said has been brought to light.'[46]

The 'sign' (*liṅga*) is a perceptual item that permits inference to a conclusion. Janaka has had the perception of Sulabhā, and he can only conclude that this diffusion of phenomenal presence across material boundaries is carnal in the sense of expressing her sexual desire. But having interpreted her extraordinary presence in his sensorium as sexual contact, he seeks to deny that he is responsive. That only leaves him suspended

[45] *ayathārtho hi te varṇo vakṣyāmi śṛṇu tan mama//saukumāryaṃ tathā rūpaṃ vapuragryaṃ tathā vayaḥ/tavaitāni samastāni niyamaśceti saṃśayaḥ//.*

[46] *duṣṭāyā lakṣyate liṅgaṃ pravaktavyaṃ prakāśitam//.*

within his reading (suffused with a sexual anxiety that Sulabhā will criticize in her peroration) of what has happened.

> [69–70] 'When a man and a woman desire each other and each gets the other, that is like nectar. When they do not get each other, or when one feels no passion, then that failure is like poison. You should not touch me. You know what is right. Adhere to the norms of your learned discipline. Your investigation of me, "Has he gained freedom or not?" is done. You ought not to conceal from me all that is hidden here.'[47]

Finally, he tries feebly to deny that she could consistently have gnostic insight (know the ultimate, *brahman*) and yet be a woman, for the two types of human being are different (and the king yet another), by apparently quoting some traditional apothegms. He would rather that she had adhered to the proper 'powers' of a woman, which is, of course, to be appealing in her bodily being to a man. He does not, however, quite deny Sulabhā her gnostic capacity, presumably because she has already demonstrated yogic power that is associated with such knowledge. We will find few texts anywhere in the classical world that grant the capacity for a woman to have the powers of a man. Janaka merely wishes it were not so.

> [73] 'Sovereignty is the power kings have, *brahman* is the power of those who know the *brahman*, and beauty, youth, and charm are the unsurpassed power women have.'[48]

Sulabhā on Rational Normativity: Ungendered Equality?

Bhīṣma immediately expresses disapproval of what has been said by Janaka, being clear that it is also directed at the gendered aspects of Janaka's diatribe. So Bhīṣma says [76] that Sulabhā was 'not shaken' (*na vyakampata*) despite the king's words, which were unpleasant (*asukha*), inappropriate (*ayukta*) and unbecoming (*asamañjasa*).

Sulabhā chooses what seems a somewhat strange place to begin her reply, and it is only obliquely that we come to see the significance of the first 'movement' in her speech. Janaka has not denied that she has the power to debate with him; even if he is unpleasant and unbecoming in his tone and charges, he does speak to her as one who expects to be spoken back to. Given this implicit framing of a shared rationality, Sulabhā chooses the intellectual high ground from which to start her reply (while her conclusion sees her move on to the moral high ground). She does this with an outline of how to debate through reason. An interesting aspect of this outline is that she does

[47] *icchatorhi dvayorlābhaḥ strīpuṃsoramṛtopamaḥ/alābhaścāpyaraktasya so 'tra doṣo viṣopamaḥ//mā sprākṣīḥ sādhu jānīṣva svaśāstramanupālaya/kṛteyaṃ hi vijijñāsā mukto neti tvayā mama/etatsarvaṃ praticchannaṃ mayi nārhasi gūhitam//.*

[48] *rājñāṁ hi balamaiśvaryaṁ brahma brahmavidāṁ balam/rūpayauvanasaubhāgyaṁ strīṇāṁ balamanuttamam//.*

not take the virtues of debate to be subordinate to authority (although she will later make clear that she does not violate the sense of rightness represented by the order of *dharma*), but something available to the trained seeker of knowledge. From the fact that she says Janaka should listen to her description, it is clear that she judges him to be untrained or insufficiently trained in this discipline of interactive inquiry.

> [78–80] 'King, a "speech" (*vāc*) is said to have an appropriate meaning, to be free of the eighteen faults that spoil words or thought, and to be endowed with the eighteen virtues (*guṇas*); and a "speech" has sophistication (*saukṣmya*), careful discrimination (*saṃkhya*), clear order (*krama*), the presentation of a conclusion (*nirṇaya*), and motivation (*prayojana*)—all five of these are aspects of the meaning to be conveyed. Listen to a careful description—in terms of sentences, words, and the meanings of words—of each one of these items, sophistication and the others, that occur over and over again.'

After defining each of these five characteristics, she then boldly claims that this is not just an ideal to strive for; she embodies them in herself.

> [86–7] 'Watch, and you will see that my speech will combine all five of these—sophistication and the others which I have just described—to form a single meaning. I am going to tell you the highest truth, king, and I shall speak to you with pertinent meaning and coherence. I will not say too little, nor too much, and I will not speak coarsely, nor unclearly.'[49]

Not only will she utilize all these aspects of reason to speak clearly and in appropriate style; her epistemic and rhetorical accomplishments have a broader existential character to them:

> [90] 'I shall say nothing whatsoever out of love, anger, fear, greed, desperation, vulgarity, shame, pity, or haughtiness.'[50]

This is a doubly striking claim from a comparative perspective. First, it argues for the incompatibility between 'reason' and 'passion' in a way that is often associated with early modern Western claims, although we will see that its motivation is something entirely different, lying in the ancient Indian requirement for detachment within the conception of absolute freedom. Second, it implies, in an obvious way, that this undesirable influence of the emotions on logical argument is evident in her male interlocutor. (Of course, we are only trying to follow the lines of this speech, so there is no call here to express the powerful criticism to which this model of reasoning can be subjected on various grounds.) It is therefore not that Sulabhā needs to deny a charge—familiar in the long history of Western philosophy—that women are creatures of passion, for

[49] *tānyetāni yathoktāni saukṣmyādīni janādhipa/ekārthasamavetāni vākyaṃ mama niśāmaya// upetārthamabhinnārthaṃ nāpavṛttaṃ na cādhikam/nāślakṣṇaṃ na ca saṃdigdhaṃ vakṣyāmi paramaṃ tava//.*

[50] *kāmātkrodhādbhayāllobhāddainyādānāryakāttathā/hrīto 'nukrośato mānānna vakṣyāmi kathaṃcana//.*

that is one charge that Janaka does not make in what otherwise descends into a diatribe against her. Instead, it is she who makes that charge against him, or at least the general charge that what is said out of emotion dilutes reason.

This claim to the capacity for reason on the part of a woman (character) bears a resemblance to an actual historical development in early modern Western thought, when Mary Astell and Mary Wollstonecraft articulate this point in a way that often has them dubbed as the first English feminists. Astell writes, 'Knowledge in a proper and strict sense... signifies that clear Perception which is follow'd by a firm assent to Conclusions rightly drawn from the Premises of which we have clear and distinct ideas. Which Premises or Principles must be so clear and Evident, that supposing us reasonable Creatures, and free from Prejudices and Passions, (which for the time they predominate as good as deprive us of our Reason) we cannot withhold our assent from them without manifest violence to our reason.'[51] As her use of the Cartesian language of 'clear and distinct ideas' shows, Astell commits herself to Descartes' metaphysical dualism; and she does so for the eminently feminist reason that she wants to assert the equality of women in the attainment of abstract knowledge, against masculinist assumptions of superior male capacity.

Now, there is a radical reading of Descartes by Susan Bardo that argues that the objectivity and purity in cognitive thinking for Descartes is conclusively 'masculine', even while it includes the emotions, the senses, and the imagination, those modes of thought that have traditionally been regarded as 'feminine', as part of a 'mature' and controlled soul.[52] On this reading, a woman's 'womanhood' stands in diametrical opposition to the impersonal, dispassionate, rational thought process. The Cartesian thinker, if she is a woman, supposedly must deny her womanhood if she chooses to enter into the traditionally masculine realm of pure reasoning and impersonal detachment. Keeping this in mind, we can turn to Cynthia Bryson's sympathetic and liberal understanding of why Astell resorts to Cartesian dualism. Astell requires an ungendered mind that can be distinguished from the already gendered body, to articulate an equality of rational capacity. 'While Locke denies race, color, or sex as excluding descriptive indicators of the nominal essence of human beings, Astell's feministic political agenda prevents her from acknowledging this directly. Rather, she holds that it is the same sort of "Lockean" thinking (calling attention to physical differences between people) that, even today, makes it difficult for many women to accept pure materialism. Feministic theorizing includes the notion that until physiological (and even racial) distinctions are considered irrelevant to people's abilities, there remains a need (for people who are not white and/or heterosexual and/or men) to believe something exists independently of the body that has the potential for total equality (an equal playing field, of sorts). This kind of dualism between the finite body and the infinite mind/soul is especially necessary for women and other groups who have been made to feel inferior in the past.

[51] Astell 1970: II, 81. Quoted in Bryson 1998.

[52] Bordo 1987: especially ch. 6.

An equality of intellect (or even an individualization of the "will") provides a positive avenue for a common entry into the field of uniformity.'[53]

By contrast, we should not see Sulabhā here as trying to claim back a sexually neutral mind for her sexually determined body, even if we are tempted to think this might be Astell's position. It should be noted that Janaka's problems with her do not seem to include the charge that as a woman she is incapable of the reasoning required for gaining absolute freedom. The narrative skilfully locates that potential for human reasoning within her introduction of the topic of proper reasoning, having left Janaka, that exemplar of the masculinist claim to knowledge, silent on how reasoning relates to knowledge at all. She is therefore able to phrase her view of reasoning as neutral to men and women. We will also see in the second 'movement' of her argument that her conception of the human being is not dualistic but compositional, and in it she recognizes the morphological differentiation of sex-properties only to render them a merely contingent aspect of human development. So her argument for equality—or neutrality—of reasoning capacity amongst human beings (although only suitably trained ones) relates to her acknowledgement of sex-differences in a very different way than Astell's in two, possibly interrelated, ways: first, she does not try to claim a capacity for reasoning that has been denied her on the basis of her being a woman; second, she does not resort to a dualist account of mind in order to get around the denial of that capacity on the basis of the body.

Here, the concrete situation of Sulabhā is critical, although it also has a larger, theoretical implication: her discourse on reason is intimately tied to her renouncer life, which—as we will see in the last section of this chapter—allows her to re-situate her place as a woman within/outside society into a life of singular agency. A fundamental criticism of early modern arguments for women's nature as rational beings is that it beds back into the social context of an asymmetric relationship between men and women. Moira Gatens quotes Mary Wollstonecraft to demonstrate this criticism. Wollstonecraft says, 'The conclusion which I wish to draw, is obvious: make women rational creatures, and free citizens, and they will quickly become good wives, and mothers, that is—if men do not neglect the duties of husbands and fathers.'[54] Gatens sees this acceptance of asymmetry—being husband/father does not intrude on men's access to the public sphere but being wife/mother does for women—as an acceptance of the limitations placed by 'women's reproductive capacity'. This, in turn, she traces back to 'the notion inherited from Cartesian dualism, that human beings are separable into a sex-neutral mind and a sexed body'.[55] Gatens' general argument, in fact, is that there will be a 'bias against women' so long as there are 'implicit associations between transcendence and the formation of rational projects, on the one hand, and immanence, the body and nature, on the other'.[56]

[53] Ibid., p. 50. [54] Wollstonecraft 1975 [1792]: 299.
[55] Gatens 1991: 25. [56] Ibid., p. 60.

In our narrative, by contrast, it is Sulabhā who places the king at the heart of the project of immanence, which is to say, the bodily project of the householder life. Transcendence is possible, in the scheme of this narrative—the scheme that narratively supports Sulabhā's perspective on the matter—only through a special negotiation away from bodily nature to gnostic detachment. It is implicit that the negotiation from bodily nature is highly gendered: as we will see, Sulabhā is clear on what she has renounced, and it is different from what a man would renounce. But the text's position is that gnostic detachment applies equally—and is sought equally—through the actual renunciatory life (albeit with the ambiguity over whether that was possible only in the Age of Right or is a possibility for fallen times too), and rigorous, reasoned argumentation.

Sulabhā then summarizes the process by which meaning (*artha*) appears [91–4]: it is when the communication is unimpaired by neither self-interest and contempt nor by too much eagerness to speak for the sake of the other side. This approach is perfectly consistent with at least one contemporary feminist argument in which 'if one construes reason broadly, appealing to gender is inappropriate'.[57] Sulabhā then concludes this, the second movement in her speech:

> [95] 'King, my speech will have this kind of meaning, and it will exhibit the full perfection of speech; you ought to listen with your mind undistracted, and focused on this alone.'[58]

Sulabhā on the Ontogenetic Body: Sex-Properties between Biology and Construction

> [967] 'King, you addressed me with the questions "Who are you? Whose are you? Where do you come from?" Listen closely, for this speech is my answer to those questions. King, the way living beings are put together in this world is similar to the way lacquer and wood are completely merged together, or the way dirt and water drops can be.'

Sulabhā's next move is a cool re-framing of Janaka's query. He has sought to hem her within the gendered identity beyond which he cannot see her. But she takes his query, couched as it is within the social norms he endorses, and reads it as one about the metaphysical implications of physical—biological—facts. Toril Moi provocatively says that there is no need 'to believe that if we accept that there are biological facts, then they somehow will become the ground of social norms'.[59] Sulabhā does something even more intriguing: she appears to subvert social norms through reference to the biological facts (as available to her). Let us see what this is meant to achieve. She starts

[57] Atherton 1993: 32.
[58] *tadarthavididaṃ vākyamupetaṃ vākyasaṃpadā/avikṣiptamanā rājannekāgraḥ śrotumarhasi//.*
[59] Moi 1999: 38.

with a lesson in metaphysics, a listing of the elements of an ontology of human existence that very loosely draws on the terminology of the early Sāṃkhya system (which is roughly contemporary to the composition of the *Mahābhārata*).

> [98] 'Sound, touch, taste, form, odor and the five senses—these ten entities, completely merged together like lacquer and wood, form a separate entity.[60] [99] And it has been determined that there is no commanding of these things; there is no awareness (*vijñānam*) in any single one of these of itself or of anything beyond itself. [101] They require other entities outside themselves—listen to these: The eye, visible form, and light are the three causes of seeing; for the other kinds of knowledge and the objects they know, the causes are like those for seeing. [102] Between the object known (*jñeya*) and the knowledge (*jñāna*) is another item called "mind" (*manas*); with it one inquires to determine what is "correct" (*sādhu*) and "incorrect". [103] And tradition teaches that there is a twelfth item called the "intellect" (*buddhi*); with it one makes decisions about matters of doubt that require understanding. [104] And within this twelfth item there is another item called the essence (*sattva*); a creature is judged to possess much of this quality or to have little of it.[61] [105] The knower of the [cognitive] field is another, the fourteenth, item here; with it one thinks, "This is mine," or does not think that.[62] [106] And, king, tradition teaches there is another, a fifteenth, item here, that is called the "integration" (*sāmagrī*) of the aggregation (*samūha*) of the separate components. [107] There is another, a sixteenth, item called "combination" (*saṃghāta*), in which the two items, "form" (*ākṛti*) and "manifestation" (*vyakti*), are located. [108] Pleasure and pain, ageing and death, gaining and not gaining, and the favourable and the unfavourable: this set of opposed pairs is taught as the nineteenth.[63] [109] There is another item after the nineteenth called Time. So it is. Understand that the origination and passing away of beings is by way of the twentieth of these. [110] There is this twenty-fold aggregation and the five universal elements and two other illuminating items, the pair made up of the two states "existing" (*sat*) and "non-existing" (*asat*). [111] So tradition teaches that there are twenty-seven items. And there is destiny (*vidhi*), virility (*śukra*), and strength (*bala*), three other items. [112] So, twenty and ten component items is the sum taught by tradition. Tradition calls that "body" (*śarīra*) where (*yatra*) all of these operate together.[64] ... [115] And that primordial nature (*prakṛti*), which is not manifested, becomes manifested by these components as I, and you, O king of kings, and these other bodily beings (*śarīriṇaḥ*).'

It is worth quoting this passage *in extenso* in order to demonstrate three interconnected aspects of Sulabhā's theory of the human being: (i) it has a carefully detailed

[60] *śabdaḥ sparśo raso rūpaṃ gandhaḥ pañcendriyāni ca/pṛthagātmā daśātmānaḥ saṃśliṣṭā jatukāṣṭhavat//.*
[61] *atha dvādaśake tasminsattvaṃ nānāparo guṇaḥ/mahāsattvo'lpasattvo vā janturyenānumīyate//.*
[62] *kṣetrajña iti cāpyanyo guṇastatra caturdaśaḥ/mamāyamiti yenāyaṃ manyate na ca manyate//.*
[63] *sukhaduḥkhe jarāmṛtyū lābhālābhau priyāpriye/iti caikonaviṃśo'yaṃ dvaṃdvayoga iti smṛtaḥ//.*
[64] *ekaviṃśaśca daśaśca kalāḥ saṃkhyānataḥ smṛtāḥ/samagrā yatra vartante taccharīramiti smṛtam//.*

account of compositional nature, one which constructs the bodily human within an ecological paradigm in which different dimensions of existence and environment determine its constitution; (ii) it is in no way susceptible to a dualist construal of the human being as a mind/body entity; and (iii) the unified explanatory role attached to the 'mind' (as the purely non-material, cogitative unity that gives reflexive identity to each human subject) found in any Cartesian-style account is distributed over different elements of the human being: there is the 'mind' as the functional organ of inquiry, the 'intellect' as the judging faculty, and the 'essence' as moral-phenomenal character, while the 'cogniser of the field' is the term for the reflexivity that permits self-attribution. (There are also more or less enigmatic items—'integration', 'combination', 'aggregates'—that refer to the combinatory nature of this account.) It would take a different enterprise to develop this into a systematic metaphysics that seeks answers for various questions that this passage provokes; is it reductive because it is analytic? Is there a glimpse of an emergentist theory of consciousness here? Is a metaphysical self ultimately asserted or denied?

This theory of human being—let us recall that Sulabhā gives it to counter Janaka's limited and limiting question of who she is—relates back to what she has previously said, and forward to what she will say. Looking back, the significance we have seen her attach to reasoning and debate is not at all removed from the question of bodily being. The instruments, content, context, and consequences of reasoning are all part of what Sulabhā clearly brings together in her description of the bodily being (*śarīrin*). This means that Sulabhā's exaltation of reasoning and debate (the realm of 'mind', 'intellect', and the rest) cannot be read as her taking refuge in a doctrine of the neutral mind as a rejoinder to the gendered limitations placed by social norms upon her body. The case for reasoning is a case for freedom in toto; when she lectures on what reasoned debate is she is also lecturing on the situation of the woman as she chooses to appear—'beautiful, young and yet an ascetic'. Looking forward, this compositional account permits her to find a striking way through the enduringly tricky issue of sexual morphology and its implications.

Sulabhā then turns from the itemization of her compositional theory of the bodily being to the specific ontogenesis of the body. The medical details are not as relevant for us as the introduction of sex properties in foetal development.

> [116] 'The *kalala* embryo arises as the particular structures that develop from the union of blood and semen, "the depositing of the drops" and so on, occur. [117] From the *kalala* embryo the *arbuda* embryo is formed; the *peśī* embryo originates from the *arbuda* embryo. Then the limbs develop from the *peśī* embryo and the nails and the hair from the limbs. [118] King of Mithilā, when the ninth month has been completed the named-and-formed one [i.e., the particular person] is produced, "female" or "male" according to its sign.'[65]

[65] *saṃpūrṇe navame māse jantorjātasya maithila/jāyate nāmarūpatvaṃ strī pumānveti liṅgataḥ//.*

The 'signs' here are inferential marks, encountering which a conclusion is drawn as to whether the foetus is male or female. These signs, then, are 'sex-properties', the biological signs of sex within the (proto-)biological account of foetal development that Sulabhā is presenting. Is this sufficient for us to conclude that sex is offered here as a given? Sulabhā's position here sits at an angle to the sort of argument made by Georgia Warnke: '[S]ex is less inborn than interpretive. Assumptions and expectations about proper and distinct gender activities erect the interpretive frameworks through which certain features and combinations of features appear to be fundamental to bodies and to comprise sex... The idea that we just are essentially male or female is... less of an idea about nature than it is an interpretation of natural properties...'[66] Alison Stone points out two things with regard to the type of reasoning given by Warnke: (i) 'some bodily properties' are 'really necessary for genital sexual reproduction', and that is why they 'become the focus of people's attention given a social norm stipulating that men and women must have reproductive sex', so the social norm is not just an interpretation of the body; moreover, (ii) there has to be some cluster of properties that has the causal effect of giving people—'fairly regularly'—the ability to reproduce.[67] Warnke also says that even if properties do cluster to make a natural sex difference, we need not classify people on the basis of this difference. Stone's comment is that we need not consider sex to be '*the* central and basic principle of human classification'. We could not stop classifying people altogether by sex: 'our sex-properties are bound to influence our behaviour in some way, even if these influences are mediated by society'; so we could 'treat sex as just one basis of classification amongst others'.[68]

I would suggest that the location of this recognition of the foetal development of sex-properties within Sulabhā's larger account of human becoming indicates an attitude consistent with Stone's. Sulabhā recognizes the morphological role of sex-properties that mark the developing human being, but gives it just one, contingent place in development. In terms of a bodily ontology, she acknowledges the morphology but simply as one factor within a developmental account that is for all human beings. Presumably, since inferences are tied to the detectable sex-marks, there is an implicit opening up to non-binary sexual morphologies; this is not entirely unexpected given the ancient Indian recognition of such possibilities, strongly de-valorized by social norms though they usually were. Even some radical feminist positions seek to work with and around morphological structures. '[T]here is a contingent, though not arbitrary, relation between the male body and masculinity and the female body and femininity. To claim this is neither biologism nor essentialism but is rather to acknowledge the importance of complex and ubiquitous networks of signification to the historically, psychologically and culturally variable ways of being a man or a woman.'[69] I must emphasize that I am certainly not claiming that the content of the speech given by the character of Sulabhā should be seen as a deliberate articulation of a position within the debate characterized in contemporary feminism as 'sex vs gender'. Rather, we should see it as

[66] Warnke 2001: 130. [67] Stone 2007: 48. [68] Ibid., p. 49. [69] Gatens 1996: 13.

part of an account that seeks to offer a rigorously universal view of what it is to be human—a complex, layered, compositional being of bodily presence—that folds into it the acknowledgement that sexual morphology is also part of that bodiliness, albeit a contingent, developmental one.

Strikingly, Sulabhā uses this carefully constructed account of human ontogenesis to deny Janaka the satisfaction of having his question answered. Janaka had wanted to know who she was in terms that indicated a social normativity in which being a 'woman' (even as renouncer) immediately had a certain constricting significance. Instead of answering within those terms, she ends this 'movement' with a rhetorical denial of the very coherence of such socially normative questions as his. It is rightly pointed out that the feminism particularly associated with French thinkers sought 'to question whether the biological category "woman" has any stable social significance, not to question the biological category as such'.[70] By accepting the biological category as a contingent feature of a larger ontology, and offering that ontology in response to a question that was in fact wholly driven by an assumed social significance, Sulabhā's questioning of social norms of gender is both oblique and deep. It is oblique because this response presents only a universal account of being human, and is not offered as a specific critique of masculinist norms. But it is nevertheless deep, because its universalism is thoroughgoing and constructed from the ground up as a self-standing account that leaves no base for masculinist norms. Of course, none of this is to deny that social norms exist. Sulabhā's assertion that their very origins have no basis in the ontogenesis she has described amounts to the rejection of 'biologism', the doctrine that social norms are derived from morphological features.[71]

> [123] 'All people perpetually come into being in this fashion—like a fine horse running swiftly!—so who are they? Where do they come from? Where do they not come from? [124] Whose is this? Whose is it not? Where does this come from? Where does it not come from? What is the connection between beings and the components that make them up in this world?[72] [125] Just as fire comes to be from the combination of the sun, a crystal lens, and some twigs for tinder, so beings come to be from the combination of their components' (*evaṃ samudayātkalānāmapi jantavaḥ*).

The Claim for an Ungendered Neutrality: Janaka's Paradigm of the Metaphysical Self

Sulabhā then turns to consider the implications of what she sees as Janaka's own understanding of how he is free.

[70] McIntosh 1991: 114.

[71] It will be clear by now why, in just following the contours of this text, it is neither philosophically possible nor exegetically necesary for me to engage with the more radical rejection of sex-properties within the thesis of the entirely constructed nature of gender, most influentially in the work of Judith Butler. This choice is determined by the task at hand and has no implications for any other comparative project.

[72] *kasyedaṃ kasya vā nedaṃ kuto vedaṃ na vā kutaḥ/saṃbandhaḥ ko'sti bhūtānāṃ svairapyavayavairiha//.*

> [126–7] 'Since you see your self within yourself by means of your self, why do you not, in exactly the same way, by means of your self, see your self in someone else? And if you are firmly resolved upon the sameness in your self and in another, why do you ask me "Who are you?" And, "Whose are you?" Why, King of Mithilā, does someone who is freed from the pairs of opposites (such as, "This is mine and this is not mine") ask, "Who are you, whose are you, and where do you come from?" '

As James Fitzgerald notes about verse 126, it is not obvious that Janaka himself has put his position that way. Some modern commentators have seen this as an (early) expression of metaphysical non-duality between all individual selves and an absolute self.[73] He suggests instead that the simpler way of reading 126 is that 'it is a stock way of saying, "Since you [claim to] have reached *mokṣa* through a kind of yoga, how is it you fail to recognize someone else who has also reached *mokṣa* through yoga?" '[74] This makes sense: it is irrelevant whether there is a non-dualist position here or not; whatever the actual metaphysics, the core point is that Sulabhā reads Janaka's claims as indicating that he is committed to understanding the self as neutral and therefore the 'same' in some way, whether ontologically identical, phenomenologically interchangeable, or intellectually equal. So it is not too much of a stretch from the exact content of Janaka's claim to Sulabhā's re-formulation of it. In any case, her interest is not in the metaphysics, but in the psychological consequences that would result from a freedom that treated everyone as the same. Or rather, she wants to establish that, even if freedom did consist in the attainment of a self whose being is neutral between sexes, classes, and other markers of difference, it certainly does not manifest itself in Janaka's attitude and conduct. One can suggest that his questions, while a standard mode of identifying a man in terms of patriliny, here imply the essential dependence of a woman on the men of her family. She implies that this is inconsistent with a genuine attainment of freedom from all pairs of opposites (including, in this case, 'I am a man and you are a woman').[75]

There is some scope for thinking of Sulabhā's position as indicating support for a conception of the self as neutral in some way; after all, we have seen her strive to command for herself, a woman, the right to rational thought equal to any man. If what is going on in this passage is purely the criticism of Janaka that he fails to attain the neutral self that Sulabhā endorses, then we should read such a self as a powerful conception for challenging the subordination of women. And again, Mary Astell's writings come to mind as comparision. Speaking of Astell's concern for 'self-preservation' (which Astell conceives as the preservation of the mind from evil, where the mind is

[73] Fitzgerald 2003: 674. [74] Ibid., p. 674.

[75] She also makes it a point about his insistence that he is both free and a king: the particularities that are inherent to the actions of a king too are inconsistent with freedom from duality or the pairs of opposites: [128–9] 'O lord of the earth, what indication (*lakṣaṇa*) is there that one is freed when he treats some as an enemy, others as allies, and others as neutrals in victory, in alliances, and in war? What indication is there that one is freed when he does not understand the [structure of]... this world and is still attached to [it]? [130] What indication is there that one is freed when he does not see sameness in kindness and unkindness, in weakness and in strength?'

truly the self), Cynthia Bryson says, 'For Astell, it ['self-preservation'] is a mind/body distinction... The disembodied mind is "who" a person is, and the gendered body is meaningless to individuality and identity.'[76] Bryson asserts that Astell's view is that 'the mind is distinct from the gendered body; the "mind," as the true "self," exists as neither masculine nor feminine'. Bryson acknowledges that Astell tacitly concedes the cultural presumption about women in order to make her metaphysical point: 'If the mind remains separated from "matter" (the body), then the physiological dissimilitude between men and women (the "sexual defect") is of no consequence, for in matters of rationalization they are equal.'[77] 'Self-determination means the freedom to create a gender-neutral "self." And while the gendered body becomes unimportant, no one can really deny the external difference between a penis and testicles, and a vagina and breasts... But, according to Descartes and Astell, the body's "housing" doesn't matter. What is important is the disembodied (gender-less) mind, the "true" self. And on that point, Astell would say that women and men are identical...'[78]

Now, Bryson's argument requires both a Cartesian self-body distinction and the claim that a bodiless self has an identity (but one that is somehow also gender-free). We will not find such a metaphysics in our dialogue, for better or for worse. Nevertheless, the psychological point in Astell's argument is that there is a way in which one must think of oneself as not essentially bound by divisive gendering. It is this argument for a certain attitude—if you see people equally through seeing them as selves, then you should not see them unequally by seeing them as men and women. So, it may well be that one way of reading Sulabhā here is that she is indeed asserting that the self is the same, and Janaka has not understood this, which is why he asks her questions premised on her not being 'the same'—i.e., the neutral self—as him.

But perhaps Sulabhā's position is more ambiguous. We must recall that in her previous moves, she appeared to have arguments comparable to Western feminist ones but which, on closer inspection, turned out to be subtly (if pointedly) different either due to the difference in intellectual context or due to a genuinely different line of thought. So too here. One way of looking at her move here is that, given the likely dominance of this doctrine of self (*ātman*) in her cultural world, it might be that she thinks it better to not deny outright the sameness of self—in effect, her equality with Janaka—in some way; she just turns the tables on him by saying his psychology undermines his claim to having attained that freedom of sameness. Nevertheless, her acceptance of this notion of *ātman* must at most be a cautious refusal to outright reject a dominant conception of selfhood. Her previous move presents the human person as a compositional, bodily one, whereas this 'self' that Janaka argues for (regardless of the many other, more complex ideas of *ātman* found in ancient Hindu materials) appears precisely to be independent of the highly contextualizing and particularized bodily being.

[76] Bryson 1998: 52. [77] Ibid., pp. 54–5. [78] Ibid., p. 56.

Therefore we should think of her, instead, as altogether rejecting the doctrine that absolute freedom consists in the realization that one is fundamentally a neutral self (*ātman*). At no point does she seem to think that there is a pure core of selfhood behind the compositionally detailed ecologically embedded, bodily person. Note here that I am not saying anything about the coherence or otherwise of the concept of a neutral self; in itself, it is a formal place-holder, and there are many varieties of arguments for and against it in the history of Indian thought[79]—none of which is particularly evident in this brief passage. It could well be argued that any account of an ungendered self is simply a coded masculinism, so that there can be no way of subverting binaries through ascent to such a self. But in any case, if this second interpretation of her move is the more plausible one, we do not need to fill in the details of the concept of a neutral, true self hinted at in this passage. We have seen Sulabhā outline what she thinks a human being is, and it does not turn on the appeal to such a self. So, when she says Janaka nowhere evidences the psychological consequences that are supposed to follow from a freedom consisting in the realization of a neutral, pure self, we really ought to interpret this as her dismissal of the plausibility of such a conception in the first place. At the same time, we should also recognize that Sulabhā's ambiguity over the nature and existence of a neutral self is not ambivalence towards a project of transcendence (indeed, as I will suggest at the end, these are two interconnected projects). In this, she is certainly not at one with contemporary secular feminist theorists who likewise deny the viability of a neutral, core self.

> [131] 'So you are not freed, and the conceit you may have in believing you have absolute freedom should be suppressed by your friends, as medicines might be used for someone who is unconscious.'

The Torments of the King, or the Immanence of Masculinist Power

Sulabhā's rhetoric at verse 131 marks the next stage of her criticism of Janaka.

> [133–6] 'King, listen to what I tell you about these and some other subtle points of attachment . . . and are relevant to absolute freedom. The king who rules this whole earth under a single parasol dwells in just one city, and in this city he stays in just one palace, where he lies upon just one bed at night, and when he rests in that bed, half of it belongs to his wife; thus is he joined to the consequences of actions by these attachments.'

> [138] 'The king is always dependent upon others, he himself attends to just a small part of things. How could the king be independent (*svatantra*), completely in control,

[79] See the papers in Kuznetsova et al. 2012.

> when making treaties and waging war? [139] He is never completely in control, even when spending time in play with his women; how could he be completely in control when he meets his councillors for advice?... [142] He is not in charge, others are always telling him what to do—"Bathe, take hold, drink, eat, pour the offering, worship the sacrificial fires, speak, listen..."'
>
> [150–1] 'Not freed from the mental torments that arise from desire, aversion, and fondness; nor from the diseases that fall upon one, like headaches, etc.; beset by many of the pairs of opposites, fearful on every side, he sees his kingdom plagued with many enemies and lies awake counting through the nights.'[80]

This is thought-provoking in comparative context, because Sulabhā's view is that Janaka who, as king, is the exemplification of the masculine ideal, exists in a deeply problematic existential condition because such masculinity is expressed only in the sensuous life. The classic feminist criticism of abstract philosophical thought is that it ends up (the aetiology varies with critics) relying on an assumption about the thinker as male. Genevieve Lloyd, for example, argues that Descartes makes an association, even if it is unintentional, between a trained mind and a conception of masculinity: this 'sexual division of labour' is one in which 'women have been assigned responsibility for that real of the sensuous which the Cartesian Man of Reason must transcend'; 'women's task is to preserve the sphere of the intermingling of mind and body', so that the Man of Reason 'must leave soft emotions and sensuousness behind'.[81] From this, she derives the case that the untrained mind, functioning in 'the realm of the sensuous' then becomes assigned to women. Seen this way (and setting aside counter-arguments about Lloyd's reading of Descartes), the claim to abstract thought is masculinist. Nancy Bauer, in tackling this kind of problem through Beauvoir, seeks to establish how there may be a distinctively feminist way of deriving abstract reason: '[W]e cannot think coherently about what a "man" is, cannot make out a coherent sex-neutral sense of the term, until we address the question of what it means to be, to be called, a woman.'[82]

If we keep this consideration in mind and turn to Sulabhā, we can note these following points. First, it is true that Sulabhā does not directly thematize abstract thought through being a woman. This goes back to my initial observation that we cannot think of Sulabhā as actually espousing what we may read as a feminist perspective.

However, and this is the second point, in the specific rhetorical line she follows, we may nonetheless find that the capacity for abstract thought is presented as a trained human capacity via a critique of a masculine way of being. In effect, Sulabhā sees Janaka as the exemplification of the untrained mind—or less dualistically—an untrained (or poorly trained) human being in search of transcendence. She takes him at his word as the exemplar of the masculinist order, the royal householder. And it is precisely the

[80] *amukto mānasairduḥkhairicchādveṣapriyodbhavaiḥ/śirorogādibhī rogaistathaiva vinipātibhiḥ// dvaṃdvaistaistairupahataḥ sarvataḥ pariśaṅkitaḥ/bahupratyarthikaṃ rājyamupāste gaṇayanniśāḥ//.*

[81] Lloyd 1984: 50.

[82] Bauer 2001: 50.

conditions of this life that are located in 'the realm of the sensuous'. To be everything a man is, he is to be lodged in emotion and sensuality; it is there that men have the power that they value: to rule, to have sex, to be served. In that realm, Sulabhā would have been a wife. Her analysis is provocatively informative, because she interprets social norms to imply that if the sensuous life, one of dependence, is to be seen in gendered terms at all, it is associated with masculinity! But this is not to suggest that she has merely reversed the sexual division of labour. From her perspective, she is trained in abstract thought directed towards a project of transcendence, and she functions in this way exactly by not being like the exemplary man. Yet she does not rule out that men can be trained, since what she has to say about renunciatory power applies to men too. In that sense, her account is neutral between men and women, but arrived at from the opposite direction to the Cartesian division of gendered labour presented and criticized by Lloyd.

Freedom: A Woman's Agency, a Particular Human Path

The final 'movement' of Sulabhā's speech is a spiritual autobiographical justification of who she is, with a contrastive criticism of Janaka for having made the accusations he has of her.

> [162] 'I have no attachment to my own body, how could I be attached to another's? You should not say such a thing about someone like me who is freed.'[83]

While the king may have been critical of a male renouncer with her powers, Janaka would not—could not—have said the same things about such a man as he has said about Sulabhā. So it is clear that it is her being a woman, young, attractive, and yet an ascetic, that Janaka has found unforgivable, not her being an ascetic per se (which would be, of course, a male ascetic). By contrast, her reply, in terms of its epistemic quality, its rhetorical prowess, and its analytic purposes, have been just what Janaka's words required. So she draws a contrast between his deeply personal—emotional, irrational—reaction to her capacities and presence, and her own cool, calm focus on the content of his statement. Compare her comportment with Beauvoir's in this striking passage: 'A wild cry of rage, the revolt of a wounded soul—that they could have accepted with a moved and pitying condescension; since they could not pardon me my objectivity, [my masculine readers] feigned a disbelief in it. For example I will take a phrase of Claude Mauriac's which perfectly illustrates the arrogance of the First Sex. "What has she got against me?" he wanted to know. Nothing. I had nothing against anything except the words I was quoting.'[84]

[83] *svadehe nābhiṣaṅgo me kutaḥ paraparigrahe/na mām evaṃvidhāṃ muktāṃ īdṛśaṃ vaktum arhasi//.*
[84] Simone de Beauvoir, *The Force of Circumstance*, vol. 2: 263–4; translated and quoted by Bauer 2001: 46.

Sulabhā then indicts Janaka for misreading her yogic communication with him. Not only did she not do what he has accused her of doing, the very fact that he did so demonstrates perfectly that he fails to have achieved that freedom he so claims to cherish.

> [164–6] 'So, king, if you stand there freed of your attachments, having overcome the bonds that fettered you, how is it you have come once again to be attached to such things as your parasol and so on? I think you did not really learn that lesson, or you learned it wrongly, or you learned something that merely seemed to be the lesson, or you learned some other lesson instead. You live according to these popular ideas, but you are bound by attachment and aversion like any bumpkin.'

She offers her own version of the nature of what she has done, going back to the significance of the temporary co-presence of their 'essence'.

> [167] 'If you are completely free, what wrong did I do you when I made entry into you with my essence?[85] [168] There is a special stricture in the rules for ascetics: They must dwell in an empty house. What violation did I commit, and to whom, when I came to stay in this empty house? [169] I am not touching you, king—not with my hands, nor my arms, nor my feet, nor my thighs, nor any other parts of my body.[86] [170] A far-sighted man from a good family who has a sense of shame should not say such a thing in public—whether it be true or false, it occurred between the two of us alone.[87] [172c] . . . you should not talk of such a joining of man and woman in public.[88] [173-4] I am going to dwell here in you, king of Mithilā, without touching you, as a drop of water on a lotus leaf stands on the leaf without touching it. Or if you do sense some touch of me though I do not touch you, how is it then that the knowledge transmitted to you by that mendicant is "seedless"?'[89]

This is a fascinating outline of an imaginary phenomenology whose formal impossibility permits us to think more deeply of the significance of Sulabhā's action, Janaka's response, and Sulabhā's critical clarification of the bodily nature of gender and human identity. As I said at the beginning of the episode, Sulabhā's action must be seen as an assertion of an alternative way of being herself. Merely to gaze back at Janaka would not remove the traces of exactly how he sees her as other. Instead, she establishes a radically different form of engagement, in which her proximity to him cannot be mediated by social norms.

This mode of engagement is, of course, ambiguous in some ways. She intends it—as she now makes clear—to be heteronomous. Their proximity of essence leaves Sulabhā

[85] *sattvenānupraveśo hi yo'yaṃ tvayi kṛto mayā/kiṃ tavāprakṛtaṃ tatra yadi mukto'si sarvataḥ//.*

[86] *niyamo hyeṣa dharmeṣu yatīnāṃ śūnyavāsitā/śūnyamāvāsayantyā ca mayā kiṃ kasya dūṣitam//na pāṇibhyāṃ na bāhubhyāṃ pādorubhyāṃ na cānagha/na gātrāvayavairanyaiḥ spṛśāmi tvā narādhipa//.*

[87] *kule mahati jātena hrīmatā dīrghadarśinā/naitatsadasi vaktavyaṃ sadvāsadvā mithaḥ kṛtam//.*

[88] *strīpuṃsoḥ samavāyo'yaṃ tvayā vācyo na saṃsadi//.*

[89] *yathā puṣkaraparṇasthaṃ jalaṃ tatparṇasaṃsthitam/tiṣṭhatyaspṛśatī tadvattvayi vatsyāmi maithila// yadi vāpyaspṛśantyā me sparśaṃ jānāsi kaṃcana/jñānaṃ kṛtamabījaṃ te kathaṃ teneha bhikṣuṇā//.*

and Janaka, if each is free as s/he claims, unmixed in intimacy. Of course, because of the magical nature of this proximity, the ordinary language description seems inadequate for its metaphorical import, and as I have suggested, we must take 'touch' (*spṛśa*) here to be some sort of label for a suprasensory proximity. Sulabhā's rigorous commitment to renunciatory freedom (articulated in 173–4) makes her view of this contact consistent with an ethical commitment to the otherness of the other. This brings to mind what Levinas has claimed for touch: 'To be in contact is neither to invest the other and annul his alterity, nor to suppress myself in the other. In contact itself the touching and touched separate, as though the touch moved off, was always already other, did not have anything in common with me.'[90] But the implication and the aetiology of this heteronomous contact are quite different in the two cases. For Levinas, contact moves in the direction of what exactly Janaka would have it be, the erotic encounter. As he says shortly after noting the alterity coded into the very structure of contact, '[i]n a caress, what is there is sought as though it were not there';[91] proximity is therefore intimacy, a deliberate search for otherness in which loss of difference is also simultaneously sought (even if impossible to find). And once he is set in that direction, his masculine reading of the erotic opens itself up to criticism. As Catheryn Vasseleu observes of this Levinasian paradigm, 'Eroticism is a loss of perspective. It does not aspire to the infinite transcendence required for desire, which is reserved for the absolute alterity of the divine... The dimension of intimacy in the midst of existence is opened by the feminine, not the dimension of transcendence.'[92] The relevant point here is not the exact nature of Levinas' contrast between erotic contact and transcendence, because the atheological freedom that Janaka and Sulabhā are discussing makes no mention of the divine (let alone its otherness). Rather, it is that, once such extraordinary proximity is read in erotic register, then it would seem to be a barrier to transcendence as Levinas would have it. And to that extent, it is just this that is implied by Janaka in his anger at Sulabhā's entry of her essence into his.

Now, it is a different project to see the caress as pleasure, an exploration of the sexuate nature of the erotic, as Luce Irigaray does in her critical engagement with Levinas. And we will turn to such a project in Chapter 4 of this book. Instead, here I want to stop and acknowledge how proximity as the contact of alterities can indeed call for an erotic reading. Janaka has made that plain, and Sulabhā acknowledges it. Not for her a disingenuous denial that there could possibly ever be an erotic construal of contact between man and woman. However, she thinks that such proximity—a supersensory contact, metaphorically evocative of, if not exactly like, the sense of touch—would neither be made nor received erotically by those who are absolutely free. Janaka's unfreedom is evident in his receiving that proximity in conventional—and thus, sexual—terms.

As we ponder this claim, her yogic capacity and her particular use of it here also start making sense. Her freedom consists in detachment. She does not cling to the

[90] Levinas 1981: 86. [91] Ibid., p. 90. [92] Vasseleu 1998: 106.

details of her existential condition (although she does not reject them; after all, she lives as a woman, as an almswoman, as a highly trained debater). It is because her freedom consists in not being bound to the material states that determine the bodily being of humans that she has the power to subvert the boundaries of those material states. She opens up what the locus of bodily being is by her freedom and her powers because she takes a detached stance about whatever happens to her, the particular bodily being that she is at any one time. For her, 'taking on' a beautiful form, or bringing her cognitive essence into contact with Janaka's are variations on a theme. Once one is free of the implications of one set of states, one can be in any other state.

She is not disembodied—her compositional account of the person has made that clear. But bodiliness is fluid, which she has demonstrated through her agency (or rather, which the text has demonstrated—as if it were a thought-experiment—by inviting us to think that we can give phenomenal content to its mysterious narrative of a yogic power). I think it is plausible to look at the magic that the narrative permits itself as a heuristic through which it destabilizes the fixity of a human's phenomenological field. This does not dispense with individual subjectivity: recall that Sulabhā is clear that there is no overcoming of the otherness of Janaka. What we have is the equivalent of contemporary thought-experiments, which tend to rely heavily on intuitions about possible technologies, to switch bodily loci, phenomenologies, modes of communication, etc. Here, we are pushed to the limits of the imagination about gender and the body: there are slippages and flows, but also fixities and perspectives. Sulabhā is somehow 'in' Janaka, but still as a woman (which is what permits the disagreement between them as to how that contact ought to be read).

Sulabhā then continues, combining her continued chiding of Janaka for his lacking the freedom that he claims, with an enigmatic description of her own path to freedom.

> [175] 'You have fallen away from the householding pattern of life without having reached absolute freedom that is so hard to understand; you exist between these two, babbling about absolute freedom. [176] There is no mixing of social orders in the passionless (de-attached, *bhāvābhāva*) union of one who is freed—who knows of unity and separateness—with another who is freed.'

Sulabhā's criticism of Janaka is that his account of the dialectic between immanence and transcendence is circumscribed by his being a man (indeed, the exemplary man); it is not therefore the master-narrative it appears to be. Her rejoinder, however, is not to say that she can speak only as a woman, but to offer her own account of transcendence, a counter-universalism of transcendence through detachment. What would it be like for a man to perform her renunciation (rather than what he would be expected to by the dominant discourse of male renunciation)? That would be the path to reach freedom for any human being. So the specificity of her bodily being as Sulabhā the woman renouncer—by which she is located in a world of meaning—nevertheless does not contain all the meaning that she has found through her acts.

> [180–2] 'So even if we are of different social orders, because our life patterns are different, and because we are completely different one from the other, how could there be mixing of our orders? I am not higher in social order than you by birth; nor am I a *vaiśya*, nor a lower sort of woman. I am of the same order as you, king, a woman of clean birth, and chaste. There was a seer who was a king called Pradhāna. Obviously you have heard of him. Understand that I came to be in his family and I am named Sulabhā.'

Sulabhā does not have an agenda here on questions of class and elitism (the *Mahābhārata* has other places where it incorporates critiques of social class, in complex and contested ways[93]). She will not be caught on the point of adherence to the right norms and social order (*dharma*) by the 'hypocritical' King who 'flies the banner of righteousness' (recall the double-meaning of Janaka as '*dharmadhvaja*'). In demonstrating her dharmic scruples, she also mentions her origins. She was born and brought up a veritable princess, no less. But then she sailed out into the waters of normative indeterminacy.

> [184] 'In that clan was I born. Since there was no husband suitable to me, I was trained in the rules for gaining absolute freedom, so, all alone, I live according to the hermit (*muni*) way of life.'[94]

She was meant for marriage, which is what social norms ask for. But at the same time, they did not rule out her taking renunciation. She will not say why there was no husband suitable for her; and oddly, it is that refusal to tell which is itself emblematic of her agency. Howsoever she arrived at the process by which she could gain training for her project of transcendence, nothing of what Janaka conjectured about her solitary state can be true. As such, at least in some ways, one must risk the anachronism of asking about the symbolic meaning of her way of life. I will do no more than juxtapose this glimpse of Sulabhā's life with Cynthia Bryson's spirited interpretation of Mary Astell: 'It is interesting that Astell had chosen neither to marry nor to acquire property during her lifetime, defying the traditional role for women and practically denying her own gender status to remain fiercely independent... Perhaps Astell's refusal to submit to the enslaving contract of marriage is the reason that some scholars describe her as a radical feminist.'[95]

We must nonetheless note that in that classical system (as indeed in any celibate religious order) the renunciation of a woman is her renunciation of reproduction, and this offers the most profound asymmetry with a man's renunciation. Any renouncer gives up marriage, true; but what man would say in that ancient context that he became a renouncer because no wife suitable to him was found? (Indeed, even today?) We can think of another of Beavoir's famous declarations. 'But if I want to define

[93] On the highly charged story of the tribal hunter-archer Ekalavya as symbol of complex liminality and the dominant classical Sanskritic world, see Brodbeck 2006; Shankar 1994.

[94] *sāhaṃ tasminkule jātā bhartaryasati madvidhe/vinītā mokṣadharmeṣu carāmyekā munivratam//.*

[95] Bryson 1998: 51, 54.

myself, I must first declare: "I am a woman"... A man never begins by affirming that he is an individual of a certain sex: that he is a man goes without saying.'[96] Sulabhā has recognized the morphological facts in her account of foetal ontogenesis; she has acknowledged the social norm that women marry. But she reconfigures the gendered assumptions of renunciation, and that too in a systematic way: she is careful to point out that her 'way of life' is consonant with *dharma*—she adheres to all the requirements of the renouncer, such as chastity, homelessness, and so on. Is the more radical subversion to deny *dharma* or to reconfigure it?

Sulabhā's autonomy is not just about the refusal to take a husband, that is to say, be free of social dependence. Although she is keen to assert that she was properly trained, the training on the renunciatory path is only to establish her in her own independent practices of conduct and intellect.

> [185–6] 'I am not concealed in a disguise, I do not confuse what is another's with what is mine; I am not creating a mixture of lawful norms, I hold firm to the practices of my own lawful duty.[97] I do not waver in my promises; I do not speak without careful examination; nor have I come into your presence without careful examination, O lord of men.'

It is significant that Sulabhā is not paired or associated with a male thinker; her reference to her father is only because she wants to make a point about her social order but nothing more. Her singularity grounds her being, and her being a woman does not make her intellectual capacities derivative of a male presence.[98] Michele Le Doeuff perhaps unfairly structures the access of women to philosophy (before the professionalization of the discipline from the mid-twentieth century) in the West to an invariable 'theoretico-amorous' relationship to a famous male philosopher.[99] Elizabeth Grosz says of this observation, 'here the female "partner" may be presumed to take on the role of body to the male philosopher's position as mind'.[100] As we see, in her dialogue with Janaka, the situation is almost perfectly reversed, for it is Sulabhā who espouses broadly the life of the mind, and it is Janaka she criticizes for his immanence, that is to say, his life of the senses. The conceptual framework of her independence, while utilizing the tension between immanence and transcendence, does not so much resist the male paradigm as upend it. At the same time, the details of both the narrative and the teaching of Sulabhā should make us cautious of too close an identification between immanence and the body, together with a correlative identification between transcendence and freedom from the body. We cannot deny that there is such a dynamic in Sulabhā's teachings; but the bodily aspects of her situation—her persistent identity as a woman as she asserts

[96] Simone de Beauvoir, *The Second Sex*, xxi; noted by and quoted in Moi 1999: 192.

[97] *nāsmi satrapraticchannā na parasvābhimāninī/na dharmasaṃkarakarī svadharme'smi dhṛtavratā//.*

[98] It is perhaps notable that the most famous independent woman thinker of Western antiquity, Hypatia, bears an astonishing resemblance to the literary character of Sulabhā, dignity and virtue being values they express by the radical removal of sexual relations from their lives.

[99] Le Doueff 1989. [100] Grosz 1994: 211–12, endnote 3.

her freedom from bodily influence, her acknowledgement of a basic yet contingent role for sex properties in the development of human beings—ought to modify such a straightforward identification.

But whatever we can say about the complex role of bodiliness in Sulabhā's project of transcendence, nevertheless, the central feature of that project is her renunciation. It was only because she was an almswoman that Janaka received her in the first place. Only then—if at least then—does the solitary woman have a place, whatever its contested position, in the classical Indian world. And the power of this renunciation is not only a social one; as Sulabhā makes clear, it is spiritual. All she is, for herself, for Janaka and others in the text, and for us, turns on her decisive rejection of sexuality.

> [189] 'As an almsman might dwell for one night in an empty house in a city, so I will spend this night in this body of yours.'[101]

In whatever bodily state and locus she 'dwells' in, it is 'empty' for her. It carries no emotional presence, no erotic charge to fill up around her. This, it must be said, makes us think carefully of the bearing of the Sulabhā story on contemporary discussions. Moira Gatens is pungent on the question of the relationship between feminism and sexuality. 'It is a striking peculiarity of much contemporary feminist writing that the essential component of female subjectivity, once it is freed from the "tyranny" of nature, is taken to be female sexuality. Michel Foucault offers an analysis of the tendency inherent in modern Western culture "to direct the question of what we are, to sex".'[102] Furthermore, Gatens points to Beauvoir's sense that the options available to 'the independent woman' are 'bleak' in the realm of sexuality.[103] It is obvious that Sulabhā is pessimistic—indeed, dismissive—about the very possibility of women's autonomy in sexual relationships. She will say at most to Janaka that 'half the bed' belongs to his wife (v. 136), but her description of the condition of immanence wholly in terms of the king shows that her view of social norms is inherently masculinist. For her, the gnoseological freedom to explore transcendence through her subjectivity intrinsically requires stepping outside sexuality. Indeed, her keen awareness of the masculinist structuring of a woman's appearance through her sexuality is made evident at the very outset, when she is said to take on the form of a supremely beautiful woman.

> [190–1] 'King of Mithilā, I have been honored by your giving me a seat, and by the hospitality of your words. Having slept well sheltered, pleased, I will go on the morrow. After he heard these reasoned and significant statements the king did not say anything further.'[104]

It is clear that Sulabhā is committed to 'absolute freedom' as a transcendence of her bodily condition. It is important that we note that hers is a double freedom. First, there

[101] *yathā śūnye purāgāre bhikṣurekāṃ niśāṃ vaset/tathā hi tvaccharīre'sminnimāṃ vatsyāmi śarvarīm//.*

[102] Gatens 1991: 130. She quotes Foucault 1978: 78. [103] Gatens 1991: 131.

[104] *sāhamāsanadānena vāgātithyena cārcitā/suptā suśaraṇā prītā śvo gamiṣyāmi maithila//ityetāni sa vākyāni hetumantyarthavanti ca/śrutvā nādhijagau rājā kiṃcidanyadataḥ param//.*

is the existential freedom of having made herself, her bodily situation, one that is expressive of her agency, in which she is in constant dialectic with her gendered history: a woman set to marry but who became a renouncer, a woman expected to be protectively constrained by male society who wanders free, a woman who was not expected to learn the mystery of existence but who was trained rigorously for insight, a woman who has attained immense powers but who is still challenged by a man for being the woman he thinks she is, a woman who finds herself needing to defend herself but can instead turn her defence into a lesson on reason and spirit, a woman whose presence is sexualized but who offers a metaphysics that cannot contain sexuality.

At the same time, and second, hers is also that very specific metaphysical freedom which she preaches: detachment from her situation, a freedom which motivated her and now permits her continued existential freedom. Janaka seeks to situate her entirely through a construal of her gendered role as a woman. In turn, Sulabhā situates him as the exemplar of immanence—someone whose being is wholly contained within the norms of gendered society. Not only that, she demonstrates that his claim to transcendence (which they agree consists in detachment from the human condition) is in fact tied back to his particular bodily situation. Now, we have to acknowledge too that Sulabhā is careful to communicate through the same teleological terminology: hence her insistence that she adheres to *dharma* and has striven for detachment. As a woman her relationship to *dharma* is different, as she well knows, so she negotiates between how dharmic norms have determined her situation, and how from that situation she has attained the metaphysical transcendence that Janaka cannot deny. By contrast, Janaka takes the standard and therefore unspoken masculinist stance that his being dharmic is the entirely unconstrained choice of his to be a dharmic king.

We should therefore not see the text as giving us as a man seeking/claiming a universal attainment of transcendence versus a woman seeking/claiming a situated version of such an attainment; nor even both a man and a woman being irredeemably situated. Rather, we should see that all chance of that universal attainment which the *Mahābhārata* here presents as metaphysical freedom is only arrived at through existential freedom. Existential freedom does make meaning only in the recognition of the bodily situation—a recognition which Janaka signally fails to have. This particular narrative is set up such that it is Sulabhā who has this insight and acts upon it. It is her situation—the woman whose presence is always already gendered—from which the possibility of detachment can be attained. Anyone else, another woman or a man, can also then set forth on the universal project of metaphysical freedom only through the recognition of the situated nature of existential freedom that Sulabhā achieves and Janaka does not. We may reject or replace the metaphysical project, or deny that there can be one. But that is not the point of my exegesis, because what I want to draw attention to is how the particular situation of Sulabhā can be read as the making of existential freedom: from gender, through body, through the very reconceptualization of what body means, and what that implies.

Concluding Puzzle

Beauvoir grants that facticity is the background against which choices are made, facts about the past, of place, of ways in which someone is viewed by others, and the perceptible physical facts of appearance. But 'facts...in themselves have no significance...[Their] meaning...is revealed as such only in the light of the ends man proposes.'[105] Whether she is criticized for this or not, she is notable for having suggested that women have the freedom to give meaning to the facticity of their having been born female (*femelle*) (the famous 'One is not born but rather becomes, a woman'[106]). Of course, her key point was that the meanings that are accepted by women come from a culture made by men, but her existential commitment to freedom appeared to make her more confident of a project of self-affirmation than the ambiguities of sexual difference appeared to permit (from the perspective of later generations of feminists).

We may draw different lessons from the Sulabhā story, especially given the uncertainties of who composed it and why that lies over what we see happening in the story; but it is striking that she constantly transgresses representations of her lived body. She is a woman throughout, but there is absolutely no direct description of her before she herself chooses to take on a particular form; just because there are other stories in which a woman changes appearance in one direction or the other between 'old and ugly' and 'young and beautiful', we should not make a presumption that this is the case here. It would have been well within the capacity of the composers to tell us that. Instead, we should take a hermeneutic cue from the silence about her prior appearance, and treat the enigma creatively, as the narrative condition of an unsayable 'bare-ness' of being. Whatever we are originally is not something we can answer anyway, for we can only point to how we find ourselves making meaning. By moving what she used to be, 'out' of the frame of the story, the narrative indicates that all we can do is encounter what is always already given. Yet, having said that, within the narrative, Sulabhā's powers do enable us to see her capable of choiceful meaning-making. But when we turn to what meaning she does express in her living body, we are taken back to the ambiguities of identity: she is as beautiful as men (and women) want a woman to be beautiful, but she lives a renouncership that necessarily takes up a male model and then subverts it. And as mysterious as her origin is her exit from the story, for we never find out 'what happens next'.

The mystery of her lived body outside the story conveys, I think it is safe to say, the difficult lesson of the epistemic limits that the construction of gender places on us. There is no 'higher' perspective, a metanarrative, to discipline Sulabhā back into a story (that will inevitably mould her back into or exclude her from the masculinist paradigm of the male renouncer). What we have, instead, is the gesture of silence towards the emptiness of the pre-constructive body. In short, we are given a lesson in a self-contained ecology of gendered phenomenology. Of course, its significance is hardly self-contained: the

[105] Beauvoir 1949 [1972]: 67. [106] Ibid., p. 295.

affective role of masculinist norms on gendered behaviour and renunciatory protocols give meaning to the episode by acting into it from the surrounding epic text, the historical context of classical India—why, indeed, the world itself. And Sulabhā's reconfiguration of her gendered phenomenology has implications for the reading of the *Mahābhārata* (which is not my concern) as well as for contemporary discussions of body and gender (which is). But by 'self-contained', I mean that this episode carries with it an account of the ecology as a whole: one within which a woman's experience as woman is already structured by her situation, but also one in which her deliberate transformation of its affective powers leaves her in the position of teaching a demanding lesson in the possible transcendence of the whole phenomenological situation by all human beings.

3

The Body in Contemplation

Buddhaghosa's *Visuddhimagga*

Contemplative Practice and Ecological Phenomenology

In this chapter, I aim to follow the process by which a certain account of the human being as bodily being emerges through a series of contemplative practices described in the fifth century by Buddhaghosa in The *Visuddhimagga* (The Path of Purification), the Theravada Buddhist text that guides the monk through stages of practice to the attainment of perfection. As in the other chapters, we will see a dialectic between a robust intuition about the meaning of 'body' and its phenomenological reconfiguration in the course of the text's pursuit of its teleology.

In comparativist terms, this chapter lies at the intersection of two different lines of discussion in Western philosophy. One is the notion of 'spiritual exercise' or *askesis*, and its role in the broader classical Greek imperative of the 'care of the self'. Famously, this goes back to a reading of that classical tradition by Pierre Hadot, and slightly later, Michel Foucault,[1] both of whom also drew fruitful contrasts with the early Christian practices of asceticism. The other is the very different concern in the phenomenological tradition—particularly in the later Merleau-Ponty—to work out an understanding of our bodily selves that overcomes the mind–body dualism of traditional Western philosophy while also avoiding (for a variety of reasons) the scientistic programme of reductive physicalism.

Of course, in a broad sense, a rigorous programme of reflexive inquiry and cultivation is integral to classical Indian philosophical thought.[2] More recently, Buddhist philosophers have drawn particular attention to Hadot's role in having brought to the fore this connection between philosophy and spiritual practice that has not always been readily recognized in relation to classical Western thought.[3] Hadot—and in a much more sustained way, Foucault—have been influential in bringing out the connection between spiritual practices and the cultivation of a form of life, so it may on occasion be helpful to glance at this Western material in order to better bring out the originality

[1] On one interpretation of the complex relationship between their approaches to spiritual exercises, see Irrera 2010.

[2] Ram-Prasad 2001. [3] McClintock 2010: 15ff; Kapstein 2013.

of Buddhaghosa's elaboration of practices set within the teleology of canonical Buddhist teachings.[4]

We have already seen in the introduction that Merleau-Ponty is useful for the aims of this book, because—especially in his last work—his phenomenological inquiry into the nature of the bodily human being sets aside subject–object duality without collapsing one into the other. In Buddhaghosa too we find a view of the human being that, while drawing on the analytic categories of 'body' and 'mind', cannot be read in terms of either duality or its overcoming. Buddhaghosa does present a phenomenological inquiry, but his purpose in doing so—as part of a doctrinally specific programme of caring for oneself (as the practitioner on the Buddhist path to perfection)—means that an ontological resolution of human experience is extraneous to his methodology. I propose in this chapter to demonstrate that this is a coherent reading of Buddhaghosa.

Buddhaghosa, then, brings together care for the self and phenomenology, and for that reason, it is helpful to advert very briefly to the separate literature on these issues in Western philosophy to the extent that it helps provide a comparativist orientation to our study. This chapter is not a study of spiritual practices as such, but rather, of a view of bodiliness that emerges through those practices; and to that extent, the comparisons will be limited. Equally, this chapter is about the details of the human being as encountered in the disciplined phenomenological practice that Buddhaghosa offers, rather than an ontological theory, and so it is not exactly like Merleau-Ponty's notion of 'flesh'; comparison will therefore be limited here as well.

In what follows, I will first give an outline of how the bodily human being emerges in the *Visuddhimagga*, and locate the contextual difference between this picture and even the radical programme of the later Merleau-Ponty. After a brief description of the *Visuddhimagga* as a whole, I will look at how Buddhaghosa introduces concentration practices, and make some comparative remarks on Foucault's exposition on spiritual exercise that steer us towards Buddhaghosa's project. In the bulk of the chapter, I will deal with four sections of the text where I think we can learn a good deal about how the body is understood in Buddhaghosa's guidance through contemplative practices. The first three—the contemplation of various types of corpses under the sign of their 'foulness', the therapeutic exploration of our somatic presence to ourselves through structured breathing, and the progressive absorption in an imaginative experience of our own anatomy for the sake of detachment—form one type of discipline, in which a larger ecology of experience weaves together the practitioner's initial sense of the separateness of subject and object. The fourth, and most elaborate, practice is a performative understanding of the constitution of experience, derived from the components given in canonical Abhidhamma texts. In this practice, detailed phenomenological analysis leads to a complex and interdependent view of the contemplative practitioner that uses and yet dissolves the differences between the dualities which appear in

[4] For a sophisticated study of the quite different bodily practice and ethics in Mahāyāna Buddhism, with framing comparisons to Foucault, see Mrozik 2007.

pre-contemplative experience. I will end by drawing some general conclusions about what we can learn from Buddhaghosa on the phenomenological body in contemplation.

We find in the *Visuddhimagga* that certain compelling categorical distinctions about objects and subjectivity with which we (in the qualified and exemplary figure of the monk or *bhikkhu*) set forth are dissolved in the disciplined practices. We find eventually an account of the experiential whole that is the monkish human being as present to himself, an account that builds up the human compositionally rather than through recourse to one or two ontological categories. Buddhaghosa wants this discovery to enable the practitioner to reach towards higher stages of spiritual attainment. I want to stay true to this motivation by pointing out that for him, the practice is a phenomenological method all the way down, never directed at—what would be a mistake—the presentation of an ontology of the human.[5] (To engage in open phenomenological analysis is the task of the human seeking perfection.) At the same time, I read him here in philosophical terms, and draw the patient reader's attention to the view of the phenomenological being that emerges in the course of Buddhaghosa's description of the path.

As discussed in the Introduction, Maria Heim and I term an 'ecological phenomenology' that method which functions with whatever analytic distinctions are relevant to the intention with which embedded and interconnected being is studied. In light of that framework, the themes of this chapter are as follows: 1. The practices of care of the subject, the contemplative exercises, are systematic and ecological. 2. They do not make metaphysical presuppositions about who is cared for, but simply let a view of the human emerge in the practice. 3. What emerges is the bodily subject which is at the same time dissolved out of intuitive—not metaphysically principled—binaries. 4. As the ecological practice details it, the tension between the objective and the lived (the non-phenomenological and the phenomenological) is explained (away) through (a) the constant saturation of the object of phenomenology with the entire existential range of that phenomenology; while conversely, (b) the most fine-grained reflexivity about that phenomenology shows that anything subjective can emerge as the object of principled practice. Together this amounts to the demonstration of an ecological phenomenology through contemplative practice. I would ask the reader to see what follows in the light of these features of the discipline of contemplative practice interpreted as ecological phenomenology.

The Bodily Human Being: The Phenomenological Emergence of the Self in Question

As mentioned above, it has occurred to some scholars that there are specific comparisons to be made between classical Greek and Indian spiritual exercises. Yu Jiangxia, for

[5] Heim, forthcoming: chapter 4.

example, has recently noted that there are possibilities for comparison between Stoic and canonical Buddhist practices.[6] Yu draws attention to a parallel role for 'body' in these practices, arguing that each focuses on the 'body' in order to come to the understanding that neither it nor the world is the true self. This is an interesting comparison, depending on some intuitions about what 'body' means in the first place. In contrast, through Buddhaghosa's use of the *abhidhamma* categories, I want to bring to attention the complexity of what 'body' means, and how the human being as a whole is invoked in contemplative practice. Through this, I hope to offer a more radical phenomenological reading of Buddhaghosa's treatment of the category of the 'body'. (I bracket here what this might imply for an interpretation of the older, canonical material.)

Bodily practices are perhaps more important in the classical West, and in early Christianity, than we might have gathered from the literature following Hadot. For example, Hadot's leading commentator, Arnold Davidson says, 'Since they aimed at realizing a transformation of one's vision of the world and a metamorphosis of one's personality, these exercises had an existential value, not only a moral one. They did not attempt only to insure behaviour in accordance with a code of good conduct but involved all aspects of one's being—intellect, imagination, sensibility, and will.'[7] Note that the human being here is identified with the notion of a personality, and spiritual exercises are taken to be a set of 'inward' transformations. But in fact, if we look at the role of asceticism in the moral theory of such a key early Christian figure as Gregory of Nyssa, we find that ascetic practice—for all its theological originality, still derived from late classical spiritual exercises of the Neoplatonic schools—is in fact centred on bodily transformation, as Raphael Cadenhead argues: 'On the one hand, "the body of *sin*" (Rom. 6:6) or "the flesh" (Rom. 8:6, 16; Gal. 5:17)—in the Pauline sense—is the locus of human rebellion against God. On the other hand, indeed precisely for this reason, the body is able to overcome passion through *bodily*, ascetical practices. The battle against disordered desire, in other words, must be fought and won in the body itself—only here and nowhere else... Gregory regards the transformative potentiality of the body as the reverse aspect of its collaboration with passion. Only *because of* its intimacy with sin, in other words, can the body be regarded as the pre-eminent *locus* of ethical transformation.'[8] Of course, there is much more to Gregory than this, in particular, that bodily sensation (*aísthēsis*), being present from birth naturally asserts itself against 'mind' (*nous*), so that ascetical practices are an arduous undertaking to move from 'sensual criteria' to spiritual sensation.[9] Indeed, this points to the possibility of fruitful comparison and contrast with Buddhist (and in light of the role of divine grace for Gregory, many Hindu) practices; and Buddhaghosa has already drawn attention in comparative study with other Christian figures.[10]

I mention Gregory to make two other points: first, as his case shows, we should be careful in not confining spiritual exercises to 'mental' activity (the mind seen as

[6] Yu 2014. [7] Davidson 1990: 476. [8] Cadenhead 2013: 288–9.
[9] Ibid., p. 292. [10] Cousins 1989; Barnes 2014.

a non-material existent that is either the essence, or one half of the essence of the human being). Second, even the integration of bodily practices into spiritual exercises is framed by the conceptual context of the undertaking, and Gregory's Christian dialectic between 'body' and 'soul/mind' is far from Buddhaghosa's *abhidhamma* categories. It is relatively clear that in Buddhaghosa's Pāli, '*kāya*' translates as 'body' and '*manas*' as 'mind'. But the fact that he uses the terminology of 'body' and 'mind' should not lead us into making comparisons on the assumption that there is cross-cultural stability to these concepts, but rather prompt us to look carefully at the content of these concepts in the *Visuddhimagga*.

This chapter—as a study of how the human being emerges as a whole, ecologically related bodily being through our examination of Buddhaghosa's own set of 'spiritual exercises'—is possible precisely because what Buddhaghosa takes to be 'all aspects of one's being' is more complex, and in a profound way, innocent of the dualistic contrast in Hadot's view of the human being (the latter made necessary, perhaps due to a certain form of dualism in the Stoics and Epicureans, the schools with which he was most interested).

Now, what sort of human then emerges in the practices outlined by Buddhaghosa? To get a sense of the larger, cross-cultural philosophical relevance of Buddhaghosa's contribution, let me turn to some brief remarks on phenomenology. We should keep in mind the discussion in the Introduction, where I suggested that because of Merleau-Ponty's pressing towards a radical notion of 'flesh' that seeks to step outside the dualism and physicalism of the Western tradition, he is a useful point of comparison when looking at those classical Indian approaches that do not function along a metaphysical-dualist trajectory. Even in his earlier mature work, *Phenomenology of Perception*, he writes, 'The psycho-physical event can no longer be conceived after the model of Cartesian physiology and as the juxtaposition of a process in itself [the body] and a cogitatio [the mind]. The union of soul and body is not an amalgamation between two mutually external terms, subject and object, brought about by arbitrary degree. It is enacted at every instant in the movement of existence.'[11] So, to reiterate, in the attempt to work out the nature and presence of the human subject in its world without being trapped in the (anti-)dualisms of early modern Western thought, twentieth-century phenomenologists sought to draw from the appearance of that world as it is given in subjectivity. From examining how things do appear, they attempted to conclude how things must do so, in such a way as to bridge the gap between the subject and the occurrence of objects in its phenomenal field.

The crucial point for us is that phenomenologists saw the body as that bridge, for while it appears as an object of experience, it is also the mode of subjective presence in the world. 'Phenomenologists distinguish the pre-reflective body-awareness that accompanies and shapes every spatial experience, from a reflective consciousness of the body. To capture this difference, Husserl introduced a terminological distinction

[11] Merleau-Ponty 1962: 88–9.

between *Leib* and *Körper*, that is, between the pre-reflectively lived body, i.e., the body as an embodied first-person perspective, and the subsequent thematic experience *of* the body as an object.'[12]

As with Husserl, Merleau-Ponty too draws on the notion of the 'lived body', which he understands as our essential 'interinvolvement' with the environment of our existence, where the lived body is not just another 'thing' in that environment to which our subjectivity can relate. But once the problem has been articulated as the task of uniting subject and object—that is to say, once the starting point has been determined to be an intuitive dualism that must be overcome—then, compelling though it is to focus on the body, a sense remains that we equivocate over exactly what it is we are talking about. 'The lived body is to be understood as someone's lived relationship to the world. It is an ambiguous unity, both subject and object, both mind and body, intertwined, understood in terms of levels, or planes of signification rather than mutually exclusive categories of being.'[13] This 'ambiguous unity' is the ontological core of Merleau-Ponty's project. 'Merleau-Ponty's notion of the lived body... provides a philosophical alternative to the objectivistic epistemology that focuses on the objective body, as seen from a God's eye perspective. The lived body is understood as a mind-body presence always directed towards the world (otherness). Therein a field arises, an "in-between", that is constituted in terms of situations to be mastered and understood.'[14] The articulation of this 'in-between' in his later work is expressed as 'flesh', the lived body existing at the point where the world and the subject become mutually constituting. The subject for Merleau-Ponty is a being who is not a subject (a transcendental ego) engaging with its objective world, but rather a being that is itself within the sensible world, as much as it senses that world. The body—now seen as at once lived and objective, sensing and being sensed—possesses 'an art of interrogating the sensible according to its own wishes, an inspired exegesis'.[15] Essentially, the subject and the world occur 'are recorded on the same map'.[16]

This very brief outline of an extraordinary attempt to find a way of thinking of our existence through and beyond dualism (or physicalism, which is the assertion that the lived body will somehow be explained eventually through objective description) prompts me to ask two questions from a classical Indian perspective that did not have to start from the problematic of metaphysical dualism. Answers to these questions point us towards how Buddhaghosa on the body might offer a picture that is both radically different from and yet relevant to the undertaking of Merleau-Ponty's phenomenology.

Before that, however, it would be useful to get a sense of how the very idea of the subjective, and the practices of subjectivity that Buddhaghosa describes and which permits us to talk of his phenomenology, occur in his work. The notion of the subjective is pervasive in Buddhaghosa's analysis, but at the very least, he cannot be committed to

[12] Gallagher and Zahavi 2014. [13] Bullington, 2013: 30. [14] Ibid., p. 36.
[15] Merleau-Ponty 1968: 135. [16] Ibid., 133.

a unitary metaphysical subject because of the Buddhist teaching against some essential self. I will not here be able to argue directly that he does not have a metaphysical position—an anti-self position such as most other Buddhist systems have—at all.[17] But indirectly, we find in his presentation of the aggregates, a certain implicit narrative of the practitioner (the monk, the ascetic) as the person who sets forth on the path with a sense of himself as having some essential marker of individuality. While the analysis of the aggregates then shows—as the contemplative practices have already implied—that there is no such stable marker, my concern in this chapter is not about the putative self but about how it is that to be human is to be tied to a phenomenal body that is both the locus of livedness—a centre of subjectivity—and the object of analysis.

Subjectivity, then, is the general name for the perspectival phenomenality of being human at all. Although even to say that much is to seek a specific theory of the subject, Buddhaghosa shows no interest in such a project. For him, the practices and processes that he expounds require a functional understanding of how to analyse different aspects of experience, for which the notion of the subjective is required: with it, the monk is able to classify what happens to him according to the categories that help him cultivate a life oriented towards the felicity of *nibbāna*. For that reason alone, it is worth considering a short passage from the *Atthasālinī*, which tersely points to the uses of the notion of the 'subjective' (literally, 'one's own' (*ajjhatta*; the resonant and widely used Sanskrit equivalent is *adhyātma*)).[18]

The subjective is that which, apprehending, 'these things that occur are myself', occurs having made attendant to itself the desire for such [locutions] as, 'We will go'. The word 'subjective' has a four-fold meaning: the subjective as range (*gocarajjhatta*), the subjective as limit (*niyakajjhatta*), the subjective in itself (*ajjhattajjhatta*), and the subjective as object (*visayajjhatta*). Subjectivity as range is seen in statements like, 'Ānanda, awareness should properly be focused by that *bhikkhu* as the subjective, namely, only on that sign of concentration that has been practiced before', and 'rapt in subjectivity, concentrated'. 'The subjective is serenity', 'With the factor of subjectivity, he dwells contemplating that factor' are [examples of] subjectivity as limit. 'The six [sensory] bases are subjective ones' and the like are about the subject in itself. 'Ānanda, this is the dwelling perfectly attained by the Tathāgata: that, by being without attention to all signs, which he has reached, [namely] the subjective emptiness in which he dwells', is about subjectivity as object. Its meaning is the sense of sovereignty... Therefore, factors that occur in one's own continuity and pertain to each person are to be understood as the 'subjective'. But what is outside of that, whether bound up with the faculties or not bound up with the faculties is called 'extrinsic'.[19] (p. 25)

[17] For a sustained argument in defence of reading Buddhaghosa's project, especially through the lens of *nāma-rūpa* (the encompassing term for the Abdhidhamma aggregates, as Buddhaghosa treats them in Ch. XVIII) as a phenomenological method and not—as the conventional modern interpretation has it—ontological categories, see Heim and Ram-Prasad 2017 [Early Release]/2019.

[18] I occasionally draw (with my own translation) on this text attributed to Buddhaghosa, simply because it is helpful in offering definitions of terms used in the *Visuddhimagga*.

[19] *Evaṃ pavattamānā mayṃ attā'ti gahaṇaṃ, 'gamissāmā'ti iminā viya adhippāyena attānaṃ adhikāraṃ katvā pavattāti ajjhattā. 'Ajjhatta'-saddo panāyaṃ gocarajjhatte niyakajjhatte ajjhattajjhatte visayajjhatteti catūsu atthesu dissati. 'Tenānanda, bhikkhunā tasmiṃyeva purimasmiṃ samādhinimitte ajjhattameva cittaṃ*

A basic awareness of agency seems to be the motivation for subjectivity. Beyond that, Buddhaghosa offers just the quoted examples as explanations for the different meanings he reads out of the term. As 'range' subjectivity is used normatively, as what the subjective ought to be about, which is the sign that results from concentration practice. It is the subjective as the attainment of meditative focus. The 'limit' is the subjective as what comes within the ambit of telic awareness. In itself, the subjective is simply the set of functional capacities provided by the organic bases that enable perceiving and thinking. As 'object' it is the goal of all the practices: something that is distinct from what is currently present to the person, but yet, on perfect attainment, will be nothing other. It is an object in the strange sense of requiring to be the focus of intention but also what is realized. Buddhaghosa then distinguishes this from all the other factors that occur in the field of awareness, calling the latter extrinsic to the subjective. Being outside the subjective is a classification of what is presented in experience. In that extended sense, there is no grip here for an ontic divide between the subjective and the objective; the subjective is just one side of the phenomenological enterprise.

Given all this, let me say that Buddhaghosa's phenomenological method is a programme for training monks to attend to what is found in their experience by utilizing the categories adverting to the various factors in/of experience that the Buddha taught canonically. The analysis of experience that he offers, then, is what I mean when I talk of 'phenomenology' in the context of Buddhaghosa. I want to argue that he is not developing an epistemology in the *Visuddhimagga*, seeking to define the nature of knowledge and offering a framework through which such knowledge can be gained. To that extent, we find something similar to the familiar contrast made by Husserl in the phenomenological project that he inaugurated. (Husserl meant by this that before the conditions for the possibility of knowledge can be determined as Kant required, there must first be a description of the consciousness that is itself the condition for that possibility. Buddhaghosa does not engage in epistemology for it plays no role in the purificatory path to Buddhist perfection.)

Having said that, two points of contrast must now be made with the Western Phenomenological tradition, focusing on the two so-called 'moments' of the phenomenological reduction that motivates it.[20] The first is that Buddhaghosa's attentive analysis of what is found in experience does not begin with the *epoché*, the bracketing of the world as it is found in experience (that is, the world that we think of ourselves as being in). Bracketing takes place within the metaphysical framework that there is a

saṇṭhapetabbaṃ', 'ajjhattarato samāhito'tiādīsu hi ayaṃ gocarajjhatte dissati. 'Ajjhattaṃ sampasādanaṃ', 'ajjhattaṃ vā dhammesu dhammānupassī viharatī'tiādīsu niyakajjhatte. 'Cha ajjhattikāni āyatanānī'tiādīsu ajjhattajjhatte. 'Ayaṃ kho panānanda, vihāro tathāgatena abhisambuddho yadidaṃ sabbanimittānaṃ amanasikārā ajjhattaṃ suññataṃ upasampajja viharatī'tiādīsu visayajjhatte; issariyaṭṭhāneti attho... Tasmā attano santāne pavattā pāṭipuggalikā dhammā ajjhattāti veditabbā. Tato bāhirabhūtā pana indriyabaddhā vā anindriyabaddhā vā bahiddhā nāma. Buddhaghosa *Atthasālinī*: p. 25.

[20] Here I follow Eugene Fink's famous and clear explication of Husserl in Fink 1995: 39–47 (especially).

world presented to experience which holds back inquiry into a transcendental subject; Buddhaghosa's approach to the world is purely for the role it plays in the ecology of the monkish life lived on the path.

The second, and necessarily related contrast is that there is no 'reduction proper' either: Buddhaghosa's practice is not driven by the goal of going back (what Husserl calls '*ruckfrage*') to the transcendental 'I' that is the 'ground-experience', that which is doing the reduction away from the human being (who is presented in experience as the accepted entity found in this world). This is not due to the somewhat simplistic point that, as a Buddhist, Buddhaghosa is committed to the rejection of any kind of transcendental self. Rather, it is because of the absence of any metaphysical requirement in Buddhaghosa's project at all. His concern to attend to the analysis of experience is for the purpose of clarifying it so that the monk may be freed from the misunderstandings about his own life that keep him entangled in the painful conditions of that life. We shall see some of how such close study of experience works for this existential project; but it does not share the metaphysical teleology of much modern Phenomenology. When I speak of Buddhaghosa's phenomenological methodology, I mean his system of analysing experience through the various factors disclosed in the Buddha's teachings.

Let us now turn to the two questions arising specifically from the role of body in phenomenology as developed by Merleau-Ponty. The first one is: why is there this doubleness (held together as *Leibkörper*)—an 'ambiguity'—between 'lived' and 'objective' body? My answer, through Buddhaghosa (as also, in different ways, in the other chapters) will be that the phenomenological field allows a shifting of focus on to different interpretations of its content, varying according to intention and the salience attended to. What we notice and why we do so determines whether bodiliness is noted in terms of its constituents (that stand for what we would otherwise be tempted to call its objects) or its implications (that fall under what Buddhaghosa has termed the subjective); but each leads back into the other, because the distinctions are analytic elements of the ecology of experience and are not to be posited as ontological elements. This is part of the conception of an 'ecological phenomenology' that has already been outlined in the Introduction and has recurred in the previous chapters. To put it concisely, the gap between lived and objective body is pointed out in the Phenomenological tradition as the metaphysical gap between the subjective and the objective, the overcoming of which becomes the aim of the enterprise. In Buddhaghosa's programme, the objective body—i.e., what is other than the different senses of the 'subjective'—is read and re-read through its livedness (in other words, subjectivity), and the lived body is traced back to the functions other than it (which we can call 'objective' in this specific sense). What folds back on itself is not a phenomenological ontology that discloses reality, but a phenomenological methodology oriented to spiritual perfection, including the emptied-out plenitude that is *nibbāna*.[21]

[21] For the range of 'felicities' in Theravāda Buddhism, including *nirvāṇa*, see Collins 1998, especially chapter 1.

Second, following from the first, what is it to say that phenomenology is a question of methodology alone and not the process to determine an ontology? Our choosing why we want to undertake phenomenological examination determines what we focus upon, and how we classify what we encounter. This is a continuous process dependent on shifts in attention. Buddhaghosa offers conceptualizations of our being as a continuous method of clarification. Such clarification is the purpose of spiritual exercises, as we will see. The analysis Buddhaghosa offers is free of what we could call the ontological reflex, the need to come up with an answer for how things really are from the way they appear. Within the extended practice for progression on the path to Buddhist perfection, Buddhaghosa nowhere articulates a reality-appearance disjunction, which alone can motivate the search for an ontology (even a naïve realist one). Disciplined attention to one's experience and consequent identification of the dynamics of its phenomenal constituents, based on the teaching of the categories by the Buddha (as laid out in the canonical *abhidhamma* materials), is for the purpose of caring for one's spiritual teleology. As such, that analysis—which is phenomenology as methodology—is for understanding ourselves wholly. But that understanding is an act of caring for the Buddhist path, not a grasp of some hidden structure of reality. In the case at hand, we have practice intended to therapeutize away attachment to dimensions of bodiliness that are held to block the attainment of understanding, but to do so through an expansive understanding of the body in experience (the lived body that is itself the object of analysis).

The *Visuddhimagga*

The *Visuddhimagga* is traditionally seen as both a systematization and an exegesis of the Buddha's teachings, which are collected canonically in the *Tipiṭaka*. The result is presented as a 'path', combining guidelines for meditative practice and explanation of key concepts necessary for such practice by monks (*bhikkhus*). The text as a whole is ostensibly divided into three parts across twenty-three chapters: virtue (*sīla*) and its cultivation through restraint; various practices of concentration (*samādhi*) (oriented specifically to the development of insight (*vipassanā*) that leads to the realization of the Noble Truths taught by the Buddha); and understanding (*paññā*), this last ranging from several alternative descriptions of the constituents of experience found in analysis, through the guidelines for how the meditator may progress through the insight gained from analysis, to the description of the nature and benefits of extraordinary (or 'supramundane' (*lokuttara*)) stages of attainment on the path to liberation. Buddhaghosa opens the text with the Buddha's reply to the question of certain deity (I.1):[22]

[22] References are in the standardized modern form of <Chapter.Paragraph>. *Visuddhimagga* is is from the Chaṭṭha Saṅgāyana collection published by the Vipassana Research Institute, Dhamma Giri, Igatpuri, India, and available at www.tripitaka.org. I have of course worked with Bhikku Ñāṇamoli's standard translation,

'Inner tangle, outer tangle, people are entangled in tangles;
So I ask thus of Gotama: who disentangles the tangle?'
'When a wise man grounded in virtue, cultivates awareness and understanding,
Then, as a mendicant ardent and sage, it is he who disentangles the tangle.'[23]

Virtue, cultivation of awareness—read as the following of concentration practices—and understanding (which we will see is itself a practice) therefore become the three interlocking sections of the text. The sections relate to each other in a dynamic and progressive way, which shows this to be a text of modular practice rather than linear reading. I will try to be faithful to this feature of this text while drawing a philosophical lesson from its overall purpose. From the Concentration section, I will look at three different practices across two chapters, that focus on the category of 'body', but in ways that invite us to start seeing it as not simply a material object self-evident in some ontology (indeed, I will interrogate the very sense that the important programme of understanding bodiliness is an ontological one at all). And from the early part of the Understanding section, I will look at the chapter on the *abhidhamma* analysis of the 'aggregates' (*khandhas*) of experience, which yield an abstract network of constituents through which an individual meditator's experience can be analysed by himself. Now we have a thematization of the human being. But as we will see, the very fact that this analysis is given as a practice of understanding—rather than an explicit theory—points to Buddhaghosa's treatment of bodiliness as a clarificatory phenomenology rather than a totalizing ontology. This is why I want to say that a view of the body 'emerges' through a study of the practices (or exercises, if you will); it is not 'given', nor is it meant to be.

I do not explore here either the *abhidhamma* in the canonical, early Buddhist texts (for which, see Nyanaponika Thera[24] and Karunadasa[25]), nor other texts in the vast *ouevre* attributed to Buddhaghosa.

I will focus on three places in which the body (*kāya*) is the focus of concentration practice, and then one of the key places where an understanding of the entirety of experience (which locates bodiliness phenomenologically) is laid out. The sequence, therefore, covers the following:

1. The taking up of a variety of types of corpses as meditation subjects under the sign of 'foulness'. This starts with objectified entities already steeped with particular

1975 edition (to which I refer for page number) as well as the 2010 edition, *The Path of Purification*, Kandy: Buddhist Publication Society. However, I have offered my own translation, practically always of the terminology, and less frequently of syntax. The reader should therefore look at the translation provided as a development from the standard version, for the specific purposes of this chapter. The Pāli is always quoted in order to anchor my translational choices.

[23] *Antojaṭā bahijaṭā, jaṭāya jaṭitā pajā;Taṃ taṃ gotama pucchāmi, ko imaṃ vijaṭaye jaṭanti. Sīle patiṭṭhāya naro sapañño, cittaṃ paññañca bhāvayaṃ; tāpī nipako bhikkhu, so imaṃ vijaṭaye jaṭanti.* (*Saṃyutta Nikāya* 1.23).

[24] Nyanaponika Thera 1985. [25] Karundasa 2010.

subjective orientation, and explored in terms of how they are to be received in a meditative life.

2. Attentiveness to [one's own living] body (*kāyagatāsati*) through direct attention to 'repulsiveness' (*paṭikūla-manasikāra*). This takes what is lived and objectifies it to prompt subjective states that can then be therapeutized.
3. Breathing meditation for the refinement of insight. This takes the control of breathing to be a means of stilling the practitioner's bodily sense of himself, and triggers a process of fine-grained awareness of how he is presented to himself.
4. The understanding of the 'aggregates' (*khandha*). This gives, according to Buddhaghosa, the Buddha's analysis of the various factors in a phenomenology, and classifies them so as to guide the practitioner's own contemplative practice.

A Brief Introduction to Concentration Practice and Its Purpose

Why are practices of concentration needed? Buddhaghosa explains the role of concentration within the three-fold nature of the text early on.

And the avoidance of the extreme called attachment to the pleasures of sense-desire is shown by virtue; that [avoidance of the extreme] called attachment to mortification of oneself is [shown by] concentration. Resorting to the middle way is shown by understanding.[26] (I.11)

In the chapter describing the basic features of concentration (*samādhi*), he defines it briefly as the 'enclosing' (*ādhāna*) of awareness (*citta*) and the concomitant mental factors (*cetasikā*) in an 'equable' (*samaṃ*) and 'right' (*sammā*) manner on a single phenomenal object (*ārammaṇa*), for the establishment (*thapana*) of that awareness. Using standard *abhidhamma* hermeneutics, he gives (III.4) its characteristic (*lakkhaṇa*)[27] as 'non-distraction' (*avikkhepa*).[28] Concentration practice, then, is given as one of the three requirements of the spiritual path.

In thinking about what these practices—in effect, our version of spiritual exercises (*askēsis*)—are for, I am drawn to Michel Foucault's contrast between an Hellenistic model of spiritual exercises and a Christian one (the third, the Platonic, we can set aside for this discussion).[29] He takes the Christian model, founded as it is on the truth

[26] *Sīlena ca kāmasukhallikānuyogasaṅkhātassa antassa vajjanaṃ pakāsitaṃ hoti, samādhinā attakilama thānuyogasaṅkhātassa. Paññāya majjhimāya paṭipattiyā sevanaṃ pakāsitaṃ hoti.*

[27] The *Atthasālinī* defines 'characteristic' in this way: 'The particular (idiotypic) or generic way of being this or that factor is called characteristic' (*tesaṃ tesaṃ dhammānaṃ sabhāvo vā sāmaññaṃ vā lakkhaṇaṃ nāma*); p. 29.

[28] Although it is not of direct interest to us, we may note that at III.5, he lists sixteen kinds of concentration, including the two-fold distinction that is systematically followed later in this text and becomes enormously influential in the later tradition, namely, between 'access' (*upacāra*) and 'absorption' (*appanā*). For the debate on *samādhi* and its relationship to 'insight' meditation (*vipassanā*), see Griffiths 1981, Bucknell 1993, and Cousins 1994–96.

[29] Foucault 2005: 255–6.

of an original Text and Revelation, to concern the use of techniques to gain self-knowledge 'whose essential function is to dispel internal illusions, to recognize the temptations that arise within the soul and the heart, and also to thwart the seductions to which we may be victim.' This calls for 'an exegesis of the self', in which 'we turn round on the self' 'essentially and fundamentally in order to renounce the self'. He contrasts this with the Hellenistic model. Of course the Christian model did involve some elements of renunciation and austerity. 'But the nature itself of the means, of the tactic if you like, put to work to achieve this objective, is not primarily or fundamentally renunciation. It involves, rather, acquiring something through *askēsis*. We must acquire something we do not have, rather than renounce this or that element of ourselves that we are or have. We must acquire something that, precisely, instead of leading us gradually to renounce ourselves, will allow us to protect the self and to reach it. In two words, ancient ascesis does not reduce: it equips, it provides.'[30]

Within broader themes in classical India, certainly in the *Visuddhimagga*, renunciation is integral to becoming equipped, so the practices explored here cut across the more familiar divide in the classical West delineated by Foucault. The renunciant monk precisely is equipped, to 'distentangle the tangle', to reach a perfected way of being. When Buddhaghosa explains what the 'tangles' are, he says that 'tangle' is a term for 'the network of craving' (*taṇhāya jāliniyā*).

> It is called 'inner tangle' and 'outer tangle' because it is born of one's own requisites (*parikkhāra*) and another's requisites, for oneself and for another's, for subjective actuations (*āyatana*) and extrinsic actuations.[31] (I.2)

Here, 'requisites' are all the things that we take ourselves to need, and our entanglement is not solipsistic, because intrinsic to what we need is what others need, and vice versa. The entanglement is found in the actual states—conditioning relationalities, functions, subject-object reciprocalities—through which our lives find expression.[32] At the same time, the concentration practices—the spiritual exercises—do require renunciation of the 'requisites' of oneself and others. One must cut off the ten 'obstructions' (*palibodhā*) of a house, family, profit, one's group, any other building, travel, relations, afflictions, books, and (the temptation to acquire and use) supernormal or magic powers (III.28). Practices therefore both equip and reduce; these are not incommensurable options.

Before we turn to the three concentration practices mentioned above, we need to look at a technical feature of concentration for a variety of the forty meditation subjects ('locus of activity', *kammaṭṭhāna*) that Buddhaghosa enumerates; it is used in two of the three that we will consider. This is the use of a particular feat of imagination, by which the focus of concentration is transformed into the relevant meditative goal. In the section on the use of the meditative visual aid of a red-brown disk of earth

[30] Ibid., p. 320.
[31] *sā panesā sakaparikkhāraparaparikkhāresu sakaattabhāvaparaattabhāvesu ajjhattikāyatanabāhirāyatanesu ca uppajjanato antojaṭā bahijaṭāti vuccati.*
[32] Hence 'actuations', which is meant to capture these many implications of the term '*āyatana*'.

(the *pathavi kasiṇa*), Buddhaghosa clarifies the terminology of what is required, in a way that becomes applicable to other contemplations.

When, while he is developing it [his contemplation] in this way, it comes into visible focus as he adverts to it with his eyes shut just like he does it with his eyes open, then the acquired sign (*uggahanimitta*) is said to be produced.[33] (IV.30)

With repeated, directed thought (*vitakkha*), the hindrances (*kilesā*)—negative attitudes and emotions—subside, and access concentration occurs. The imitative sign (literally, 'counter-part' sign: *paṭibhāganimitta*) arises at this point.

In the acquired sign, the faults of the [earth-disk] aid are understood well. But the imitative sign…stands forth as if breaking out, leaving behind the acquired sign, and a hundred times, a thousand times more purified.[34] (IV.31)

He compares the power of the imitative sign in relation to the other to the moon's disk coming out from behind a thundercloud, and to cranes flying in front of clouds. The imitative sign does not have colour or shape, and is not apprehended by the senses, but it is purified and conceptually manipulable for sharpening of attention so as to attain the required attitude.

For it is born only of the conception of one who has attained concentration, consisting in being just an attendant of appearance.[35] (IV.31)

This is to suggest that the practice should be understood in terms of shaping phenomenal content between attentive focus on the experiential event and the contemplative focus on its imaginative impression. The imagination, then, becomes a means of re-configuring phenomenology: it attends upon the appearance that is the acquired sign, but it also then leaves it behind, exceeding—in the purity of its focus—the original experience that is subject to the vagaries of the hindrances. The practice outlined by Buddhaghosa bears startling resemblance to Edmund Husserl's phenomenological method of 'free-fantasy variation', 'the method of eiditic description', which is 'a transfer of all empirical description into a new and fundamental dimension'.[36] But for Husserl, this is the method to move from 'fact' to 'essence'; and while it may be possible to see the potential for an ontological approach in such Buddhist practices, it is notable that Buddhaghosa here articulates it purely as part of the method for developing feelings that are desirable on the path to perfection.

Even when there are exceptional instances where the acquired sign and the imitative sign are identical (*ekasadisa*)—as Buddhaghosa explains, in the case of a single bone

[33] *Tassevaṃ bhāvayato yadā nimīletvā āvajjantassa ummīlitakāle viya āpāthamāgacchati, tadā uggahanimittaṃ jātaṃ nāma hoti.*

[34] *uggahanimitte kasiṇadoso paññāyati. paṭibhāganimittaṃ…uggahanimittaṃ padāletvā nikkhantamiva tato sataguṇaṃ sahassaguṇaṃ suparisuddhaṃ hutvā upaṭṭhāti.*

[35] *Kevalañhi samādhilābhino upaṭṭhānākāramattaṃ saññajametanti.*

[36] Husserl 1960: 69. For an analysis of this idea, see Zaner 2010.

during contemplation on foulness in a corpse, where a whole skeleton is not available—the emotional response to each sign is to be different, pointing to the transformative purpose of the concentration practice:

> And the acquired sign of even a single bone should be disgusting and frightening, whereas the imitative sign produces happiness and joy because it brings about access concentration.[37]
>
> (VI.80)

Imagination is a key step in the reconfiguration of ordinary ways of interpreting experience. The imitative sign is also an imaginative sign, and imagination is not opposed to phenomenology. The whole point of the sign is to be able to experience (literally, undergo (*anubhava*)) in a special and 'purified' way what was originally presented to the senses. Only through a sharp division between the mental—the place of imagination—and the sensory—the place of phenomena—can imagination be contrasted to phenomenology. What we should think of instead is that there are different modes of configuring phenomenality. The basic contrast is between 'tangled' phenomenology and 'disentangled' phenomenology, to draw on the Buddha's words. Imagination and understanding are two key modes, in interaction with others that we will soon examine—spatial enactment like careful walking, practical procedures like informing the teacher, verbal repetition, and so on—that together constitute the practices.

This outline of the signs indicates the direction of my reading throughout the rest of the chapter: Buddhaghosa is concerned to sustain a practice of examination of the phenomenological field. The implicature of this technique of signs in his phenomenology of the bodily human being will become clearer as we turn to the concrete cases of practice where the technique is used.

Contemplating the Corpse: The Ecology of the Meditative Object

The first of the concentration practices that focus on the nature of bodiliness is the contemplation of the corpse. The purpose of it is renunciatory for sure, as it deliberately seeks out an object that prompts a strongly negative feeling. In its dramatic choice, it is comparable to what it meant for the Christian ascetical masters to 'hate the world': 'Thus, to hate means to oppose an obstacle, an excessive attachment to life here below or a fear of death—all of which makes the spirit captive.'[38] But for Buddhaghosa, of course, the purpose of this deliberate provocation in oneself is also for the attainment of a radically contrary attitude.

[37] *Ekaṭṭhikepi ca uggahanimittena bībhacchena bhayānakena bhavitabbaṃ. Paṭibhāganimittena pītisomanassajanakena, upacārāvahattā.*

[38] Evdokimov 1998: 204.

Loathsome though this object is, still it arouses delight and joy, thinking of its advantages thus, 'Surely by entering this path, I will be liberated from ageing and death', and giving up the torment of the obstacles [on the path].[39] (VI.87)

Apart from the obvious analogy to a sick man's acceptance of purges and emetics, Buddhaghosa more sharply compares this recognition to a scavenger seeing flowers in the garbage and thinking only that it will make him money. The technique of developing the acquired sign in order to have the imitative sign emerge in one's awareness is not a narrowly defined mental exercise. It is embedded—and possible only—in a larger hermetic ecology of discipline and self-cultivation. Only within this ordered life can the technique lead to accomplishment.

When the scion has practiced with the meditation subject under already enlightened ones, taken up the hermetic option, worked out the primary elements, discerned the synergetic entities, defined name and form, eliminated the concept of essentiality, done the duties of the ascetic, lived the life and developed what is to be developed, when he contains the seed, and is with highest knowledge and few defilements, then the imitative sign arises in his looking at the place to be seen.[40] (VI.43)

We will later on encounter some of the requirements stated here, provided they are relevant to the task at hand. But we can see that the natural way in which a technique for a recognizably 'spiritual exercise' is taken to require a complex lived context indicates that we must at all times think of Buddhaghosa's approach as a holistic one when it comes to what is 'in the mind' and what is 'about the body'.

Turning now to the contemplation of foulness, ten precisely typologized corpses—defined as bodies that are foul (*asubha*) and without consciousness (*aviññāṇa*)—are listed: bloated, livid, festering, cut up, gnawed, scattered, hacked and scattered, bleeding, worm-infested, and skeletal (VI.1). At VI.12, the example of the bloated contains four requirements for this contemplation, which apply to the other types of corpses. These demonstrate the ecological nature of the practice, and we will look at them carefully. Here is what the teacher should explain to the practitioner:

The directions for going to get the sign of foulness; characterizing the surroundings of the sign; the eleven ways of apprehending the sign; reflecting on the path on which he has come and gone, together with the process of absorption.[41] (VI.12)

What should be notable here is not only the fact that the focussing of awareness and the transformation of affect should be placed within a set of practices that cut across

[39] *Paṭikkūlepi ca etasmiṃ ārammaṇe 'addhā imāya paṭipadāya jarāmaraṇamhā parimuccissāmī'ti evamānisaṃsadassāvitāya ceva nīvaraṇasantāpappahānena ca pītisomanassaṃ uppajjati.*

[40] *Yo pana purimabuddhānaṃ santike āsevitakammaṭṭhāno parihatadhutaṅgo parimadditamahābhūto pariggahitasaṅkhāro vavatthāpitanāmarūpo ugghāṭitasattasañño katasamaṇadhammo vāsitavāsano bhāvitabhāvano sabījo ñāṇuttaro appakileso kulaputto, tassa olokitolokitaṭṭhāneyeva paṭibhāganimittaṃ upaṭṭhāti.*

[41] *asubhanimittatthāya gamanavidhānaṃ, samantā nimittupalakkhaṇaṃ, ekādasavidhena nimittaggāho, gatāgatamaggapaccavekkhaṇanti evaṃ appanāvidhānapariyosānaṃ.*

the categories of mind, body, and environment, but also the precision and elaborate care with which Buddhaghosa delineates these practices. Concentration is not just a mental act with some surrounding performance (of gesture, posture, or movement); it is constituted by such performance. In order to get a proper sense of the ecology of concentration, and the interdependent interaction of the putatively distinct categories of subject and object, it is worthwhile looking closer at how these different dimensions of phenomenological life are explored in Buddhaghosa's instructions.

In the matter of (1) directions for going (*gamanavidhāna*) to the corpse, there are many requirements to take into account, some of which are as follows. How to go: go by paths where one does not see the opposite sex (as these practices apply to almswomen too) (14). Whom to tell: Tell an elder in the monastery, so that if the practitioner is seized by fear in the charnel ground, the elder will send other novices to help (16–17). What to take: amongst other things, take a staff to ward off dogs that may be lurking in the charnel ground (23)! Where to stand: neither leeward nor windward to the corpse; in the former case, the stink will distract him from his visual focus, and in the latter, perhaps ghouls will think the smell comes from him and harm him (26).

With regard to (2), on characterizing the surrounding signs (*samantā nimittupalakkhaṇa*), we have description laden with suggestions of Buddhaghosa's personal experience of specific landscapes. The corpse may be defined precisely by its lack of relationality, but as the sign, it is integrated into the phenomenal field. If there is a rock in the eyeline, its features—size, colour—and location in relation to the corpse should be determined (*vavatthita*); if an anthill, likewise; if a tree, then which species it is, and its features and relative location; this bush, that creeper (28–33). Buddhaghosa says that the practice, combining (*samāsetvā*) the sign and object should repeatedly determine it through associative pairing, as 'this is a rock, this is a sign of foulness', and so on, thereby locating the corpse in the particular and dense environmental context in which it functions as a sign (34). Further on too, the environment continues to play a part in the practice. The practitioner should map out the path from the charnel ground, the direction it goes, where it turns, and the features along it like hills and stones and bushes. And once he has left the ground, he must walk up and down in his place of meditation, oriented to the path from the charnel house. But should there be an obstruction, like a fence or a ravine, that stops him from walking up and down facing in the direction of the path, 'he should turn his thoughts in that direction' (53–5).[42] The ecological nature of even the sign of that isolated entity, a decomposing corpse, is motivated by an epistemic therapy of deranged emotion. Asking himself explicitly why the surrounding signs must be characterized—thereby indicating that he is well aware of the challenge his account offers to narrower notions of meditation practice—Buddhaghosa says it is for non-delusion (*asammoha*). But this is not some abstract state of epistemic consciousness, as it might be with some other systems. Buddhaghosa instead considers the likelihood that, left with a bloated corpse in the charnel ground,

[42] *cittaṃ pana taṃdisābhimukhaṃyeva kātabbaṃ*.

the practitioner may imagine that it can move and chase him, and he can be gripped by panic, his hair standing on end with fear. This meditation subject is the most frightening (*atibherava*). But focusing on the entirety of the corpse's environment with firm mindfulness, the practitioner should remove his fear: no dead body gets up and chases one, it will not move any more than that stone or creeper, and the fear is just born of one's conception (*saññaja*), generated by conception (*saññāsambhava*). And then he can laugh away his fear, with his prior delusion, that he was in danger from a corpse, removed (56–7).

He then explains (3) the eleven kinds of apprehending the sign (*ekādasavidhena nimittaggāho*), required for the practice to work:

> Having done this [associative pairing] with the specific sign and its object, again, he should bring to mind its having its own particularity (literally, its being its own being), its own state of being bloated which is not shared with anything else; it is said that he defines it by the fact of its having become that particularity.[43] Having defined it thus, he should apprehend the sign in the following six ways: by colour, by mark, by shape, by orientation, by presentation, by delimitation.[44] (VI.35)

'Mark' is explained as being about the age of the person who died, as indicated by a study of the corpse; 'presentation' concerns how it is laid out in view, while 'delimitation' here is about fixing the boundaries of the corpse and determining its exact extension.

With pedagogic pragmatism, Buddhaghosa offers these six ways of apprehending the sign first, and then five more in case the first six are not successful in bringing forth the imitative sign. These five further apprehensions should be through the joints of the corpse, its openings, its concavities (eye socket, roof of mouth, base of neck), convexities (knee, chest, forehead), and finally, the body in toto (45–9).

Finally, there is (4) the reviewing of the path come and gone.[45] The intensity of the meditation on the imitative sign is likely to be diminished by both ordinary social comportment and by the performance of monastic duties. Buddhaghosa sternly warns that one does not ignore a layperson's greeting, or refuse to answer a question (even if only to acknowledge ignorance!), or be inhospitable to a visiting monk, only thinking, 'I have a meditation subject.' So too with the myriad of duties, at the shrine, in the refectory, to the teacher, and the rest. But it must be admitted that the imitative sign may indeed fade away (60–1). Then the strength of a carefully cultivated imagination becomes important: for when the imitative sign has thus faded, the monk should go back to his quarters, and undertake a review (*pacchavekkhana*). He must carefully re-trace the entire journey from starting out from the monastery, through every turn

[43] *Evaṃ sanimittaṃ sārammaṇañca katvā pana sabhāvabhāvato vavatthapetīti vuttattā yvāssa sabhāvabhāvo anaññasādhāraṇo attaniyo uddhumātakabhāvo, tena manasikātabbaṃ.*

[44] *Evaṃ vavatthapetvā vaṇṇatopi liṅgatopi saṇṭhānatopi disatopi okāsatopi paricchedatopīti chabbidhena nimittaṃ gahetabbaṃ.*

[45] *gatāgatamaggapaccavekkhana.*

of the path and past every aspect that was noted of the surroundings, to the place where the corpse was contemplated, all the way onwards through the return to where he is currently seated cross-legged (62–3). So we are once again to notice that it is not just the 'object' in isolation that is the focus or the sole means to the retrieval of the imitative sign.

The first point I therefore want to draw out of this exercise is the deeply ecological conception of even the most abstract mental process. To paraphrase Alva Noë, another of the contemporary philosophers discussed in the introduction, meditation too is 'out of our heads'. The second point is consequent on the first. The corpse is the most complete objectification of body possible: the opposite of the lived body is not merely the objective body but the dead body. Yet, when we look at the motivation, context and purpose of the meditator's clinical gaze, we find the practice to be a subjectivation of the dead body. This is brought out through a consideration of the spiritual purpose of the meditation on foulness: the dead body in its context is re-conceptualized into the framework of the lived body.

> Even like the dead body, the living one too is foul; it is just that the characteristic of foulness is not obvious because concealed by adventitious ornamentation.[46] (VI.88)

The aesthetic of adventitious ornamentation—brushing teeth and washing mouth, wearing appealing clothes, salves and scents and flowers—explains how the body, that as object has yielded the sign of foulness, is appropriated in 'I' (*aham*) and 'mine' (*mama*) (90). The typical expression of this state for Buddhaghosa is sexual appeal (*rata*). A swathe of 'livedness'—the steeping of experience in meaning—is explained as a contingent interpretation of phenomena that can, and in meditation practice will, be re-oriented completely. That dominant expression of living—sexual attraction—is powerful only because of an appropriation of elements of experience into a narrative of possession ('I' and 'mine'). But this exercise brings out a different phenomenological interpretation: there is nothing to lust for here. The quite general implication is that the consideration of the body as corpse signals the contingent nature of our phenomenal investment in our (constitutively bodily) existence. In short, there are no divisions between what is given in—and how we take our experience of—body. All that matters is figuring out how to read the relationship between the various aspects of experience; and the stern meditation on foulness indicates the goal of such figuring out.

In order to drive home the point that the meditative perspective ranges across the same, interconnected, ecological elements of experience, Buddhaghosa draws on the standard canonical use of the instantly recognizable experience that people develop a variety of negative emotions towards things that are routinely taken out of the body, like hair, teeth, nails, spittle, and excrement. He uses this to challenge the stability of the self-other distinction. People no longer desire to have what is now separate from

[46] *Yatheva hi matasarīraṃ, evaṃ jīvamānakampi asubhameva. Asubhalakkhaṇaṃ panettha āgantukena alaṅkārena paṭicchannattā na paññāyati.*

the body: they are 'troubled, ashamed, disgusted' (*aṭṭiyanti, harāyanti, jugucchanti*) by these things.

> But so long as any of these remains [in the body] then—even though it is just as repulsive—wrapped in the darkness of unwisdom that is suffused with tenderness and passion for oneself, they take it that it is 'desirable, agreeable, permanent, pleasurable, and oneself'.[47] (VI.91)

So there is an arbitrariness to the ordinary intuitions we have about what is lived and what is objective. The point of a corpse—that is to say, when a body is not a person—is that it occupies a very precise position: it was once the locus of a lived body. Its inanimate nature is peculiar, moving in attention between being like a stone and being like what I will be (about which BG is clear, VI.87; 90–1). So one can say it represents a highly charged phenomenal membrane: not because it is the dreadful divide between the subjective and things in the world, but because it is that permeable surface of interpretive sensibility through which the duality of the subjective and its objects is diffused.

By shifting our attention from corpse to our own body at the end of the chapter, Buddhaghosa sets us up to treat our living body in the same way in the other meditations that are focussed on bodiliness. Just as our existential attachment ranges out to the corpse amongst the creepers, so it also pulls away from our own assumed selves, first in minding what is given in phenomenality as ourselves, and then—in the understanding of the aggregates—to that phenomenality itself.

Attentiveness to the Living Body: Between Revulsion and Concentration

Another important—and perhaps logistically more accessible!—exercise is '*kāyagatāsati*', attentiveness concerning [one's] body. With some hesitation, I deviate here from the conventional translation of 'sati' as 'mindfulness'. As Bhikkhu Bodhi observes wryly, 'We take the rendering 'mindfulness' so much for granted that we rarely inquire into the precise nuances of the English term, let alone the meaning of the original Pāli word it represents and the adequacy of the former as a rendering for the latter. The word "mindfulness" is itself so vague and elastic that it serves almost as a cipher into which we can read virtually anything we want. Hence we seldom recognize that the word was chosen as a rendering for *sati* at a particular point in time, after other terms had been tried and found inadequate.'[48] He points out that the meaning of the word is more fully brought out in the term 'bringing to attention', as the development of the notion of focus from the more general use of 'remembrance' or 'memory'.[49] I shall call it 'attentiveness' (despite its running close to another loaded translation, 'attention'

[47] *Yaṃ yaṃ panettha avasesaṃ hoti, taṃ taṃ evaṃ paṭikkūlampi samānaṃ avijjandhakārapariyonaddhā attasineharāgarattā 'iṭṭhaṃ kantaṃ niccaṃ sukhaṃ attā'ti gaṇhanti.*

[48] Bhikkhu Bodhi 2011: 22. He traces its first use to T.W. Rhys Davids in 1910.

[49] Ibid.

for *manasikāra* (mental acting)), as a way of deliberating estranging '*sati*' from a great deal of contemporary usage, with its—perhaps subliminal—dualist suggestion of a mind that has a particular relationship with its body.[50]

This concentration exercise concerns one's own body, under the 'thirty-two aspects (*ākāras*)', organized as the focus of 'attention to the repulsive' (*paṭikkūlamanasikāra*) (VIII.44). Of course, as we saw Buddhaghosa himself acknowledge towards the end of the previous practice, human beings normally have an attachment to their own living body (over which ranges the lived body) that is the opposite of revulsion. The very categorization of this exercise under 'attention to the repulsive' gives away its teleology. The 'thirty-two aspects' is a traditional list (*Majjima Nikāya* iii.90) of physical body matter as identified through attention to: head hairs, body hairs, nails, teeth, skin, flesh, sinews, bones, bone marrow, kidney, heart, liver, abdomen, spleen, lungs, bowels, entrails, gorge, faeces, bile, phlegm, pus, blood, sweat, fat, tears, grease, spittle, nasal mucus, oil of the joints (synovial fluid), urine, and (Buddhaghosa gives this separately, and like most classical traditions, does not identify it with cognition) brain-matter.

This exercise is introduced through the requirement of a 'seven-fold skill in learning' (the *uggahakosallas*) (VIII.48). This is a phenomenological method aimed at peeling away that ordinary subjectivation of anatomical constituents of the living body. There is (i) verbal repetition (*vācāya sajjhāya*) (49), literally the recitation of the thirty-two aspects. To bring home the weight of acquiring this skill, Buddhaghosa refers to a tradition of the practitioner beginning the exercise by doing only the recitation for four months. The skill is acquired through structuring the recitation. The repetition should go forwards and backwards (*anulomapaṭiloma sajjhāya*) (50), through ordered sets organized around some principle—the skin, the kidney, the lungs, and the brain pentads (albeit the 'brain pentad' includes bowels, entrails, gorge, dung, and brain), and the fat and urine hexads, with the repetition bringing the preceding sets into it, and culminating in the final hexad, which is followed by all the previous ones (51–6). There is (ii) mental recitation (*manasā sajjhāya*) next (57). This is followed by concentration through analysis of the aspects according to (iii–vi) colour (*vaṇṇata*), shape (*saṇṭhānata*), orientation (*disata*), presentation (*okāsata*) (58). Finally there is concentration (vii) according to delimitation (*paricchedata*), which is of two types:

> Here, (i) delimitation through sameness is to be understood thus: this, with such a name, is delimited through [this] beneath, above and across. (ii) Delimitation through difference should be understood with such cases of non-mixture as body-hair is not head-hair and head-hair is not body-hair.[51] (59)

[50] For a perspective that contrasts the Pali Abhidhamma and the later, Sanskritic Abhidharmakośa, arguing that the former offers a constructivist metaphysics that eventually leads to a non-duality of subject and object, see Olendzki 2011. As will be evident, in adhering to Buddhaghosa's account, I find the discussion to be about a certain discipline of phenomenology (directed to a doctrinally accepted state of perfection) rather than any concern for offering a Buddhist metaphysics of experience. Whether this is true of the Pali abhidhamma as a whole or whether it is just the way Buddhaghosa uses it is another question.

[51] *Tattha ayaṃ koṭṭhāso heṭṭhā ca upari ca tiriyañca iminā nāma paricchinnoti evaṃ sabhāgaparicchedo veditabbo. Kesā na lomā, lomāpi na kesāti evaṃ amissakatāvasena visabhāgaparicchedo veditabbo.*

Once the teacher has conveyed the seven-fold skill in learning, he must introduce the practitioner to the ten-fold 'skill in attention' (*manasikārakosalla*) (61–79). This consists in attention (i) as to order (of the aspects); (ii) moving not too quickly (from one to the next); (iii) not too slowly; (iv) warding off distraction; (v) overcoming the designation (of the particular aspect) in thought (so as to only think of its repulsiveness); (vi) moving successively (from one to the next aspect); (vii) absorption or enstasy (*appanā*); and (viii–x) energetically engaging in concentration practice in accordance with three relevant original teachings of the Buddha (in the *suttas*). Each of these skills advances the practitioner's development of the attitude of revulsion to what he has hitherto taken to be components of his sense of himself as a living being.

The striking feature of this exercise is the deliberate refusal to make any distinction between what might ordinarily be considered disgusting—the things ejected from the body normally, like urine and faeces, and in sickness, like phlegm and blood—and those that are simply of forensic value in our grasp of information about ourselves, like lungs, kidneys or the heart. Consider, in Ñāṇamoli's translation, paragraphs 111 and 113:

'This is the heart flesh. As to colour, it is the colour of the back of a red-lotus petal. As to shape, it is the shape of a lotus bud with the outer petals removed and turned upside down; it is smooth outside, and inside it is like the interior of a *kosātakī* (loofah gourd). In those who possess understanding it is a little expanded; in those without understanding it is still only a bud. Inside it there is a hollow the size of a *punnāga* seed's bed where half a *pasata* measure of blood is kept, with which as their support the mind element and mind-consciousness element occur…As to direction [i.e., what I have translated as 'orientation'], it lies in the upper direction. As to location [i.e., "presentation"], it is to be found in the middle between the two breasts, inside the body. As to delimitation, it is bounded by what appertains to heart…'

As is also obvious, the often anatomical precision of the description is woven together with evocative metaphors and observational remarks. Thus anchored in more familiar parts of experience, the descriptions—which refer to things that are inaccessible to himself in the practitioner—they function as pedagogic tools to ease the development of the imitative sign. Here is another example from Ñāṇamoli's translation (133):

'These are the water element that trickles from the eye. As to colour, they are the colour of clear sesame oil. As to shape, they are the shape of their location. As to direction ['orientation'], they belong to the upper direction. As to location ['presentation'], they are to be found in the eye sockets. But they are not stored in the eye sockets all the while as the bile is in the bile container. But when beings feel joy and laugh uproariously, or feel grief and weep and lament, or eat particular kinds of wrong food, or when their eyes are affected by smoke, dust, dirt, etc., then being originated by the joy, grief, wrong food, or temperature, they fill up the eye sockets or trickle out. And the meditator who discerns tears should discern them only as they are to be found filling the eye sockets. As to delimitation, they are bounded by what appertains to tears…'

When the practitioner has moved systematically, with all the requisite skills, from the head hair to the urine, then he thinks of the whole of himself as he is, from the outside. The exercise therefore aims for the rigorous objectification of what was hitherto held naturally to constitute the foundations of one's phenomenal self-presence. It is completed with a final shift to a displaced perspective, in which the inner is seen as the outer, the lived unity as merely an assemblage of occurrences.

If he [then] were to focus attention externally too, when all the parts have become manifest in this way, then human beings, animals, etc., as they move about, are divested of their aspect of having an essence, and stand forth as just a complex of parts. And when they swallow food and drink, it looks as if it is being put in amidst the complex of parts.[52] (140)

In technical terms, in this exercise, the attendant presence (*upaṭṭhāna*) of the thirty-two aspects of the living body are apprehended variously (according to colour, orientation, etc.), and together constitute the acquired sign. The attendant presence of the attitude that they are repulsive in all aspects marks the imitative sign (141). That is to say, what emerges in the imagination—through the attentiveness paid to the various aspects of that complex—is the clarified feeling that the bodily complex is repulsive. The imitative sign's being a 'purified' version of the acquired sign (as explained under the previous exercise at IV.30–1) is now layered further: purification is identified specifically as the development of the appropriate emotional response—revulsion—to the content of the acquired sign.

Now, if the concentration practice is through some other mode of attention, then the purification of the acquired sign into the imitative sign can be constituted by other means too. Buddhaghosa returns to the same thirty-two aspects of the body as the meditation subject but through another concentration subject, the analysis of constituents (*sasambhāravibhatti*) at XI.47. He says that here, instead of awareness being stabilized by means of revulsion (*paṭikūlavasena cittaṃ ṭhapetabbaṃ*), it is done by means of the components (*dhātuvasena*) presented in experience. By this he means that each component is analysed as merely in a contingent co-presence with the others; this understanding replaces how we think of ourselves as distinct individuals, in whom the components are in organic relationships with one another. For example (59), the heart and the rib cage are like a piece of meat and a cart in which it is placed: 'these things are devoid of any mutual thought or consideration' (*aññamaññaṃ ābhogapaccavekhaṇarahitā ete dhamma.*) The heart is 'just a single constituent of this body', (*imasmiṃ sarīre pāṭiyekko koṭṭhāso*), an instance of the earth element. To take another example, tears (75) are similarly devoid of mutual consideration with the eye socket.

[52] *Sace pana bahiddhāpi manasikāraṃ upasaṃharati, athassa evaṃ sabbakoṭṭhāsesu pākaṭībhūtesu āhiṇḍantā manussatiracchānādayo sattākāraṃ vijahitvā koṭṭhāsarāsivaseneva upaṭṭhahanti, tehi ca ajjhohariyamānaṃ pānabhojanādi koṭṭhāsarāsimhi pakkhipamānamiva upaṭṭhāti.*

We should understand that what he is doing here, as with revulsion, is to lay out a practice whose purpose is to take the organicity of the body and isolate each of the body aspects, with the result that each aspect is reduced to its character as a contingent form of an inert element. The resulting absorption in the body as analysed components then reconfigures phenomenology, from the somatic subjectivation that characterizes entanglement in the body's world, to the serene joy of understanding that is disentangled from that world. At one and the same time, there is a richly valued phenomenal actuation—the occurrence of 'joy'—but also a discarding of ordinary suppositions about the bases of phenomenality itself (namely, the subjectivation of bodily aspects). The hermeneutic of this type of concentration practice is that it takes what is constitutive of the subject's sense of being a person and—literally and figuratively—anatomizes that subjectivity.

We can see this practice as a progression from the meditation on corpses. But it also reverses the direction of attention from the subjective to the extrinsic aspects of phenomenology. In the foulness practice, we saw the apparently disconnected, 'objective' corpse turn out to be important as the locus of where the lived body (of the practitioner) expressed its livedness: its environment gave an ecological dynamic to the life of the practitioner. It did so at the very beginning of the practice, by offering the provocation of disgust in a way a slice of decomposing animal matter would not (quite) do. But it did so at the end too, where it showed how to develop the capacity to therapeutize traumatic emotional responses. So the objective body turned out to be also woven into the livedness of the lived body. Now, with the repulsiveness practice, the lived body is disaggregated in imagination—through the imitative sign, as one cannot actually look at one's own heart or lungs—so that its agglomerated objectivity is realized in attentiveness.

The point about the symmetry between these two practices is that the same things happen, but in the opposite direction to the other. In the first practice, from what looks like it is far from you, an 'objectified entity', the corpse, you begin moving towards closer attention to your phenomenal field, until the corpse you have encountered so carefully becomes a matter of intense phenomenological relevance to you. In the second, you start with the pre-given subjectivation of your anatomy, the way the lived body expresses ownership, and move away into disassembling it into components of your phenomenal field and nothing more. Crudely, the object becomes subjectified, and the subject becomes objectified, thereby comprehensively undermining any ontological reflex towards duality: what shifts are the contours of your phenomenology, in accordance with your attentiveness. Together these practices take what would be a fairly intuitive and densely biological description, and transform it into guidance for enacting a heightened awareness of the ecology of body livedness. In this respect, there is a resonance here with the programme of explaining bodily livedness in the texts treated in the previous chapters.

If these practices make the monk perform a bodily search for perfection, the *abhidhamma* analysis to which we eventually move treats the understanding of that bodiliness itself as a performance.

The Fungibility of Bodily Categories: The Lesson from Breathing

Before we finally turn to the *abhidhamma* analyses that constitute the practice of understanding, let us look at the practice of attentiveness to breathing. As we will see, it will show that for Buddhaghosa, attention to biological components of body is not indicative of a simple commitment to a material account of it. Rather, the ordinary category of the 'material' body—the *kāya*—turns out to be subject to the manner in which it is attended to in phenomenological analysis. In breathing practice components presented as material are treated as phenomenal objects of attentive experience rather than as buildings blocks of an ontology. Phenomenal objects are utilized to sharpen our capacity to pay attention to what we find in experience, so that there is a change in our emotional attitude towards who we take ourselves to be; and that change is what puts the practitioner on the path to perfection. Although that teleology is not my concern here, it is helpful to remember **why** he is doing all this, because that will sensitize us to **how** he deals with the practitioner's bodiliness.

At VIII.145, Buddhaghosa introduces the concentration through breathing (*ānāpānasatisamādhi*) as taught by the Buddha (given in the *Samyutta Nikāya* v, 321–2; and the *Vinaya Piṭaka* iii, 70), which has sixteen stages. Breathing is correlated with awareness of different subjects of meditation, from the mere fact of breathing long or short, through awareness of various bodily constituents to various positive emotions, and thence to higher existential states like impermanence, cessation and relinquishment.[53] He also quotes extensively (168) from the earlier canonical *Paṭisambhidā*. With the practice of long in- and out-breaths over specific stretches of time (called *addhāna*), zeal (*chanda*) arises. As the breathing becomes more subtle (*sukhuma*), gladness (*pāmujja*) arises. Further subtlety of breathing—in the literal sense of controlled and regulated breathing—results in awareness turning away from the breathing, so that 'equanimity is established' (*upekkhā saṇṭhāti*). (He has previously defined 'equanimity' as that which watches as it arises (*upapattito ikkhati*), and that which sees without partiality (*apakkhapatita*) (IV.156).) Such care (*upaṭṭhāna*) constitutes attentiveness, and the contemplation (*anupassanā*) that occurs in equanimity is itself right cognition (*ñāṇa*) of oneself. 'By that attentiveness, with that right cognition, he [the practitioner] contemplates the body'.[54] Breathing practice maps the synergic body (*kāyasaṅkhāra*)—the body present lived as the interaction of various constituents—because the practice calms it (*passambhati*) (175).

Throughout this practice, Buddhaghosa uses the terms 'coarse' (*oḷārika*) and 'refined' (*sukhuma*) to measure the progressive shifting of the practitioner's understanding through various layers of meaning about bodiliness. VIII.176 is particularly helpful for understanding that Buddhaghosa is not talking about an ontological continuum, as

[53] For the breathing practice in Theravāda more generally, see Ñāṇanamoli 1973.
[54] *Tāya satiyā tena ñāṇena taṃ kāya anupassati.*

the traditional translation of these terms as 'gross' and 'subtle' might suggest, although '*sukhuma*' in particular lends itself to 'subtle' and other translations too.

And here, both coarseness and refinement, and calming, should be understood properly. Previously, at a time when the monk does not apprehend properly, his body and awareness are coarse, because anxious. And while the coarseness of body and mind has not been quietened down, the in-breaths and out-breaths are coarse... [He then breathes through his mouth.] But they become peaceful and quiet when body and mind have been apprehended. When they are quiet, then the in-breaths and out-breaths occur so subtly that he has to ask himself, 'Are they occurring or are they not?'[55] (176)

We must bracket what Buddhaghosa means here by 'body' and 'mind' until we turn to the analysis of the aggregates. In the meantime, we must note that the terms 'coarse' and 'subtle' are used in a quotidian way, as a matter-of-fact description of breathing. Nevertheless, the experiential dimension of this description should be noted, as the last sentence demonstrates. It is already clear that we are not here dealing with what would be an incoherent ontological claim, namely that bodily constituents are entities that literally change from being gross to subtle as analysis proceeds. Instead what we have is the description of a phenomenological progression through ever more discerning attentional shifts.

This is best seen in 180, which outlines the process of 'insight' (*vipassanā*). To begin with, when the practitioner sees the synergic body (*kāyasaṅkhāra*) as just what his bodiliness is, he is in a state of non-apprehension (*apariggaha*), so that the body with regard to itself is coarse (*oḷārika*); but when he apprehends the basic elements (*mahābhūtas*)—i.e., when he understands that the synergic body is constituted of these elements—then he sees it refined (*sukhuma*) in relation to his previous (uncomprehending) view of it. Then a sequence follows in which at each point of insight the synergic body is 'refined' in relation to the previous point and 'coarse' in relation to the succeeding one. Thus, the sequence starts from initial non-apprehension to discerning the syngeric body as determined by the basic elements; then it progresses through seeing it as constituted through contingent formations (*upādirūpa*); through any formation (*sakalarūpa*) at all; as formation-free (*arūpa*); as interdependent between formation and formlessness (*rūpārūpa*); as constituted by conditions (*paccaya*); through seeing naming and forms within their conditions (*sapaccayanāmarūpadassane*); then, as seen through insight into the characteristics of phenomenal objects (*lakkhaṇārammaṇ ikavipassanā*); next, with insight lacking strength (*dubbala*); and finally, with strong (*bala*) insight. Progressive calming—a quietening of anxiety—happens through each shift in apprehension from coarse to refined insight.

[55] *Tatra evaṃ oḷārikasukhumatā ca passaddhi ca veditabbā. Imassa hi bhikkhuno pubbe apariggahitakāle kāyo ca cittanca sadarathā honti oḷārikā. Kāyacittānaṃ oḷārikatte avūpasante assāsapassāsāpi oḷārikā honti... Yadā panassa kāyopi cittampi pariggahitā honti, tadā te santā honti vūpasantā. Tesu vūpasantesu assāsapassāsā sukhumā hutvā pavattanti, 'atthi nu kho natthī'ti vicetabbatākārappattā honti.*

Although we will look more closely at the idea of 'formation', it is not possible here to examine each of these stages in greater detail. I only want to draw attention to two inter-connected features of this practice. The first is that breathing is transformed into a device for the exploration of body as phenomenal field. For Buddhaghosa, the Buddha finds no gap between a physical act and a transformation of consciousness, but moves back and forth between the development of two sides of a single technique: on the one side is breathing, and on the other is the accompanying change of focus, although they are inseparable in the practice itself. In a theme that will become very clear in the analysis of the aggregates, it is not as if the tradition is incapable of making the analytic distinction between the material and the mental. But it does not see them as ontic, as two orders of being that need bringing together. It treats them as different aspects of what is encountered in experience, and can therefore be manipulated for phenomenological cultivation of the perfected life. The second point is that this phenomenological cultivation consists in increasingly fine-grained understanding of what is encountered in attention to the bodiliness of the practitioner. In short, the body is a phenomenal whole, which is understood through rigorous practices that range across that whole, through what are initially presented coarsely as world, body, and mind.

Re/constituting Bodiliness I: Understanding as Practice

In the formal three-fold schema of the book that Buddhaghosa gives, we now move from Concentration (which contains many other practices and the description of their spiritual benefits) to Understanding. However, as we have already noticed, key explananda in the concentration practices point forward to the chapters on Understanding. It is clear that the scholar's linear reading does not capture the interconnections between the sections of the text, since the practitioner moves back and forth between them. But even more striking than the mere interconnections is Buddhaghosa's presentation of 'understanding' (*paññā*) as itself a performance, a continuation of practice. In the rest of this chapter, we will consider much of Chapter XIV, on the aggregates of the *abhidhamma* system, which forms the first chapter of the section on Understanding. To put it gnomically, this is a phenomenological performance, because understanding [noun] is understanding [verb]: what sounds like a state is in fact a way of being.

In what sense is it understand*ing*? It is understanding (*paññā*) in the sense of being an act of understanding (*pajānana*). What is this act of understanding? It is cognizance (*jānana*) of a pre-eminent mode, distinct from conceptualizing (*sañjānana*) and cognizing (*vijānana*). For although conception and cognition and understanding are equally states of cognizance (*jānana-bhāva*), nevertheless conception is only the mere conceiving of an object as, say, 'blue or yellow'; it cannot bring about the penetration of its characteristics as 'impermanent, painful, and not-self'. Cognition has cognizance of objects as 'blue or yellow', and it brings about the penetration of its characteristics, but it cannot bring about, by ascetic practice, the appearance of the path. Understanding has cognizance of object in the way already stated, it brings about the penetration of the characteristics, and it also brings about, by ascetic practice, the manifestation of the path.[56] (XIV.3)

In fact, then, the contemplative or ascetic practices and understanding are integral parts of the same process. This explanation that understanding is performative must alert us to the difference between the way knowledge-as-practice is treated by Buddhaghosa and the way knowledge is related **to** practice in Western classical and Christian traditions. Foucault, for example, succinctly puts the care of the self for the Stoics to consist in the sequence, 'After *methēsis, askēsis*'; that is, first learning, then exercise.[57] Similarly, in early Christian thought: 'The remedy for this state of affairs [of loving the world too much, before God] is not more information, the remedy is therapeutic asceticism. This implies that the task of liturgical renewal is not primarily gnostic, done with study, but ascetic, done in the heart.'[58] But both these traditions—or more precisely, traditions as they have been interpreted in contemporary Western thought—offer a telling contrast to Buddhaghosa's model. I mention them because it is all to easy to overlook the subtle way in which Buddhaghosa treats as one two concepts that we might be tempted to keep apart.

In the rest of the chapter, we will look at the understanding of the aggregates (*khandha*s), which form the basis of the traditional teaching of *abhidhamma*.[59] The five aggregates are *rūpa*, *viññāṇa*, *vedanā*, *saññā*, and *saṅkhāra*. I am in broad agreement with the view expressed by Rupert Gethin: '[T]he five *khandhas,* as treated in the *nikāyas* and early *abhidhamma,* do not exactly take on the character of a formal theory of the nature of man. The concern is not so much the presentation of an analysis of man as object, but rather the understanding of the nature of conditioned existence from the point of view of the experiencing subject. Thus at the most general level *rūpa*, *vedanā*, *saññā*, *saṃkhāras and viññāṇa* are presented as five aspects of an individual being's experience of the world; each *khandha* is seen as representing a complex class of phenomena that is continuously arising and falling away in response to processes of consciousness based on the six spheres of sense... For any given individual there are, then, only these five *upādānakkhandhas*—they define the limits of his world, they are his world. This subjective orientation of the *khandhas* seems to arise out of the simple fact that, for the *nikāyas,* this is how the world is experienced; that is to say, it is not seen primarily as having metaphysical significance.'[60]

[56] *Kenaṭṭhena paññāti? pajānanaṭṭhena paññā. Kimidaṃ pajānanaṃ nāma? Sañjānanavijānanākāravis iṭṭhaṃnānappakārato jānanaṃ. Saññāviññāṇapaññānaṃ hi samānepi jānanabhāve, saññā 'nīlaṃ pītaka'nti ārammaṇasañjānanamattameva hoti. 'Aniccaṃ dukkhamanattā'ti lakkhaṇapaṭivedhaṃ pāpetuṃ na sakkoti. Viññāṇaṃ 'nīlaṃpītaka'nti ārammaṇañca jānāti, lakkhaṇapaṭivedhañca pāpeti. Ussakkitvā pana maggapātubhāvaṃ pāpetuṃ na sakkoti. Paññā vuttanayavasena ārammaṇañca jānāti, lakkhaṇapaṭivedhañca pāpeti, ussakkitvā maggapātubhāvañca pāpeti.*

[57] Foucault 2005: 311. [58] Fagerberg 2013: 67.

[59] As mentioned before, for the standard view of the Abhidhamma see Karunadasa 2010. My treatment of Buddhaghosa's deployment of *abhidhamma* may well be unrecognizable from the perspective of the standard account.

[60] Gethin 1986: 48–9. It should be noted that Gethin gives a more metaphysical interpretation elsewhere.

This is certainly the case with Buddhaghosa. The thrust of my argument is that by adopting so rigorously phenomenological a method, we may clarify that Gethin's mention of 'subjective orientation' does not contrast with some other, 'objective', orientation that another putative teaching might be thought to provide or which the *abhidhamma* might be supposed to fail to provide. To conceive of the *abhidhamma* aggregates (and, to reiterate, let me confine myself here to Buddhaghosa's rendering of it) as having a subjective orientation might implicitly shift our reading to an ontological register, as if there were some possible method (left unexplored) to delineate the objective while this only offers an exploration of the subjective. Reading Gethin carefully, we can see that such a temptation is to be resisted. Rather, what it means is that the treatment of the *khandha*s leaves no space for us to assume that what we have is an ontology elsewhere. Buddhaghosa's usage of the *abhidhamma* as phenomenological method demonstrates that experience provides in itself the reflexive materials for insightful orientation to experience as a whole.

The *abhidhamma* operates across the endless abstract factors (*dhamma*) that make up the content of experience, and for Buddhaghosa it was taught by the Buddha from out of his understanding of all the rich and varied experience he had undergone through the many lives leading up to his enlightenment.[61] With this formal template, the practitioner is able to attend to the content of his own experience, and proceed to analyse it carefully in order to understand in what his being consists. (And by 'being' I mean merely the livedness of a person, with no implication of an essential identity—for, of course, that is just what the Buddha warned against.) This is broadly comparable to Husserl's distinction between the noematic and the noetic. To simplify, the noema 'is an "idea" or abstract structure common to different acts of the same type'.[62] The intentional act of attending to an experience contains its noesis, its sense-giving (Sinngebung). 'It is this part of the noesis that gives the act its directedness toward a specific object and determines just how that object is represented in the act; and it does so by giving the act a "Sinn", i.e., a "meaning" or "sense". Correlated with this "real" constituent of the noesis is the Sinn or meaning itself—the subject's "sense" of an object. This meaning or sense is the main constituent of the act's noema . . . This meaning-component of the noema, or "noematic Sinn" as Husserl calls it, is then an "ideal" or abstract entity, whose role is to determine just which object an act represents and precisely how it represents it.'[63] We could say that the *abhidhamma* is literally the collection of noematic Sinn, the 'ideal' *dhamma*s, as abstracted by the Buddha, which correlates with the real or actual and particular noetic acts on the part of the one who contemplates particular experiences and attaches to them the meaning given by the Buddha.[64]

[61] Heim forthcoming, chapter 4.

[62] McIntyre and Woodruff Smith 1989: 159.

[63] Ibid., p. 159.

[64] Compare, too, what McIntyre and Woodruff Smith say about Husserl's earlier terminology: 'The real content of an act is something that necessarily belongs to that act alone: just as different acts are numerically distinct events, occurring at different times or even in different streams of consciousness, so are the component events that make up these different acts. Nonetheless, there is a sense in which two persons, or

Fundamentally, then, to study these formal categories is to enact a reflexive contemplation of oneself; but we take the scholar's liberty of studying them as they are not to be studied, that is, as giving us a picture of what it would be like to see a human being in the formalized terms of the Buddha's experience (according to Buddhaghosa).

Re/constituting Bodiliness II: Formation (*rūpa*)

The first of the five aggregates traditionally given is '*rūpa*'. It is potentially misleading to think of *rūpa* as 'matter/materiality' as the conventional translation in the *abhidhamma* context has it, given that already in early Buddhism *rūpa* primarily occurs in the context of the analysis of '*saviññāṇaka kāya*'. Rupert Gethin translates the latter as 'body-endowed with consciousness',[65] but more directly, it can be translated as 'cognizant body', to ensure that no body *versus* non-body metaphysics is accidentally implied. It merely indicates the difference between the practitioner and a corpse, which latter is *aviññāṇa* (*vide* VI.1). As we will see in the descriptions that follow, '*rūpa*' is both 'form' (the basic meaning) and 'formation'.[66] It is about what occurs in experience; not because Buddhaghosa distinguishes between what occurs in experience (the 'form' of it) and some sort of thing (i.e., matter) outside of it, but because his attention—driven by the need to teach contemplative practice—is always on the experience: so much so that he is never concerned to come to conclusions about things other than as they are experienced.

Buddhaghosa gives an evocative and explanatory (if philologically doubtful) derivation of *rūpa* (XIV.34): the 'one-fold' definition is that it is any factor (*dhamma*) that is 'impinged upon' (literally, 'molested' or 'vexed': *ruppana*) by its conditions. What is

the same person at different times, can be said to have the same experience, i.e., experiences with the same content. In that sense, we can speak of acts of the same kind, e.g., two perceptions, as having the same quality and acts with the same intentional character as having the same matter. But then we are speaking of quality and matter, not as components of an act's real content, but as constituents of what Husserl calls its intentional content. This intentional content is not literally "in" the act as its actual constituents are; rather, it is an abstract or "ideal" structure that different acts can "share". The real content specific to a particular act, Husserl believes, is in every case a particular and individual exemplification or realization of such an abstract structure, which can also be realized in the real contents of other acts of the same phenomenological type' (p. 158). If we thought that abstract structure to have been determined in the Buddha's omniscience, then we have a startling comparison with this theory: the endlessness of our specific experiences of *dhammas* is structured by the Buddha's *abhidhamma*.

[65] Gethin 1986: 36.

[66] The brilliant translator, Ñāṇamoli is well aware of the problem, and crisply makes the point about dualism, and yet his justification for choosing nonetheless to translate *rūpa* as 'materiality' (and *nāma*' as 'mentality') is entirely unclear to me. He says in the Introduction to the translation, '"[M]entality-materiality" for *nāma-rūpa* is inadequate and "name-and-form" in some ways preferable. "Name" (see Ch. XVIII, n.4) still suggests *nāma*'s function of "naming"; and "form" for the *rūpa* of the *rūpakkhandha* ("materiality aggregate") can preserve the link with the *rūpa* of the *rūpāyatana*, ("visible-object base") by rendering them respectively with "material form aggregate" and "visible form base"—a point not without philosophical importance. A compromise has been made at Chapter X.13. "Materiality" or "matter" wherever used should not be taken as implying any hypostasis, any "permanent or semipermanent substance behind appearances" (the objective counterpart of the subjective ego), which would find no support in the Pali' (p. xxxviii).

thus formed—a formation—is *rūpa*. When looking at these formations, we must keep in mind that Buddhaghosa is talking about the constituents of experience, and therefore that an object (*ārammaṇa*) is a phenomenal object. But by this I do not mean to imply a reality–appearance disjunction. If we always keep in mind that Buddhaghosa's task is to develop the monk's capacity to understand himself on the path to perfection, then we will see that such a distinction is of no purpose to him. So, while an object is phenomenal because it is the experience that is being studied through the formal terms of the *abhidhamma* categories, there is no harm in talking about the object per se. Indeed, the advantage to such talk is that we do not have constantly to repeat the formula that when talking of these formations, we mean what is shaped in experience. I proceed with this 'disquotational' use in mind: the 'object-in-experience' can be talked about merely as the 'object'.

Buddhaghosa then offers 'the two-fold definition' of *rūpa*. Here, *rūpa* is divided into two types: (i) elemental (*bhūta*) and contingent—which is to say, derived because clung to (*upādāya*).[67] I will not here explore the implicitly spiritual implication that these forms are forms because of the existential desire from which freedom is sought through the Buddha's path. But what is made clear here is the fundamentally phenomenological nature of these forms—they are classified according to how we are in experience, namely, as those who cling to what we think we have. The elemental is of four kinds: earth, water, fire, and air (35). Self-evidently, it refers to the materials out of which it is traditionally held that all objects are made. The forms that are contingent (upon our existential reflex of clinging to an assumed reality) are of twenty-four kinds: eye, ear, nose, tongue, body, the visible form (*rūpa*), sound, odour, taste (*rasa*), the feminine faculty (*itthindriya*), the masculine faculty (*purusindriya*), life faculty (*jīvitindriya*), the heart-substance (*hadayavatthu*), bodily intimation (*kāyaviññati*), verbal intimation, the spatial component (*ākāsadhātu*), the lightness of formation (*rūpassa lahutā*), its malleability (*mudutā*), its pliability (*kammaññatā*), growth, continuity, ageing, and impermanence; and material food (36). These formations are also contingent in that they are derived from the elements, and are dependent for their specific form upon particular interactions between the elements that generate them.

It is clear that we need to look more carefully at some of the contingent formations at least, since it is these that most obviously provide the components of bodiliness. In what follows, we should be careful when thinking of '*kāya*'—normally translated as 'body'—as standing univocally for the entire composite entity. In the context of *rūpa*, *kāya* is used in a specific way, as that which gains 'intimation' (*viññatti*) 'by touching' (*phusitvā*). As it is one of the 'forms contingent upon clinging' (*upādāyarūpa*) amongst eye, nose, etc., and *kāyaviññatti* is paired with 'verbal intimation' (*vācaviññatti*), the former cannot refer to 'body' as a whole. At the same time, it is more than 'skin' (which in many other classical systems is listed as the organ of touch). It should be taken as

[67] After Ñāṇamoli at XIV.35: 'derived [by clinging] (*upādāya*)'.

referring to that wider notion of 'touch', as an awareness that saturates the body, thereby not being localized to particular regions of it as the other senses are.[68]

While looking at each of the twenty-four would take too long (better simply to read the *Visuddhimagga* itself!), I want to mention and comment on a few in order to convey the detailed, rhizomatic (multiple, interactive) and context-sensitive way in which Buddhaghosa proceeds to make the practitioner learn how to contemplate on the multiple ways that he is present to himself in experience.

The twenty-four kinds of contingent formations function in phenomenological analysis through the use of the notion of 'sensitivity' (*pasāda*), the receptivity of awareness through bodiliness. The list of the functions[69] of the five sensory formations—in terms of sensitivity—is correlated with a list of the structural locations of each sensory sensitivity. The nose (39) has the characteristic of sensitivity to the impact (*abhighāta*) of smell, and the desire to smell is the source of the activity by which smelling originates. Then, to correlate with 39, the nose (50) has an inside shaped like a 'goat's hoof', and is both the substantial basis (*vatthu*) of, as well as the entrance (*dvāra*) for nasal cognition. Similarly, at 41 with the body (and we see the narrow meaning of 'body' here): it has the characteristic of sensitivity to the impact of the tangible (*phoṭṭhabba*), the desire for touch being the source of its activity. And in turn, the location of that bodily sensitivity (52) is to be found throughout the body, so long as there are 'formations that are "clung-to"' (*upādiṇṇarūpaṃ*), that is, when desire drives the search for sensation. (Phenomenology includes moral phenomenology, where the moral is that which arcs towards perfection, which is free from desire.)

Each of the other formations contains within it a recognition of some formal aspect of how a human appears to himself and how other humans appear to him. So, for example, we have (58) the sex faculty: for women and men, this faculty presents as the cause of the 'mark, sign, behaviour and mettle' (*liṅganimittakuttākappānaṃ*) of being female or male. Incidentally, whereas the Pali Text Society Dictionary has '*kutta*' as generally pertaining to a woman, Buddhaghosa's use of it with men too points to his understanding of it as being about any gendered behaviour. In both cases, this faculty 'pervades the somatic whole' (*sakalasarīrabyāpakaṃ*); being a woman or a man is not a question of parts.

Even more abstract is the faculty of life (*jīvitindriya*) (59) whose 'characteristic is the maintenance of conascent formations' (*sahajarūpānupālalakkhaṇaṃ*). Its function

[68] Again, since it would take us into another complex comparative investigation, I cannot say more than point to the rich possibilities here of the *abhidhamma* identification of body as itself the place of touch for the discussions inaugurated by Derrida. Derrida uses his insight into the traditional Aristotelian understanding that touch is necessary for the other senses (Derrida 2005: 46–9) to argue that the work of a soul, as that which renders the body's sense organs functional, is undermined by the idea of touch as that which renders other sensations intelligible. One doubts, though, whether Buddhaghosa would follow Derrida into claiming for touch the notion of 'spectrality', a gap between function and non-function that appears from the deconstruction of the traditional Western binaries. Buddhaghosa has the advantage of not having to wrestle with those binaries as metaphysical categories in the first place.

[69] The *Atthasālinī* (p. 29) offers the following definition of '*rasa*': 'That which ought to be done or that which attains is called "function"' (*kiccaṃ vā sampatti vā raso nāma.*)

is to make these formations that are born together to occur (*pavatta*) at all. Here too one spots the advantage of Buddhaghosa's discerning restriction of analysis to the functional.

And although it has the capacity characterized as maintenance and so on, it only maintains conascent formations at that present moment, as water does lotuses, etc. Though factors (*dhamma*) arise due to their own conditions, it maintains them, as a wet-nurse does a prince. And it occurs itself only through its connection with the occurrent factors, like a ship's captain; it does not cause occurrence after dissolution... Yet it must not be regarded as devoid of the power to maintain, bring about, and make present, because it does accomplish each of these functions at a stated moment.[70] (59)

On the one hand, it is important to associate phenomena with life, in the formal terms that distinguish body from corpse; so we have what life means for contemplative analysis. On the other hand, since that is all that is needed for the path, we need not expect either a scientific or a metaphysical drilling down to what life 'is'.

Then, as with other classical cultures, Buddhaghosa's system also associates the heart with the location of thought (60): the heart substance has the characteristic of being the support (*nissaya*) of the mind component (*manodhātu*) and the component of mental cognition (*manoviññāṇadhātu*). As we will see, these two are crucial to coordinating the data of the sense-organs (while also indicating how strictly functional is the conception of 'mind' in this system). The heart substance's function is to preserve (*ādhāraṇarasa*) them; it manifests itself continuously in carrying (*ubbāhana*) them.[71]

At this point, it would help to look ahead to XIV.97, which explains the difference between 'mind' and 'mental cognition'. 'The mind component has the characteristic of taking cognizance of the visible, etc., [the data of the sense organs] immediately after visual cognition, etc., itself',[72] and its function is reception (*sampaṭicchana*). 'Mental cognition' is different: 'the component of mental cognition, with the operation of investigation, has the characteristic of taking cognizance of the six [types of] phenomenal objects';[73] its function is therefore investigation (*santīraṇa*).[74] We will return to these items under the next aggregate, 'cognition' (*viññāṇa*). Of course, we are tempted

[70] *Santepi ca anupālanalakkhaṇādimhi vidhāne atthikkhaṇeyeva taṃ sahajarūpāni anupāleti udakaṃ viya uppalādīni. Yathāsakaṃ paccayuppannepi ca dhamme pāleti dhāti viya kumāraṃ. Sayaṃ pavattitad-hammasambandheneva ca pavattati niyāmako viya. Na bhaṅgato uddhaṃ pavattati... Na ca anupālanapav attanaṭṭhapanānubhāvavirahitaṃ, yathāvuttakkhaṇe tassa tassa sādhanatoti daṭṭhabbaṃ.*

[71] Again, *Atthasālinī* (p. 29), on 'manifestation', or 'phenomenon': 'Accessibility or result is called manifestation' (*upaṭṭhānākāro vā phalaṃ vā paccupaṭṭhānaṃ nāma*).

[72] *cakkhuviññāṇādīnaṃ anantaraṃ rūpādivijānanalakkhaṇā manodhātu.*

[73] *saḷārammaṇavijānanalakkhaṇā... santīraṇādikiccā manoviññāṇadhātu.*

[74] Compare, on the notion of the heart as having the core functions of a 'control-centre' for perception, movement, and motivation in Stoic thought, Gill 2010: 87ff. But because Stoic thought depends on the sharp ontological division between *physis* (nature) and *psyche* (even if both are in some sense 'physical') that I argue is not of concern to Buddhaghosa, and the sort of division that is not evident in *abhidhamma* phenonemology, a full comparison between the specific features of the two systems would take us far away from our present concerns.

to investigate further what 'support' and 'carrying' can mean here, while the implication of some idea of supervenience is tantalizing. But if we adhere to the project at hand, then all we need is to accept that they are to capture the pervasive felt sense of this organ within the chest as the place of receiving and thinking about one's world.

My intention here has not been to give a comprehensive account of *rūpa*, but to indicate through examples of it—some, like the senses, obvious; others, like 'life', intriguingly less so—that this aggregate offers a critical dimension of the human being in experience. The balance of the obvious and the unobvious is important. Buddhaghosa is not revisionary in his delineation of experience: the formal template that the list offers is for ordinary experience. The recognizability of the formations is what motivates the practitioner. (We will see under the cognition aggregate that there are advanced, unordinary experiences that perfected ones (*arahant*s) have, but these are specifically separated out from what is common to all.) The Buddha's insight was that these aspects of being human would not only be of benefit to the humans whose attention was drawn to them, but that utilizing them rigorously for the practice of understanding would lead them on the path to perfection. Consequently, there is something intuitive about many features of our experience of the formations, since they advert to what we already know vaguely about ourselves and can therefore sharpen through attentiveness. But burgeoning attentiveness begins to draw us away (as in an existential sense it will the practitioner) from these intuitions towards subtler, less obvious, and therefore startlingly fruitful aspects of who we are.

For my purpose, this examination of the formations has shown that our lived body—what is reflexively available in experience—does range over familiar things we think about as our 'body', what we conventionally call the 'material' body. It is self-evident to all but a pathological (rather than methodological) sceptic that the material is present in the phenomenological. At the same time, it should now be clear that the formations are present phenomenologically: the focus of this practice of understanding is not the determination of the nature of that which is 'other than' the subjective, but rather, the constitution of subjectivity itself. At the same time, phenomenology itself shows a doubleness, between formations that structure our experience, and other aggregates that offer the conditions of reflexive awareness of those structures. The remaining four aggregates, to which we now turn, belong to this other side of phenomenology.[75]

Re/constituting Bodiliness III: Cognition (*viññāṇa*) and Other Aggregates

It will require a different undertaking to study how the notions of 'cognition', 'feeling' and 'conception' are defined in the larger Buddhist (and classical Indian) tradition;

[75] Hence the title of Heim and Ram-Prasad 2017 [Early Release]/2019: 'In a Double Way'. 'Thus one should define, in a double way, name and form in all phenomenal factors of the three realms . . .', XVIII.24.

Buddhaghosa himself does not seek to develop any formal theory, but rather fills in the content of these notions through the specific *abhidhamma* terms. So, we will follow him here in his usage, and thereby get a sense of how he uses these terms in the particular.

The cognition aggregate has a richer, more complex typology in the *abhidhamma* than the formation aggregate, and the remaining three follow the same pattern, as Buddhaghosa himself says: 'Here, once the cognition aggregate is understood, the rest are easily understood too' (XIV.81). In themselves, these aggregates—but especially cognition and feeling, lend themselves to a study of the 'moral phenomenology' of Buddhaghosa's presentation of *abhidhamma*.[76] However, here I want to think of them primarily in relation to the formation aggregate. This is because the significance of these aggregates for the purposes of this chapter is two-fold. First, through them, Buddhaghosa lays out the phenomenological method. If so far we have seen how his approach is implicit in practice, now we see him explore the constituents of the reflexive analysis through which phenomenology becomes the 'path of purification' (*visuddhimagga*). Second (and this follows from the first), we see how, despite the analytic distinction between the 'body' formations and the 'mental' aggregates, the *abhidhamma* aggregates altogether contain within them a constant percolation of causal references between each other, destabilizing any intuitions we moderns may have about a body–mind divide. They thereby provide a fluid account of how the body occurs in phenomenology.

The cognition[77] aggregate, as too the remaining three, are divided at the most abstract level into three types—good (*kusala*), bad (*akusala*), and indeterminate (*abyākata*). Of course, other translations are possible too. To give a general sense of this classification, we may note this from the *Atthasālinī*: 'By 'good' is meant the good that disturbs what is abominable. Or again, 'good' is health, blamelessness, and accomplishment through skill' (p. 29).[78] The bad is simply what is not that; the indeterminate is neither.

The *abhidhamma* classification of the cognition aggregate is embedded in the larger programme of progressing through the different stages of meditative attainment (the *jhānas*). In modern scholarship, it is usually given as a long table along the two axes of the three-fold typology (given above) and the four spheres/realms (*avacara*)—the sensory/sensual (*kāma*), form (*rūpa*), formless (*arūpa*), and supramundane (*lokuttara*).[79]

[76] Heim 2014: 91ff. Heim's perceptive work has influenced my general approach to Buddhaghosa's treatment of the *abhidhamma* categories.

[77] We must note that, at 82, Buddhaghosa explicitly equates *viññāṇa*, *citta*, and *mano* (and hence *mānasika* and *cetasika* are both 'mental'). But in fact, while it is simplest to translate both the latter two as 'mind', the first most naturally translates in context as 'cognition'. The synonymy indicates the dynamic and functional sense in which 'mind' is to be read in this context, far from the dominant Cartesian sense of the immaterial subject in which it continues to be used today, even (or in a particularly puzzling way) by those who are officially committed to a reductive physicalism, like most practising psychiatrists: see O'Sullivan 2015 as an example of an entire discourse built on this anomalous usage.

[78] *Kusalanti kucchitānaṃ salanādīhi atthehi kusalaṃ. Apica ārogyaṭṭhena anavajjaṭṭhena kosallasambhūtaṭṭhena ca kusalaṃ.*

[79] See Ñāṇamoli's Table III in Ñāṇamoli 1975: 881.

I will deal with the terminology only to illustrate how the classification functions, and confine myself to aspects of it that have a bearing on my concerns: namely, the phenomenological practice encoded here, and the way the classification points to the bodily human who is encountered in that practice.

First of all, I want to present the classification given in XIV 83–110, not in the familiar tabulation alone but also, in the case of the Indeterminate type of cognition, a tree diagram. This tree turns out to have iterative elements, which pictorially captures the reflexive and progressive nature of the cognitive analysis of cognition.

The tabular aspect of Figure 3.1 concerns the division of all cognitions into Good, Bad, and Indeterminate. As will be obvious, the complexity of classification concerns the Indeterminate, in which the spheres originally classified as Good are iterated at crucial divisions of the stems. I will look primarily at the Sensory sphere and its crucial reproduction under the Indeterminate type of cognition. It is in their combination that the ordinary human life is found, the place where the possibility of contemplative progression is traced out.

Of the four spheres of Good cognition, the latter three are mapped on to the doctrinal states of spiritual progress. The Form sphere is associated (86) with the various constituents (*angas*) of the meditative attainments (the *jhānas*): the initial application of thought (*vitakka*), sustained inquiry (*vicāra*), exuberant delight (*pīti*), agreeable, easeful pleasure (*sukha*), and concentration (*samādhi*).[80] The Formless sphere (87) is associated with further, more abstract, doctrinally determined stages of attainment,

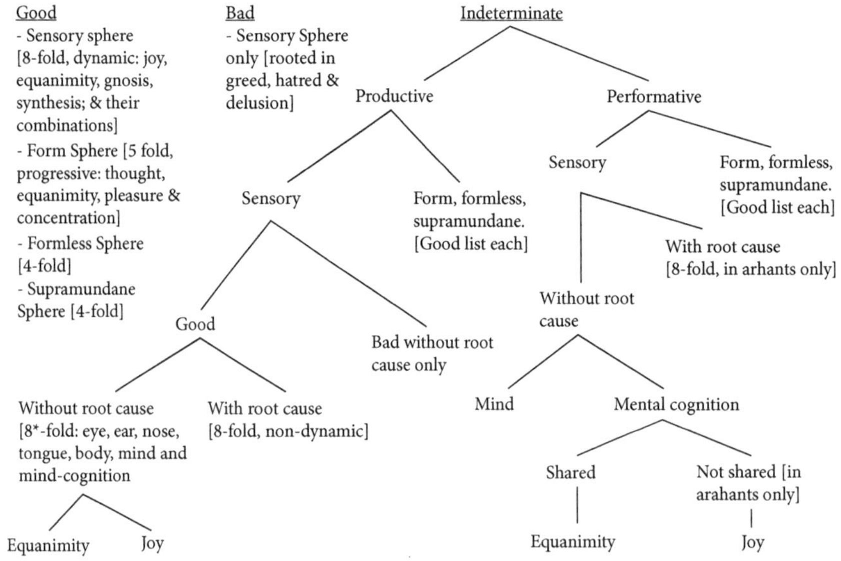

Figure 3.1 Tree diagram of the three types of cognition

80 See Gunaratna 1985 for the canonical material through the *Visuddhimagga*.

like infinite awareness and the like, while the Supramundane (88) concerns the 'four paths', each more advanced than the previous, towards liberation.[81] We may note that they occur at different points of the Indeterminate Cognition tree too, thereby indicating that the ordinary practitioner who starts with Indeterminate Cognition can advance to their attainment: what we have is a flow-chart of human becoming, as much as a typology of human being.

In what follows, I concentrate on the manner in which the Indeterminate tree (the third column) is foliated primarily by the various branches of the Sensory Sphere. Here we get the material relevant to this chapter; but we need to pay some attention to the (as it were) mind-boggling details to which Buddhaghosa adverts in describing them, for that is how the bodily being emerges in the *Visuddhimagga*—obliquely and in the details.

Good Cognitions within the Sensory Sphere (*kāmāvacara*) are classified according to the occurrence of four factors and their combinations: joy, or literally, well-mindedness (*somanassa*);[82] balance or equanimity (*upekkha*); insightful knowledge or gnosis (*ñāṇa*); and whether prompted by oneself or others, synthesis (*saṅkhāra*)[83] (83–5). Buddhaghosa is sensitive to the implications of this being the sphere of '*kāma*', which means 'desire'. The *Atthasālinī* sums up the synonymy of the senses and desire, such that the sensory sphere is also the sphere of the sensual.

> The sensory has a two-fold classification: the substance-sensory and the hindrance-sensory. Of these, the hindrance-sensory means excitable passion, the substance-sensory is the round of the three worlds. The hindrance-sensory is the sensual because it [sensorily] desires; while the other is sensual because [sensorily] desired.[84] (p. 28)

Any analysis of 'hindrance' (*kilesa*)—also 'corruption', 'affliction', 'defilement', etc.—would take us too far away from the present topic; Buddhaghosa evocatively but unspecifically says, 'the hindering of virtue (*sīla*) is the breaking apart, and the like, of it'[85] (I.143); the breaking of virtue consists in breaching the various forms of restraint that define it. The result is the hindering of progress on the path. The negative qualities that hinder spiritual progression together effect the functioning of the senses: what is sense is what is desired. Desire constitutes the sensory; and the word for desire becomes the word for the sensory.[86]

[81] Bond 1988.

[82] We should remember here that we have already seen that 'mind', which is 'supported' by the heart, is not restricted to thinking but also extends to less deliberative forms of awareness.

[83] Buddhaghosa's contrast is between synthetic well-mindedness, when a man requires prompting by himself or others to produce the right attitude in his conduct, and the natural familiarity (*jātaparicaya*) of children with good conduct (85).

[84] *uddānato dve kāmā, vatthukāmo ca kilesakāmo ca. Tattha kilesakāmo atthato chandarāgova vatthukāmo tebhūmakavaṭṭaṃ. Kilesakāmo cettha kāmetīti kāmo; itaro pana kāmiyatīti kāmo.*

[85] *khaṇḍādibhāvo sīlassa saṅkileso.*

[86] For an elaborate development of a theory of desire and perception in the Phenomenological tradition (quite untouched by Buddhaghosa!) see Barbaras 2005.

The Bad Cognitions also have a complex typologization. They all fall under the Sensory Sphere. Consequently, what is rooted in greed is itself classed according to the four factors and their combinations as already seen in the Good cognitions of the Sensory sphere. That rooted in hate is accompanied either by grief ('ill-mindedness': *domanassa*) or anger, either synthesized or natural; and delusion, always accompanied by *upekkha*—which here cannot mean equanimity as such, but lack of commitment—is associated with either uncertainty or agitation.

The Good and the Bad are the touchstones for the moral constitution of cognition; as such, they are tabulated in lists. It is helpful to think of the Indeterminate class of Cognitions as cognitions in the making, the type that humans ordinarily have, from which the practitioner starts on the path. This is why I have sought to present this class as a tree, branching out to cover the agentive, moral complexity of being human. It is then notable that the four non-Sensory spheres, whether Productive or Performative, all eventually lead iteratively back to Good Cognition.

By contrast (and this is what is relevant to our present analysis), there is a proliferation of complexity—a foliation of types of cognition—along the sensory stems. The Sensory leads us back to somatic formations (*rūpas*)—eye, ear, nose, tongue, bodily touch—and we can see how the analytic distinction apparent in classifying these two aggregates separately does not in fact encode a dualism of body and mind at all (nor of course, reducing 'mind' to 'body' in a monotonic physicalism). Instead, they become different aspects of how the human being experiences himself (in the person of the monk).

Indeterminate Cognition is therefore the locus of attentive practice (94), and it contains two branching formulae: one is the Productive (*vipāka*): it produces—i.e., both generates and results in—consequentiality (*kamma*). The other is the Performative (*kiriya*): it is doing cognitive work, but work that does not produce *kamma*. Performative Indeterminate Cognition therefore does not hinder perfection, unlike Productive Indeterminate Cognition.[87] We should expect, then, that much of cognitive life will occur in the left-branching stems, *kamma*-produced/producing and in the Sensory Sphere. The challenge for the practitioner will be to shift activity into the Good stem under it and away from the Bad stem. But just by laying out the constitution of these stems, Buddhaghosa shows us what makes the human being.

The way visual-cognition and the rest are treated here (96–9) shows that it is just the entities presented under Formations (*rūpa*) that are now approached through the category of Cognition: there is therefore a shift of analytic perspective on the human being, rather than a division of the human into two parts.

What is introduced here are 'mind' with the function of 'reception' (*sampaṭicchana*) and 'mental cognition' with the function of 'investigation' (*santīraṇa*).

[87] On an elaboration of the technicalities of this concept in *abhidhamma*, see Wijeratne and Gethin 2002: xx.

> The mind component has the characteristic of taking cognizance of the visible, etc., [the data of the sense organs] immediately after visual cognition, etc., itself.[88] The component of mental cognition, with the operation of investigation, has the characteristic of taking cognizance of the six [types of] objects (i.e., including the mental).[89] (97)

It is clear here that these two components of the Productive Sensory Sphere are the key factors in the generation of a phenomenology, through (i) having phenomena and (ii) analysing them, respectively.

The significance of the phenomenological method becomes clearer when we turn from the Productive to the other branch of the Indeterminate, namely, the Performative. This, as cognitive activity purified of the possibility of generating binding consequences, is obviously the type that the advanced practitioner seeks to reach.

We then notice that (setting aside the doctrinally abstract Form and Formless spheres), the Sensory Sphere under Performative Cognition now only contains mind and mental cognition. Since it is they that receive and investigate experience, their function is clear: they are required to push the awareness of experience towards perfection. This heightened function is evident in Buddhaghosa's re-formulation (from the one at 97) at 107 of 'mind' and 'mental cognition' on this purified branch of Indeterminate cognition.

> The mind component has the characteristic of being the forerunner of visual cognition, etc., and the cognizance of the visible, etc.; its function is to focus. It is manifested as the confrontation of visibles, etc.[90] (107)

Similarly reformulated is the component of mental cognition—albeit specified here as of the type common to all (*sādhāraṇa*): it is characterized by having cognizance of the six types of objects; and 'its function is to determine and focus on the five [sense-organ] entrances and the entrance to mind' (108).[91] (The uncommon type is restricted to perfected persons (*arahants*), characterized by joy and the capacity to look smilingly even on forms that are not sublime.[92])

We can spend less time on the other aggregates, following Buddhaghosa's own instructions that they have the same typology at Cognition. And indeed, at 127, the description of Feeling (*vedanā*) loops back to Cognition's tabulation and tree given at 83. Of course, for those studying these topics individually, there is much of interest; as too with how his understanding of the relationship between Cognition and Feeling might contribute to philosophical debates about emotions and the body.[93]

[88] *cakkhuviññāṇādīnaṃ anantaraṃ rūpādivijānanalakkhaṇā manodhātu.*

[89] *saḷārammaṇavijānanalakkhaṇā…santīraṇādikiccā manoviññāṇadhātu.*

[90] *cakkhuviññāṇādipurecararūpādivijānanalakkhaṇā manodhātu, āvajjanarasā. rūpādiabhimukhabhāv apaccupaṭṭhānā.*

[91] *kiccavasena pañcadvāramanodvāresu voṭṭhabbanāvajjanarasā.*

[92] Ñāṇamoli 1975: 513, fn. 41.

[93] Maiese 2014, is an example in the Western tradition of trying to overcome the traditional dichotomy there between cognitive (abstract, intellectual) and feeling (bodily, non-intentional) theories of emotions; enactive theories such as hers, that explore the bodily and environmental experience of emotion, could be enriched by a Buddhaghosan approach that drew on his distinctive use of *abhidhamma*.

For the purposes of our chapter, I just want to mention one particular aspect of this aggregate. At 128, we have a correlation from Formation and Cognition aggregates to Feeling. Pleasure (*sukha*), and sorrow (*dukkha*) are explained as bodily enjoyment (*kāyika assāda*) and bodily affliction (*kāyikābhāda*) respectively, making them somatic states. Correspondingly, joy (*somanassa*) and grief (*domanassa*) are said to be mental (*cetasika*) enjoyment and affliction respectively. Pleasure (*sukha*) has the characteristic of 'experiencing a desired tangible [datum]' (*iṭṭhaphoṭṭhabbānubhavanaṃ*); its function is to intensify what is associated [with it]' (*sampayuttānaṃ upabrūhanaṃ*); it is manifested as bodily (*kāyika*) enjoyment (*assāda*). It is immediately occasioned by the bodily faculty (*kāyindriyapadaṭṭhāna*). Pain is the opposite, it makes what is associated with it fade, and manifests in bodily affliction (*abādha*). Joy (*somanassa*) has the characteristic of experiencing the desired object (*iṭṭhārammaṇānubhavana*). Its function is to savour together the aspects of an object (*iṭṭhākārasambhoga*), and is manifested as mental (*cetasika*) enjoyment. It is immediately occasioned by calmness (*passaddhipadaṭṭhāna*). In turn it is contrasted with 'grief' (*domanassa*) in a similar way.

This alignment is already signalled under the Cognition Aggregate at 99, where it is said that somatic cognition (*kāyaviññāṇa*) is conjoined with happiness (*sukha*) and mental cognition (*manoviññāṇa*) with joy (*somanassa*). Two different phenomenal aetiologies and their respective functions are delineated here. These are phenomenologically subtle observations about how we can undergo positive feelings in different ways, because they arise and register differently. To clarify this analysis, distinct labels are attached to them. By now, we must surely be able to resist the temptation to think that what is meant here is that somehow a body–mind divide generates two different types of emotional feeling in a person.

This reading of two ways of feeling is articulated in terms of two different aspects of the whole human being. There is an attractive parallel in the classical Greek world. The Stoics appear to make a distinction between *hēdoné* or *voluptas* and *eupátheia* or *gaudium*, normally translated as 'pleasure' and 'joy' respectively. The former is the good feeling that comes from external goods, the latter out of the consistency of one's own experience.[94] Although Foucault translates both *voluptas* and *gaudium* as 'pleasure', he makes a distinction that resonates with ours: *gaudium* 'is defined by the fact of not being caused by anything that is independent of ourselves', whereas *voluptas* 'denotes a pleasure whose origin is to be placed outside us and in objects whose presence we cannot be sure of'.[95] We can make a comparison to the extent that there is a sort of positive feeling that is robust and settled, whereas there is another that is provisional, uncertain; and of course, the one is valued more than the other in some way. But there is also a limit to the comparison. The Stoics make this normative distinction on the basis of a subject–object ontology: there is a complex, thinking *psyche* (even if it is in

[94] Wildberger 2014: 452. [95] Foucault 1986: 66.

some sense physical) which alone can generate *gaudium* for itself, whereas *voluptas* can unbalance the emotions because of the variable external world being its source. Buddhaghosa, on the other hand, focuses on what I have called phenomenal aetiologies, how and where these feelings are felt. The evaluative distinction unfolds only through the larger purposes of these two feelings (a further study of which will take us too far from our topic). In brief, the Stoic distinction is based on an ontological commitment, Buddhaghosa's on a phenomenological methodology, although both generate an evaluative distinction.

The presentation of Conception (*saññā*)[96] and Synergies (*saṅkhāra*), again while full of exegetical possibilities for other purposes, do not add to ours.

To sum up the sections on 'Reconstituting Bodiliness', Formation (*rūpa*) crucially splits into extrinsic (*bāhira*) and subjective (*ajjhattika*). The other aggregates split between I. the formal qualities—Good and Bad—that indicate stages in spiritual progression through the *jhāna*s within a normative framework, and II. the phenomenological analysis of Indeterminate Cognitions/Feelings, etc., which can be assessed and reconfigured in accordance with those normative qualities. The latter proceeds through the Sensory-sphere stems of both the *kamma*-Productive and *kamma*-free Performative branches.

So it is not just the case that phenomenology is double-sided in its formation, between (i) what is 'subjective' and 'sensitive' on the one side, and (ii) what is 'extrinsic' (and 'insensitive') on the other. Furthermore, the subjective/sensitive Formations are also to be seen in terms of what they produce and how they function normatively (where the norm is what conduces to spiritual progress through stages of attainment). The latter perspective is offered through Cognition, Feeling, Conception, and Synergic Aggregates. This means phenomenology is double-sided yet again between (i*) the perspective on subjectivity through the Formations and (ii*) that through the other Aggregates. As I said before, my approach here is a formulation, in the specific context of bodiliness, of Maria Heim's general interpretation of *abhidhamma* in Buddhaghosa.[97] This is a radically different way of approaching the *abhidhamma* material than has been the case so far, where the presupposition of dualism has frequently framed the analysis of the very structure of the aggregates, even when there have been scholars who have understood the need to see *abhidhamma* as fundamentally an alternative to the mind–body dualism with which the Western tradition has wrestled.[98]

[96] The standard translation, which Ñāṇamoli also uses, is the plainly wrong 'perception'. Rupert Gethin refers to the first comment on *saññā* as being 'idea' by Wayman, in Wayman 1976. Gethin also refers to exactly this paragraph in the *Visuddhimagga* in Gethin 1986: 36, n. 10.

[97] Heim forthcoming.

[98] We have already noted Ñāṇamoli's own influential usage of materiality as the standard translation of rūpa in his translation of the *Visuddhimagga*. For a study explicitly framing the study of *rūpa* as a contribution to a pre-given 'mind–body problem', see Harvey 1993.

Ecological Phenomenology in Contemplative Practice

Foucault distinguishes between (i) 'our habitual categories of thought' in which it is asked 'can there be knowledge of the subject which is of the same type as knowledge of any other component of the world, or is there another type of knowledge required which is irreducible to the first?', and (ii) the fact that 'The question never arises of whether the subject is objectifiable' in classical thought.[99] 'But when the question of the relations between the subject and knowledge (*connaissance*) of the world is posed... there is the need to inflect knowledge (*savoir*) of the world in such a way that it takes on a certain form and a certain spiritual value for the subject, in the subject's experience, and for the subject's salvation.'[100] By way of comparison, Buddhaghosa's use of *abhidhamma* does indeed look at the world in terms of its value for the subject's experience, as the focus of an analysis of its own constitution.

Now, Foucault also delineates what he calls the Hellenistic model as one in which 'knowledge of the self' (the self standing in for 'the human subject, the human soul, human interiority', etc.) was 'not an alternative to the knowledge of nature.'[101] Instead, there was a 'certain relationship of reciprocal links between knowledge of nature and knowledge of the self'. There is some structural comparability here. But Buddhaghosa's approach in fact stands outside the implicitly metaphysical formulation of the process as one between nature and self. Instead, he proceeds with his *abhidhamma* in a rigorously phenomenological way: at all times, what he is doing is analyzing the constitution of what is available in experience. The bodiliness of the subject emerges at this juncture: for, having started with the presumption of the subject (the person who is the practising monk), the purificatory path proceeds through unpacking what that subject is in terms of what is given in his experience, so that the dissolution of the presumption itself becomes the critical step on that path; and the subject is a bodily subject to the extent that subjectivity is composed of a variety of categorizable entities that are reflexively detectable. There is then no binary divide between a subject and a world that is bridged through a body that partakes of both (as we find in Merleau-Ponty's 'lived body'). Or perhaps we should say, there is no concern for the possibility of such a divide and the need to bridge it. But to be ametaphysical about the bodily subject is not to step back from understanding how that bodily subject occurs to itself in experience; and because Buddhaghosa sees such understanding as critical to the quest for Buddhist perfection, it becomes the focus of his text.

To reiterate the argument of ecological phenomenology, and what has become evident in Buddhaghosa's text, it is perfectly possible to make analytic distinctions such as dead/alive, inside/outside, body/world, consciousness/object. But the very process of meditative attention and guided phenomenological classification shows that it is intention—purposive orientation—that brings about any one rather than another mode of self-realizing being. As subject there are objects, as person there is world,

[99] Foucault 2005: 317–18. [100] Ibid., p. 318. [101] Foucault 2005: 259.

as consciousness there are states, as feelings there are prompts, as mind there is body. As there is an intended perspective, so there is an understanding of the perspectival subject. We may claim on Buddhaghosa's behalf, although it is no business of his, that there is no purpose to an ontology that overcomes dualities, when dualities are only localized taxonomic systems. I have sought to argue through Buddhaghosa (we could say, through his 'inspired exegesis') that we can learn much from a sharply analytic capacity to parse human nature and situation. His project is to bring about (Buddhist) wisdom, and he does this through his meditative focus on aspects of the human situation. It seems that in doing so, he offers a map of that situation, the human being constitutively located within and deriving from an infinite phenomenal reality.

Reading through the materials that Buddhaghosa gives us, we are able to re-conceive bodiliness. This understanding of the whole human being is one where:

(i) its wholeness is provisional and phenomenologically open, although its motive agency persists throughout in the search for wisdom;
(ii) the phenomenological categories do not inscribe a subject-object distinction to overcome, but conceptualize subjectivity itself as constituted through the items that occur in experience; yet
(iii) this is not a purely reductive enterprise, because the horizon of wisdom always lies beyond any particular part or parts of the categories.

Bodily being is analysable in an infinite number of personal ways within any set of formal categories (in the present case study, Buddhaghosa's interpretation of those given in the Buddha's teachings). Such a perspective allows us to re-think from basics as to how we might talk about the human as a bodily being which, although sensitive to Buddhaghosa's precise techniques, nevertheless has developed into a quite general theory of the ecological nature of human self-understanding.

4

The Body in Love

Nala and Damayantī's Love/Making in Śrī Harṣa's *Naiṣadhacarita*

Bodiliness and the Erotic

Our final chapter moves away sharply from the language, context, and purposes of the previous one, to focus on what may properly be called 'erotic phenomenology'. (Of course, what is meant by that will be an intrinsic part of our study.) At the same time, it continues the book's theme on the way human subjectivity is articulated through bodiliness. I will look here primarily at Canto XVIII of the twelfth-century composition, the *Naiṣadhacarita* (traditionally the last of the genre of the 'great poem' (*mahākāvya*) in Sanskrit literature). It is a sustained description (153 verses in the vulgate) of the night after the wedding in which Princess Damayantī dramatically chooses King Nala as her bridegroom over the gods who have also come to woo her. It is sustained in the sense that it speaks of their lovemaking, not in vignettes, but as a continuous narrative; and while naturally it has tropic resonances with that great *mahākāvya* which too has a sustained treatment of the erotic relationship, Kālidāsa's *Kumārasaṃbhava*, it is entirely confined to the earthly love of two human beings (even if they have extraordinary qualities that hint at the divine) and without any of the cosmogonic significance of its predecessor's story of the divine couple, Śiva and Pārvatī.

I approach this complex text, which is seldom studied in contemporary Indology, in a spirit quite different from the traditional attention that has been paid to its literary and aesthetic qualities.[1] The metaphysics of the *Naiṣadhacarita*—whether explicit or implied—has traditionally been commented upon, for its author also wrote that formidable and critical work of Advaita Vedānta, the *Khaṇḍanakhaṇḍakhādya*.[2] My philosophical approach here is not an exposition of those passages where Śrī Harṣa specifically deals with metaphysical views. And although I am sympathetic to such an approach, I do not follow Maya Tevet Dayan's sensitive case for the deeper reality implied by key literary devices utilized by Śrī Harṣa.[3] Instead, I want to read the love

[1] For a subtle and comprehensive analysis of the reception history of the *Naiṣadhacarita*, see Patel 2014.
[2] On this text, see Ram-Prasad 2002.
[3] Tevet Dayan 2010.

and lovemaking that emerges in Śrī Harṣa's exquisite detailing of the couple and their palatial environment as depicting an ecological phenomenology of the erotic. This approach is my own, and not part of the agenda explicitly found in the text or traditionally brought to bear on it. But I would argue that it is in keeping with the intention of this book to look at what we may make philosophically of the bodily human being in texts that are primarily concerned with doing something else. However, this is not to say that I am unmindful of the contemporary scholars who have dealt with the literary and aesthetic traditions of the genre of *kāvya* within which the text falls, as I have greatly benefitted from their work in locating the text in its context.[4]

The details of Śrī Harṣa's depiction of the royal couple help in a critical but fruitful engagement with key ideas on the erotic in the phenomenological tradition (where once more we will encounter Merleau-Ponty and the recent critical tradition following him). First of all, the location of a fulfilling (and provisionally fulfilled) desire within a sophisticated world of affect, metaphor, nature, and atmosphere demonstrates that the erotic is as much a part of ecological phenomenology as other contexts explored in this book. Secondly, the deployment of a wide range of ornamental figuration (*alaṅkāra*) enables Śrī Harṣa to explore the many senses and sources of human feeling, so that an examination of his multimodal depiction of the erotic permits us to query the ontological reflex in contemporary erotic phenomenological debates about touch and vision. Finally, while as typically heteronormative as other major literary compositions on love, East or West, Śrī Harṣa's poem is remarkably subtle in re-working the standard gender tropes of the tradition, in order to suggest a serious mutual subjectivity between Nala and Damayantī. Through such a reading of the voluptuous yet often silly, powerful yet playful, light-hearted yet poignant narrative of this Canto, I would like to argue that the *Naiṣadhacarita* yields an appealing if somewhat elusive notion of bodily subjectivity. In it, bodiliness is the medium for a dialectic between a pre-given subjectivity that is received by the other and a re-made subjectivity formed through being received by the other.

The *Naiṣadhacarita*

The story of Nala and Damayantī is recounted in the *Mahābhārata*.[5] King Nala of Niṣadha learns of the beauty and virtues of Damayantī from a golden Indian goose (*haṃsa*) and sends it as a messenger to her; and upon hearing the bird's description of him, Damayantī in turn falls in love with him. Her father declares the royal ceremony of *svayaṃvara*, in which a princess takes a husband of her own choice.[6] The four great Vedic deities—Indra, king of the gods; Agni, god of fire; Varuṇa, god of waters; and Yama, god of death—desire her. Cruelly, they ask Nala to go as their emissary to her.

[4] Most helpfully, the wide-ranging essays in Bonner, Shulman, and Tubb 2014.

[5] On the proliferation of the story of Damayantī and Nala, see the collection of essays in Wadley 2011.

[6] On the complex nature, origins and types of this much-storied type of marriage, see e.g., Jamieson 1996; Allen 1996.

He tries to demur, saying he cannot penetrate her inner quarters, but Indra gives him the gift of invisibility. Nala presents himself anonymously, and dutifully praises them to Damayantī, but she steadfastly refuses to consider anyone but Nala. At the ceremony, the gods cunningly take the form of Nala himself. But she notices their non-human qualities—they do not blink, their feet do not touch the ground, their garlands do not wilt—and chooses the real Nala. The great gods concede, but not two semi-divine beings, Kali and Dvāpara, personifications of the current and previous degraded Ages (*yugas*), who are late to the scene. Nala runs a perfect life, but one day he forgets to wash himself fully in ritual and Kali enters him and the mind of Nala's brother, Puṣkara. Thus poisoned, the brothers play dice and Nala recklessly gambles away everything except a piece of cloth each for himself and his wife. Damayantī rejects Nala's plea to withdraw to her father's house, and accompanies him out of the kingdom, leaving their two children with her parents. A bird flies away with Nala's cloth, and the couple are forced to share the single garment that is left. In desperation at the plight in which he has placed her, Nala one night tears off part of her cloth for himself and abandons Damayantī. In the forest, he rescues a snake that bites him and transforms him into a deformed dwarf, but then reassures him that this transformation is only to enable him to enter into the service of King Ṛtuparṇa of Ayodhyā without being recognized. The snake also gives him a magical garment that will re-transform him at the right time. So Nala enters royal service as a cook and charioteer. Damayantī wanders around until her beauty and presence find her service with the queen of Cedi. But a courtier of her father's recognizes her and takes her home. In search of her husband, she sends messengers everywhere, with the question, 'What kind of man abandons his wife in the middle of the night, and takes half her cloth covering?' When she hears that a deformed cook in the Ayodhyā palace responds, 'The kind who wants to make his headstrong wife return to her father's palace', she suspects that it is her husband. She announces a second *svayaṃvara* ceremony, to which King Ṛtuparṇa of Ayodhyā is driven by his dwarf cook-charioteer, Bāhuka. Damayantī meets him and asks him, 'Why would a man send his wife back to her father?', to which he replies it would be because he had gambled his kingdom away and could not support her. She knows then that this is Nala; and judging it to be the right moment, he puts on the magic garment given by the snake, and returns to his original form. In the meantime, he has taught King Ṛtuparṇa how to train horses, being taught in return how to play dice cleverly. Nala and Damayantī return to Niṣadha, where he engages his brother in another game of dice, and with his new-found knowledge, defeats him. But he magnanimously forgives Puṣkara and shares the kingdom with him. Nala and Damayantī can now continue with their loving marriage after all these trials.

Śrī Harṣa confines his great poem to just the beginning of the story, ending with the happy day following the couple's wedding.[7] Twenty-two cantos extend many times this

[7] As with all scholars since his great work, I am of course indebted to Krishna Kanta Handiqui's translation, critical notes and extracts from commentaries in Handiqui 1965. I follow his numbering, although for the text, I use both Shastri 2002 and electronic text kindly provided by Andrei Klibanov.

first, small part of the tight narrative of the original whole in the *Mahābhārata*; the narrative is only one aspect of the detailed exploration of mood, tropes, and images, conveyed through an exuberant and sophisticated use of the full range of literary craft. The narrative details are roughly the same, save for some specific details.[8] Nala and Damayantī are already in love from reports of each other when the poem begins, that is to say, before the goose acts as messenger; and Nala's passage through the palace when invisible includes a complex meeting with Damayantī in which their imagination of each other, unbeknownst to them, actually maps on to their real presence, as he sees an image of her as she is, and she imagines him just where he actually, invisibly, is.[9]

Most significantly, the *svayaṃvara* in Canto XIV is presided over by the goddess of learning, Sarasvatī who, in a literary tour de force of simultaneous double-meaning (*śleṣa*) exalts the four great gods to Damayantī through verses that can at the same time also be read as descriptions of Nala.[10] (So dazzling is this passage that it is celebrated as a separate composition in itself, 'The Five Nalas'.) This happens at the juncture when Damayantī cannot distinguish between the divine imitators and the real Nala. She is not initially able to penetrate through to the goddess's real meaning. She implores the gods themselves to help her, and they are moved by her piety to grant her wisdom (straight-thinking, *sādhu-dhī*). She sees that the verses together can only refer to Nala, and begins a process of decipherment.[11] Then she notices the signs of difference between gods and human, as in the original story, together with another, evocative one (XIV.21): perspiration, a sheen that looked as if it sought to abate within him the heat of separation from her. (This sign is evocative because perspiration is a key marker of the fluid exchanges that we will see in their lovemaking; or rather, upon coming to the perspiration of their lovemaking, the reader is reminded of how perspiration signified Nala as her human love, for gods do not sweat.) There are whole cantos devoted to the wedding celebrations, and a didactic interlude in which the now-benevolent great gods stop the latecomers, Kali and Dvāpara, in the course of which the latter two represent a materialist and anti-Vedic philosophical position that is rebutted by the great gods. The remaining five cantos cover the wedding night, and the following day, when prayers are said, boon companions share some fun with the couple, and the two watch the moonrise the following night.

[8] A thumbnail sketch is given in Jani 1996.

[9] Immo Pekkarinen points out (Pekkarinen n.d., § 'Femininity and Exteriority'), in relation to Emmanuel Levinas's assertion that 'Gyges is the very condition of man', that 'Gyges, who, according to myth, could see while himself remaining unseen, is the paradigmatic representative of a separated and egoistic subject, who hides his face and keeps his egoism'. It is surely worth further thought that, having given his hero this classic masculine power, Śrī Harṣa then has him struggle with whether he is seeing Damayantī or not, and have her pierce his invisibility even while being sure it must be an illusion. The separation of the male ego is comprehensively demolished in Śrī Harṣa's no doubt Advaitic play on the less-than-real nature of individuation.

[10] Malamoud 2014.

[11] On Damayantī's interpretive process and the metapoetic implications of Śrī Harṣa's verbal puzzles, see Bronner 2010: 87–8.

Some Remarks on the Narrative Context of Love and Lovemaking

In talking of body in erotic phenomenology, I take seriously, the 'love' in Nala and Damayantī's 'lovemaking'; and that requires me to say something about 'love'. Sheldon Pollock argues that the classical Indian aesthetic tradition likely makes a distinction between love and the erotic: 'We no longer have acceptable words for describing sexual love... "Erotic" is all that is left, and I have adopted it perforce for *śṛṅgāra*, since that rasa[12] is concerned above all with physical desire, and not primarily with "love" (later writers such as Kavikarnapura make this distinction crystal clear).'[13] In his treatment of Kavikarṇapūra (mid-sixteenth century),[14] Pollock seems to suggest that the 'crystal clear' distinction has to do with the fact that *śṛṅgāra* has to be kept distinct from *anurāga* or alternatively, *prema*, which most naturally translate as 'love': Kavikarṇapūra claims, following Pollock's translation, that the encompassing *rasa* is 'love', which is, most obviously, different from the provocative claim made by Bhoja in the eleventh century that *śṛṅgāra* (which Pollock in the context of Bhoja generally translates as 'passion') is the foundational '*rasa*', the aesthetic essence upon which all other artistic expression of emotions is based.[15] It is broadly understandable that Kavikarṇapūra and other theologians of aesthetics wished to make a distinction between the hitherto 'secular' depiction of *śṛṅgāra* and their own depiction of the love of the cowherdesses (*gopī*s) for Kṛṣṇa as code for the human adoration of the divine. Also, over time another *rasa* had been postulated, '*vātsalya*', which best translates as 'parental love' and is obviously again outside the domain of the erotic. So the situation with the terminology and classification of the aesthetic essences—*rasas*[16]—grew quite complex after 1,200-odd years of theorization.

Without wishing to make an intervention in the study of aesthetics, I will only look at what is depicted as the relationship between Nala and Damayantī in a text which Śrī Harṣa explicitly says at the end of the first canto is beautiful with the oblique course of the erotic (*śṛṅgārabhaṅgyā... cāruṇi*).[17] In other words, what constitutes the content of the erotic relationship between Nala and Damayantī? It is, of course, true that the erotic *rasa* is correlated with the 'stable emotion' (*sthāyibhāva*) of '*rati*', which Pollock translates as 'desire'.[18] Ingalls preferred 'sexual excitement' for '*rati*' but used 'the erotic' and 'love' interchangeably for '*śṛṅgāra*'.[19] When we look at the complex play of passion and commitment that we find in the attraction Damayantī and Nala have for one another, as the merest outline of their tale conveys to us, it would seem that 'love' most naturally describes their relationship.

[12] Literally, 'juice' or 'flavour' but translated as everything from 'mood' and 'sentiment' to 'aesthetic essence'; I strongly recommend that the reader consult Pollock 2016 to begin to see the philosophical and literary implications of this master-concept.

[13] Pollock 2016: xvii.

[14] Ibid., pp. 290–9.

[15] For a better understanding of whom, too, we have Pollock to thank, in Pollock 1998.

[16] An influential translation of '*rasa*' is 'mood', mainly due to Ingalls 1965.

[17] I.145.

[18] Pollock 2016: 327, under Glossary.

[19] Ingalls 1965: 13; 15.

In short, 'love' is the right English word for the full range of the erotic relationship between Nala and Damayantī. Obviously that is not to rule out that 'love' applies to other types of human relationships. As for the question of the love of God, of course Christian theologians do use the concept of the 'erotic' (indeed perhaps taking it to be the foundational *eros*), and a different comparative undertaking is required to explore the various ways in which Hindus mapped the relationship between such key concepts as 'devotion' (*bhakti*), love as *prema*, and *śṛṅgāra*. All I want to argue here is that the erotic on its narrowest construal, which pertains only to the emotional life around sexual attraction and is frequently the dominant concern of the literary evocation of *śṛṅgāra*, is the core but not the entirety of the relationship of Nala and Damayantī. And rather than treat that relationship rather artificially as a combination of sexual passion and a less intensely involved conjugality, it is more compelling to consider it organically (as it emerges in the long narrative of their adventures together and apart), and treat it as a matter of love.[20]

Seen that way, *śṛṅgāra* here is something more like our contemporary sense of the romantic, albeit a weighty one: irreducibly containing the sexual core of the narrowly erotic but encompassing too a wider, more durable passion for the other's presence. When I henceforth talk of the erotic, I mean here the whole range of romantic love; the erotic as the passion for the other's presence, not only the emotions around sexual passion. I would like to suggest that the lyrical depiction of the latter in this text gains its power from the audience's knowledge of the former as it is found in the 'whole' story of Nala and Damayantī.

For the poem's audience, the framing of the original or 'whole' story is always present.[21] Canto XVII ends with the activities of Kali, the semi-divine king of Discord (traditionally, the son of Anger (*krodha*) and Harm (*hiṃsā*), who, in an incestuous relationship with his sister Calumny (*durukti*), fathers Fear (*bhaya*) and Death (*mṛtyu*)). As will be recalled, he is met by the gods on his way to the *svayaṃvara* and told by them that Damayantī has already chosen Nala, an outcome that he cannot bring himself to accept. Śrī Harṣa merely hints at what is to come, as Kali searches through Nala's city looking for some flaw, individual or civic, through which he can insinuate himself, destroy Nala, and take Damayantī. We know, outside the poem, that this will eventually happen and that the couple will face immense sorrow and severe trials. Within the poem, Kali cannot find anything, and bides his time, dark as a glossy deer in the moonlight (XVII.220). Śrī Harṣa leaves Kali there and turns in the next canto to the first night of lovemaking. This juxtaposition is highly suggestive in light of what I have conjectured about passion and love. The audience knows that the enjoyed erotic (*saṃbhoga śṛṅgāra*)

[20] To take liberty with the contrast attributed to the nineteenth-century actress Beatrice Stella Tanner Campbell, this is about both the 'hurly-burly of the chaise lounge' *and* 'the deep, deep peace of the double bed'.

[21] Since the poem covers only the first part of the Mahābhārata story, naturally enough there has been a long debate on whether the *Naiṣadhacarita* is incomplete or was deliberately crafted to cover only this first part; see Jani 1957. I shall treat the poem as a complete text, but one that functions with deep awareness of the longer story.

is not only the fulfilment of the passion that has been thwarted (*vipralambha*) by their being hitherto apart; it is the affirmation of the deeper meaning of that passion, which is a fidelity to the other that will keep them in love through all their coming trials.

To Begin With: Lover Unmet, Love Reciprocated

The poem begins with Nala and Damayantī longing for the other. Damayantī has (only) heard repeatedly of him (I.33), but in her mind's longing made him her husband (*manorathena svapatīkṛtaṃ*; I.39). And likewise, 'Nala too heard from people of her virtues' (*nalo'pi lokādaśṛṇodguṇotkaram*: I.42) and was pierced by the flower-arrows of Kāma (46). From the beginning, then, it is given that hearing speech—the sensory modality together with its linguistic object—is capable of causing the birth of love. This is not only because, metanarratively, we might expect it of a poet setting out to demonstrate the power of language to transport people to the deepest place of aesthetic delight. Within the story itself, it inaugurates an exploration of how subjectivity is mediated between the dull tyranny of distance and the sparkling freedom of imagining about the other from what one has heard. This is not the more common form of longing, which is the separation of people who have been lovers, where memory and sexual love (both signified by one name of the god of love, *smara*) run together. Here, language—in the form of the lyrical communication of the goose—brings together what is as yet apart, and the hearing is the first creator of an erotic phenomenology that will gradually become richer and denser. An interesting verse introduces the theme of modesty and shyness whose role in Damayantī's demeanour plays out in their love-making; but here, it applies to Nala.

> Famed as foremost amongst those who had triumphed over the senses, the lord of the earth was embarrassed as the sheer power of the love god—enemy of Śambara the demon—over him gradually became clear.[22]

Śrī Harṣa teasingly juxtaposes that much vaunted spiritual ideal of freedom from the senses—woven, as his audience will know, into the very texture of his other great work, on the content and purposes of Advaita Vedānta analysis—with the joyful eruption of love. Here the tension between the ideal of detachment and the life of the senses is a fruitful one, in literary and phenomenological senses. (We recall the contrasting, desolate version of that tension in Janaka, as it emerges in Sulabhā's critique in the second chapter.)

The initial, vague account of how they hear about each other gives way next to a much more detailed plot device: the efforts of the golden goose messenger. When Nala first traps it but takes pity and releases it, it repays him with an eloquent description of Damayantī; and then flies to her in order to tell her about him in turn. The impact of its

[22] *avāpa sāpatrapatāṃ sa bhūpatirjitendriyāṇāṃ dhuri kīrtitasthitiḥ /*
asaṃvare śaṃbaravairivikrame krameṇa tatra sphuṭatāmupeyuṣi // 1.53.

words is at once continuous with and yet marks a sharp development from their first hearing of the other. It is still about the capacity of verbal description to spark an imaginative love; but now the sharing of the messenger's presence indicates the establishment also of a shared field of attraction. It is as if they are now connected through how they report on their feelings, which thereupon intensifies and clarifies those very feelings. When the golden goose has finished his lyrical description of Damayantī, Nala says:

> 'A hundred times I have heard of her, she is strong medicine that infatuates the three worlds; but now with your celebration of her, it is as if I have obtained her with my own eyes.'[23]

Hearing of the other has given birth to longing, but there is a long way to the fulfilment of all the senses: no doubt now that sight comes next, for it marks a difference in the shared field of attraction. What Nala has heard in detail from the goose makes him feel as if he has seen Damayantī, implying that to see is what the lover wants next. I draw attention here to the malleable significance of distance, for affect does not entirely obey the boundaries within which we might think ourselves confined by our skin. But affect does, of course, obey those boundaries implicitly, as we see eventually when we consider how all the sensory modes matter in the erotic, widely construed (a claim that will drive us to engage critically with contemporary debates on vision and touch). Sight does matter, touch does matter (more or less dependent on context), and perhaps taste most intensely (even if briefly) of all. But all that will have to wait as we are confined with the lovers (to be) to hearing, and to the imaginative possibilities of thought that the richness of the hearing has come to permit.

Now thinking of her as if she had been seen by him, Nala uses his skills as a painter to draw a portrait of her. As the goose later reports to Damayantī:

> 'When the king drinks in your picture, unblinkingly eager, a dispute breaks out over his tear-fall between visual love and unblinking stare, each one saying, "those tears are mine".
>
> You are in his heart, daughter of Bhīma, even if you are outside. Is there any way in which you are not his very life-breath? It is not strange that his mind spreads through your portrait, your being his only thought.'[24]

We begin to fill in a gradually developing erotic phenomenology as the feeling of the other's presence spreads out through the range of subjective states: tears, the gaze upon the indirect presence in the portrait, that mysterious physiology of heartache that all cultures have commented upon, the heightened sensitivity to oneself brought about by

23 *śataśaḥ śṛutimāgataiva sā trijaganmohamahauṣadhirmama /*
adhunā tava śaṃsitena tu svadṛśaivādhigatāmavaimi tām // II.54.

24 *pāturdṛśālekhyamayīṃ nṛpasya tvāmādarādastanimīlayāste /*
mamedamityaśruṇi netravṛtteḥ prīternimeṣacchidayā vivādaḥ // III.104
tvaṃ hṛdgatā bhaimi bahirgatāpi prāṇāyitā nāsikayāsyagatyā /
na citramākrāmati tatra citrametanmano yadbhavadekavṛtti // III.105.

changed breathing. Truly, love and death call equally upon contemplation; we have seen breathing put to anti-erotic practice in Buddhaghosa's meditative technique.[25]

We also have that elusive but evocative activity of 'mind' that we have come across in such varied contexts in this book. Inside and outside are distinguished only to be blurred, as is always the case with affect: 'What his heart incants secretly, that his face speaks of openly...'[26] With the characteristic mock-dramatic flourish that Śrī Harṣa uses to convey a truth while amusing with over-elaborate wordplay, the goose concludes his report on Nala's condition thus:

> 'Alack and alas, the valiant king sinks, defenceless, like a tusker in the clay of deep delusion on the island of deliquium, set in the Yamunā river of incessant sorrow that flows from your absence.'[27]

It is important that there is symmetry in the feelings that they have for each other, and the way their entire being is affected in the same way. When the goose speaks to Damayantī, she declares herself completely:

> 'How can the mind's desire, that the mind will never abandon, ever be expressed? What girl is it who will shamelessly own up to wanting to catch the moon, that king of the twice-born, with her own hands?'[28]

Indeed, if Nala was ashamed of his loss of self-control, Damayantī is willing to confess her shamelessness, precisely because she wishes to contrast herself with the expectation that a high-born woman is to be modest. In the distance between them that has yet to be closed, only her consciousness ranges over what is to be, just as his does.

> 'I have heard of him, in my distraction seen him in the quarters of the sky, and thought of him uninterruptedly in the thick flow of my consciousness...'[29]

Longing outruns the trivial restrictions of fact. 'Ardency waits not for time, as the keen intellect waits not for the teacher's instructions.'[30]

We have, then, two telling features in this rendition of the birth of a love constrained by distance and yet stronger than it. First, it is important to see that erotic phenomenology takes subjectivity whole: love ranges across the human being, engaging the senses, thoughts, breath, heart, the understanding of what the heart feels. We are perfectly able to distinguish between the different aspects of bodily being (the 'analytic distinctions' that have been seen frequently in past chapters), but phenomenology is organic

[25] I thank Laurie Patton for the observation on love and death.

[26] *hṛtasya yanmantrayate rahastvāṃ tadvyaktamāmantrayate mukhaṃ yat /* III.107a.

[27] *bhavadviyogācchidurārtidhārā yamasvasurmajjati niḥśaraṇyaḥ /*
mūrcchāmayadvīpamahāndhyapaṅke hā hā mahībhṛdbhaṭakuñjaro'yam // III.113.

[28] *manastu yaṃ nojjhati jātu yātu manorathaḥ kaṇṭhapathaṃ kathaṃ saḥ /*
kā nāma bālā dvijarājapāṇigrahābhilāṣaṃ kathayedalajjā // III.59.

[29] *śrutaḥ sa dṛṣṭaśca haritsu mohāddhyātaḥ sa nīrandhritabuddhidhāram /* III.82a.

[30] *...gurūpadeśaṃ gratibheva tīkṣṇā pratīkṣate jātu na kālamartiḥ //* III.91b.

despite these many organs of subjectivity. It is also ecological: the qualities of love run right across, between, over and through the boundaries of self-containment, in the dense warp and weft of reception and affect, so that being oneself is not a self-containment but a dynamic openness. This establishes a thematic of this chapter, and one that will become ever more evident in lovemaking.

Second, what strikes us as the quaint, yet arresting account of how this love is born also gives us perhaps the most important point about its nature. In this genealogy of love, sincerity of mutual commitment is assured through the manner in which Nala and Damayantī come to feel for each other, a manner that a more prosaic attitude might suggest is implausible, to say the least. The insight here goes deeper than a routinized realism. Jean-Luc Marion has made a dramatic and much-discussed claim about love.

> In fact, the more I sincerely love (or think I love, which amounts to the same for me), the less the identity or the presence of the loved one is required. I can love a woman or a man that I know only superficially, or that I do not know at all (based on his name, his reputation) or even about whom I know nothing. I can love someone who is absent most of the time, and who will probably always remain thus… Because I love, what I am in love with does not have to *be* at all, and can thus dispense altogether with maintaining the status of a being.[31]

Kyle Hubbard remarks on this that:

> Marion appears more concerned with the lover's purity than with the identity of the beloved. Marion's claim that loving an anonymous beloved is the most sincere form of love obscures the nature of love in a few ways. First, it can lead to a view of love that is so focused on the purity of the lover's motivation that it forgets the other's needs. Marion certainly is correct that I do not love another person if my sole focus is to get her to love me in return or to get something else from her. However, if I am so focused on my own purity as a lover, then I can easily forget the beloved's needs. This is especially the case if the beloved is an anonymous beloved whose only identity is in my own mind.[32]

(I take it that 'identity' here means a formal existence in the imagination, not tied to any concrete features of bodily being.)

Sincerity is clearly what is conveyed by Nala and Damayantī's feelings for one another and certainly we can say that it is based only on name and reputation. For all they know at that point, the other might remain absent forever. In these ways, they fulfil this radical requirement of not loving for something in return. But might Śrī Harṣa's depiction be subject to Hubbard's criticism? I think not. For we do not have with Damayantī and Nala that self-involved purity of motivation, which Hubbard rightly rejects; it would simply be antithetical to the very nature of the erotic, where passion is impossible without seeing oneself only in relation to the other. And that, precisely, is what Nala and Damayantī desire when they imagine that they are married to the other. At the same time, Hubbard overstates the case by saying that the opposite

[31] Marion 2002: 44. [32] Hubbard 2011: 143–4.

of self-involved purity is to think of the other's needs. Of course, that is in any case not yet possible for Nala and Damayantī at this stage; but more importantly, such a requirement would move too far in the opposite direction from Marion, for it calls for just that sort of presumption that overruns the modest hope each has of what to expect from the other. It surely is important that neither asks of himself or herself how they are the right person for the other. What we have, in fact, is a situation akin to a different—possibly over-charitable[33]—reading of Marion, given by John Milbank.

> [A]gainst any...eulogizing of the purely unilateral, Marion fully insists that the lover who advances goes on *hoping* for a reciprocating response even though he in no way demands it, requires it, or expects it...*Hence the lover goes on hoping for a response, not only in order to receive acceptance, but also to receive confirmation that his act of love is truly love.*[34]

In a profound sense, then, it is important for us, who are told the truth by the poet, to know from the beginning that the feelings of Nala and Damayantī are mutual: for that is what makes it love, and not the mere infatuation that others have for either of them (e.g., the gods for Damayantī). And the goose is key to the truth inside the story, when each finds out about what the other feels.

For this reason, it is important that the way they finally come to their mutual and public affirmation of love is through the *svayaṃvara*: she chooses a mode of marriage by which she is able to choose him; he chooses to present himself; and she chooses him of those present. (And, of course, such a wedding is required for both the pull of their story and the occasion for the literary brilliance of the 'Five Nalas' set of verses.) This is the fulfilment of that mutual hope and reciprocal agency which is love. Technically, since both are marriageable, Nala could have asked Damayantī's father for her hand at the very beginning; but Śrī Harṣa sets that possibility aside rather disingenuously, referring to the specific vow of never begging that binds him against his own longing:[35]

> 'Even though afflicted by the god of love, the powerful hero did not ask the King of Vidarbha for his daughter; the proud would rather give up life and happiness than give up the one vow, to never ask.'[36]

We should remember too that that relationship is about love not just in their falling in love and in their making love, but what follows. After they are wed, Nala teases

[33] See Jonna Bornemark's angry demolition of Marion's reading of the erotic phenomenon: 'He claims that in the erotic encounter the flesh of the other makes room for him...Her flesh is "allowing me to come in, by letting itself be penetrated"...This inactivity of Marion's woman is further reinforced when he adds that it is her passivity, which increases an arousal "more powerful than every activity".' Bornemark 2012: 258.

[34] Milbank 2007: 261; emphasis in original.

[35] So from the very beginning, we see that 'conflict of emotions, a clash of love and duty, rare in Sanskrit poetry' that Handiqui notes in the Preface to his translation: Handiqui 1965: xi.

[36] *smaropatapto'pi bhṛśaṃ na sa prabhurvidarbharājaṃ tanayāmayācata /*
tyajantyamūñśarma ca mānino varaṃ tyajanti na tvekamayācitavratam // I.50.

Damayantī for feeling sad at the sight of birds parting from their mates. But the poet reminds us:

> But thoughts, perturbed without cause, in fact speak of things that are yet to come.[37]

The audience knows of how the story will go beyond the poem, and that therefore all this electric attraction and joyful carnality are the beginnings of an arc that will tend towards the deepest love, across loss, humiliation, and hopelessness. The peculiar manner in which they first fall in love inaugurates the integrity of their relationship.

The Ecology of Erotic Phenomenology: General Considerations

With this understanding of life and love established, we can now focus on Canto XVIII, following the wedding, and look in greater detail at how the major themes of this book—on ecological phenomenology, on its multimodal nature, and the implications this has for our understanding of bodiliness—are manifested in the tender, intense, yet often light-hearted rendition of lovemaking.

We must begin by recollecting that the purpose of this chapter is to explore, through this most intense of experiences and the significance of body in it, the larger issue of how to think about us as bodily beings in relation to the world. While the intersubjective aspect of ecological phenomenology will naturally dominate this discussion, it is important to start with the general point that an ecological reading does share with certain strands of the Phenomenological tradition a commitment to thinking of subjectivity in terms of its world. Merleau-Ponty was clear about such a commitment. The world is 'the permanent horizon of all my cogitations and as a dimension with respect to which I never cease to situate myself'.[38]

Others in the mid-twentieth-century tradition also had the sense that there were significant ways in which the understanding of the human subject was not about bracketing the objects of its attention (as they thought the Husserlian project meant to) but quite the opposite. 'The world is our home, our habitat, the materialization of our subjectivity. Who wants to become acquainted with man, should listen to the language spoken by the things in his existence [i.e., to what things mean to him]. Who wants to describe man should make an analysis of the "landscape" within which he demonstrates, explains, and reveals himself.'[39] More recently, and although—perhaps inevitably—still tied up in Cartesian language while moving on from the Cartesian body, Luce Irigaray articulates the relationality of body in a way that echoes our ecological metaphor.

> Our body is not only set down or situated in space, placed side by side with other bodies, or other things. It is also intertwined with them, and interlacing of those within it. It thus constitutes

[37] *kvāpi vastuni vadatyanāgataṃ cittamudyadanimittavaikṛtam //* XVIII.69.
[38] Merleau Ponty 1962: vii–viii. [39] Van Den Berg 1955: 32.

a place made from flesh which no longer greatly resembles Descartes' *partes extra partes* space. But this is not simply due to the fact that it is a body; it is rather because it always is in relation with. And that which philosophy lacks, even more than a thought about the body, is a thought about our body-soul as being essentially relation-with.[40]

Ecological phenomenology shares the same metaphor-laden intuition as these earlier insights, but it also seeks to develop a more fine-grained account of the ways in which this situated subjectivity, and the analysis of 'landscape' work together, because it holds that the importance of the ecological landscape lies in contextuality and not in a post-dualist metaphysics of 'man' and his 'materialization of subjectivity'. It conceives subjectivity as formed in the contextual totality of experiences.

The context is the specific type of experience that occupies the attention of the phenomenologist: so far, we have looked at illness and wellness, the formation of and reflection upon gender, and contemplative practices directed towards a disciplinary transformation of life. In each case, while analytic distinctions between various aspects of the subject—such as mind, intellect, senses, and sense organs, etc.—are certainly available, it becomes clear that not only is a metaphysical divide (and its healing) between immaterial mind and material body beside the point for an ecological phenomenology, but that the subjectivity is not limited to the infusion of life into a presupposed, pre-given, and bounded object, the body. (Ecological phenomenology therefore does not work within the *Körper-Leib* distinction (i.e., between body as object and the lived body), as we have already seen in previous discussions in this book.) Instead, ecological phenomenology suggests that our reflexivity is determined by a dynamic range of functions and connections, whose totality is given only by a specific context (and therefore varies between contexts).

This philosophical perspective suggests three interrelated things for the reflexive subject itself. First, 'body' is not a self-evident entity within whose bounded range all experiences are stably located. Second, correspondingly, the very nature and grasp of bodiliness is sensitive to the nature of the experience that is sought to be understood by the subject undergoing it.[41] Third, and most importantly, the totality of an experience ranges across the various analytic elements we use to talk about the human being, and so in that holistic sense, subjectivity simply is bodily subjectivity, for there is no mind apart from body and (in the opposite direction) what is body can also be what is world.

Renaud Barbaras has recently argued that thinking of phenomenology as the study of life requires moving away from the duality that will not go away in Western thought; neither corporeality nor consciousness can be the focus of study.

[40] Irigaray 2004: 403.

[41] It would be useful to remember from the introduction that the examples studied in this book abstract away from the continuity of life in which experience is the pell-mell undergoing of change; the constraints of phenomenological study that helps with theorization no doubt is at an artificial remove from the fluidity of the unexamined life.

Despite all the ways we might restrict its use, the body implies an inevitable dimension of *körperlichkeit*, which necessarily brings back into play the side of consciousness—when what is at issue is to think phenomenality. It follows that in order to think belonging we must *push the body out of the picture*. It is not the case that because we have a body we belong to the world. On the contrary, it is insofar as we belong to the world that we have a body. This reversal implies that the meaning of the body must be derived from the meaning of belonging. But, as well, the vocabulary of consciousness must be abandoned, since to speak of consciousness is to situate the subject of the correlation in a relation of difference, which is indeed one of exclusion in relation to corporeality. Conceived through an exclusionary difference, consciousness immediately stops us from finding the possible foundation of belonging.[42]

He suggests instead that 'life' and 'movement' become radically new subjects of study instead of body or consciousness. Ecological phenomenology can be thought to go in the opposite direction, by continuing to use 'body' and 'consciousness' as analytic elements of study, but within the notion of bodiliness and not as the two conceptual bases of being. It is true that there is a shared sense between these two programmes that 'the meaning of the body must be derived from the meaning of belonging'. We should indeed push both body and consciousness out of the picture; but only if, by that, we mean that we must stop thematizing the one through the other. But as have seen through the course of this book, if we begin with various senses of belonging—each 'meaning of belonging' given by the context of our attention—then both body and consciousness are brought back into the picture, although as analytic functions of phenomenological description, and not as native ontological existents. Perhaps nothing enacts this better in words than the depiction of the erotic in the *Naiṣadhacarita*.

Social Order in a Capacious Ecology

Now, having said that we must be attentive to the context, we should begin our reading by noting that such attentiveness calls for a capacious sense of what constitutes its ecology. Let us begin with the initial verses of Canto XVIII.

Then, after he had won her, Nala had the daughter of Bhīma, that best of wives, enjoy the intimacies of love. She was for him the boat to the farther side of the waters that make the third end of man.

He was a knower of self; thus, although day and night he partook of pleasure together with her, he accrued no sin. The mind clear with understanding is not besmeared even when captivated by the oneness of sensuality.[43]

42 Barbaras 2011: 9 (emphasis in original).

43 *so'yamitthamatha bhīmanandinīṃ dārasāramadhigamya naiṣadhaḥ /*
tāṃ tṛtīyapuruṣārthavāridheḥ pāralambhanatarīmarīramat // XVIII.1
ātmavitsaha tayā divāniśaṃ bhogabhāgapi na pāpamāpa saḥ /
āhṛtā hi viṣayaikatānatā jñānadhautamanasaṃ na limpati // XVIII.2
Henceforth, verse numbers given without the Canto are all from XVIII.

We will see that Śrī Harṣa will make creative use of the erotic context to delineate many shifts in their sense of self that occur between the lovers.[44] But in order to get to those shifts, and as I will suggest, their potential to subvert models of gendered interaction, we need first an acknowledgement of the formulaic power of the dominant teleological paradigm within which the poet and his audience function. The paradigm is the four-fold 'ends of man' or 'objects of human pursuit' (*puruṣārthas*): ordered social and personal virtue (*dharma*), material wealth (*artha*), pleasure (*kāma*) and liberation from the conditions of existence (*mokṣa*). The most complete and elaborate requirements in accordance with this paradigm apply to high-born males, such as a king. We do not need to delve into the historical and philosophical details of this hoary formulation that conceptualized an hegemonic understanding of life. In referencing it, however, Śrī Harṣa immediately orients his audience to the context of the sexual pleasure he is going to describe: it falls within the legitimate objectives of the paradigmatic life of the high-born man. There is, of course, the historical consideration that this is a brahmin writer at a royal court, of whom we would scarcely expect anything else than an automatic framing of sexuality within the dominant paradigm of order. More germane to us is the situation within the narrative: we expect this royal couple, even when they come to the marriage bed at long last, to take it for granted that their pleasures will be assimilated into the norms of the rightful life. This does not mean only the force of patriarchal conformity; far from it. As we look in detail at the lyrical description of their lovemaking, we will find ourselves asking how we are to interpret the ways in which perspectives shift and emotional qualities switch between the partners, for they seem not to sit so easily within a masculinist view of sex.

Already here, it must be added, Śrī Harṣa slips in hidden indicators of a more fluid context within which we are to see the lovers: the word for 'water', *vāri*, is also a name for the goddess Sarasvatī, who we have already seen play such a critical role in the poem. Maya Tevet Dayan has argued persuasively in her illuminating study that, 'indications of a hidden identity between the goddess Sarasvatī and Damayantī appear throughout the text'.[45] The ecology is more than it seems. Nevertheless, as we saw with the duties of physicians, the status of kings and renouncers, or the rules of monks in their monastaries, a social paradigm is part of the ecology of experience. We must acknowledge that how the couple act and feel—in conformity with or in subversion of it—is affected by the paradigm's complex and powerful expectations.

Just in case the context of orderly virtues of conduct does not suffice to indicate the complexity of the situation, Śrī Harṣa also references a concern for which he was already famous, the role of spiritual knowledge—the insight into the ultimate nature of self-consciousness—that is the telos of the system of Advaita Vedānta, on which he had

[44] For an analysis of Nala's shifting sense of self in the original Mahābhārata story, somewhat adjacent to rather than directly contradictory to my account here, see Shulman 2001. He comments in passing that he is concerned with issues different from 'the series relating to Nala's love for Damayantī and its recurrent trials'; Shulman 2001: 151.

[45] Tevet Dayan 2010: 25.

written his philosophical book, if the traditional chronologies and biographies are to be trusted. It is another matter as to what he meant by the claim that the erotic life is metaphysically possible and structurally compatible with the cognitive attainment of self-realization; for he seems to stand against the role of strict renunciation of all social values (thus, the first three of the four ends) that had been asserted strongly by most[46] previous Advaitins. Again, for our purposes, we only need to keep in mind that social and moral norms too are enfolded into the forms of experience—even the erotic. Lisa Folkmarson Käll extends Merleau-Ponty in just this way. 'When Merleau-Ponty writes that erotic perception in the most manifest way lays bare our relation to the world, this also involves our relation to its social, cultural and historical dimensions and does not refer to some "pure" and socially undistorted immediate corporeal attachment to the materiality of the world.'[47] Ecological phenomenology seeks precisely to work with the variety of relationships to be found in the specific affective dynamics that form bodiliness in various contexts; and here we see examples of the cultural forces at play in the situating of the erotic relationship between Nala and Damayantī.

The 'World' of the Lovers

Having noted these preliminary considerations about the ecology of erotic phenomenology, we can turn to that ecology's next significant feature: the literal environment of the lovemaking, starting with its enabling materials. The material environment is integral to the pursuit of sensory pleasures. James McHugh has explored the culture of consumption which developed over the centuries within 'the discourse of connoisseurship' for what he calls the 'pursuit of erudite pleasures'.[48] Literary representations of the erotic include perfumes and other exotic stuffs, and in the discourse of which this poem partakes, these materials instantly conjure up a specific erotic sensorium. In it, we find the presupposition of an elaborate economy of wealth, service, and attention to the sensory prompts of the erotic. (The audience will be mindful of an alternative environment that is also a literary trope of the erotic: reed beds, fields, open skies, deep forests, simplicities required due to adultery or poverty or some other exigency.[49]) Once in place, they have the literary function of alerting the audience to the presence of pleasure.

From our phenomenological perspective, we notice that they are vectors of eroticism, for their affective presence shapes the specific contours of royal lovemaking on the wedding night. (Might we wonder if, in far different circumstances long after the poem

[46] But by no means all Advaitins: There is a long-standing folk tradition that Vācaspati Miśra named his renowned sub-commentary on Śaṅkara's commentary on the *Brahma Sūtra*s the *Bhāmatī* after his wife, to compensate for the fact that he had once become so engrossed in writing it that he failed to recognize her. This persistent tale makes for the richly ironic observation that one of (what retrospectively came to be thought of as) the two major schools of Advaita—whose founder had so powerfully argued for the necessity of renunciation—gained its name for an apparently uxorious reason.

[47] Käll 2012: 232.

[48] McHugh 2011.

[49] Many of the short poems and fragments in Selby 2000 richly illustrate these contrasting environments.

ends, they awakened to each other's nakedness in the forest when they shared one piece of cloth between them? And did they finally return to each other as on this first night, enriched by sorrow, to the riches of this palace?)

> The interior was perfumed always by finest dark *agaru* wood, and cooled by a breeze dense with the camphor and sandalwood powder placed upon the latticed windows.
>
> There in the palace, a place was undarkened by great-fragranced oil lamps, their wicks laced with that incense called 'the arrow of the love-god'. The outsprung lamp-light was like the dazzle of the love-god's throbbing arms.[50]

The materials are part of it but, of course, what they do to the senses and how they create and resonate with the erotic mood of the lovers is more important still. In groundbreaking recent work, Yigal Bronner and Gary Tubb have both touched on the interconnected and evocative functions of certain literary qualities. Bronner in fact talks of these literary functions as forming 'an ecosystem of love'.[51] He notices the formation of exocentric compounds in the works of people like the sixth-century writer Subandhu that result in 'lines... that tend to begin with some outside influence on one or more entity, and end, through a chain of "ecological" reactions, in its impact on the outside environment'.[52]

Analysing a verse on the advent of spring described by Subandhu's eponymous heroine, Vāsavadattā, Bonner writes:

> [T]he soft southern breeze (*komala-malaya-māruta*), known for its intoxicating sandalwood scent, mobilizes the world of love. It shakes the mango trees (*uddhūta-cūta*), whose flowers then flow with sap (*prasava-rasa*). Feasting on this nectar, the cuckoos burst into a frenzy of intoxicated sweet coos (*āsvāda-kaṣāya-kaṇṭha-kala-kaṇṭha-kuha-kuhārāva*), which fills every corner of the heavens (*bharita-sakala-diṅ-mukhaḥ*)... Subandhu begins by describing two external actors, the wind and the mango tree, coming into contact, and ends with a much longer description of an output, the perfervid but pleasant melody of cuckoos... [He] crafts a tightly constructed system of echoes, rhymes, and metrical patterns (for example, *mala... mala*, *ūta... ūta*, *kaṇṭha... kaṇṭha*, *kuha-kuha*), which also highlights the existence of a centre (*rasa... rasa*), where the sweet substance of love is consumed and from which it is reproduced with even greater intensity.[53]

He argues that 'force (*ojas*) and sweetness (*mādhurya*) not only coexist in Subandhu's compounds that depict love, but also seem to depend on each other': for example, in another verse, there is the echo of *rasa*—essential flavour—in *sārasa-rasita* (crane-cry), 'quite possibly alluding to the flavour they consumed and reproduced'. Bronner concludes that, 'As Subandhu portrays it, love has an amazing capacity to reproduce

[50] *dhūpitaṃ yadudarāntaraṃ ciraṃ mecakairagarusāradārubhiḥ /*
jālajāladhṛtacandracandanakṣodamedurasamīraśītalam // 5
kvāpi kāmaśaravṛttavartayo yaṃ mahāsurabhitailadīpikāḥ /
tenire vitimiraṃ smarasphuraddoḥpratāpanikarāṇkuraśriyaḥ // 6.

[51] Bronner 2014: 250ff. [52] Ibid., p. 252. [53] Ibid., p. 252.

itself and repeatedly trigger a dense ecosystem of flora and fauna, substances and sounds, tastes and scents. This erotic transformation, which spreads in ever-widening circles, is what many of Subandhu's compounds are all about.'[54]

Bronner is primarily concerned here to interpret the writerly techniques that inform the aesthetics of literary creation. But the implication is that such an aesthetic is possible only because in the poet's world, the erotic emotion is in fact caused, formed, expressed, and conveyed within the dynamic factors that constitute the world within which it occurs. The literary analysis works because emotion is an ecological reality waiting for the writer to refract through words about human subjects located within the work.

Bronner's insight shifts from being of literary to phenomenological value when seen in the context of our study here. There is no doubt that Śrī Harṣa draws upon this tradition, and there is a constant filtration of affect and interpretation, as the rich and richly suggestive palatial environment yields semantic charge to the reading of mood, and mood colours the sensory engagement with the environment. Earlier on, when protesting to the magical goose that she could not possibly become anyone else's bride, Damayantī presents the impossibility as unnatural. It is impossible to think of 'the night having a beloved (*kāntā*) other than its beloved moon (*soma*; but also *kāntā*)'. It is as if 'the lotus (*sarojā*) were connected to something other than the sun'.[55] She returns with a variation on the theme of the sun and the moon and the lotus: Why would the lotus (*nalinī*)—that blossoms with the sun—dally with the nectarine moon, even if it was indeed full of nectar?[56]

Now, walking together through the palace to the bedchamber, the lovers have that feeling that songsters far away and a long time later would make familiar as 'love is in the air', and 'birds and bees do it'. The sharp attention to natural detail is notable, as too the implication of the ways in which lovemaking can and will proceed. (It scarcely need be said that the literary qualities that Bronner identifies in the earlier writer are more than evident here, as they are everywhere in this supremely language-engrossed work—so engrossed that Tevet Dayan can reasonably claim that it is metapoetic and linguistically metaphysical at the same time.[57] But it would require a different undertaking to bring out those literary qualities; I merely invite the reader of Sanskrit to take time to read aloud the text and be tugged happily into its clever embrace.)

There their eyes took in coupling swans ornamenting a pond in their carnival of love, and too, lustful mynahs and sparrows returning to sexplay again and again.[58]

Then, later in the canto, Śrī Harṣa teasingly works through the following metaphor to erase fixed distinctions between fabricated and living beings, through resonances between affect and effect.

[54] Ibid., p. 254. [55] III.75–6. [56] III.80. [57] Tevet Dayan 2010: 25.

[58] *yatra mattakalaviṅkaśīlitāślīlakelipunaruktavattayoḥ /*
kvāpi dṛṣṭibhiravāpi vāpikottaṃsahaṃsamithunasmarotsavaḥ // XVIII.16.

The fire of her passion was smothered by the suppressive power that was the decoction of her shyness, but was re-kindled by the magic invocations of her lover.[59]

It is pleasing that here we are no longer tied to familiar modern contrasts of the material and the mental, but instead follow the metaphor as a suggestive expression of emotion in context. That context can function not only with materials, living forms, and their blurry boundaries. Śrī Harṣa also draws on another technique of *kāvya*, in which analytic distinctions necessary for metaphor are invoked only to make us rethink whether they are metaphors at all or, in fact, evocations of an ecological whole in which subjective states run through, between, and across boundaries hitherto thought of as dividing inside from outside.

In the context of a literary analysis that implies and evokes the ecological connections between the state of the environment and of the subject, Gary Tubb has talked about the techniques of 'atmospherics'.[60] Again, as with Bronner, I present the literary analysis and suggest that it can illuminate the phenomenological case I am making in my reading of the *Naiṣadhacarita*. Tubb's analysis is of the ninth-century *Rāmacarita* of Abhinanda. Abhinanda, he says, often connects the actions of his characters and the experiences of his readers through 'references to atmospheric stimuli', a telling example being his use of 'the cumulatively demoralizing effect of the dampness of the monsoon, a palpable emotional fact familiar to anyone who has lived in India', when talking of Rāma's depression during the long wait for the battle to kill Rāvana and rescue Sītā. Lakṣmaṇa tells him, 'Shake loose the dreadlock that cling to the slopes of your shoulder, soaked by the drops that have fallen from the leaftips of the sal trees . . . ', 'air out these arrows with their soggy fittings; take out your long bow from the old wet cloth of its sheath'. Or 'at the other end of the humidity scale', the troop of monkeys searching for Sītā 'could not find even a vine with a shred of shade, much less Sītā'; 'they encountered rocks as cruel as Rāvaṇa, but nowhere did they come across a stream as cool as Sītā'.[61]

Tubb notes this within a more general observation of 'varying poetic techniques',[62] and not in terms of the philosophical account of subjectivity that I am trying to get at here. Nonetheless, it is telling that the scholarship on *kāvya* reveals just the sort of descriptive awareness of the ecology of emotion available in the tradition that Śrī Harṣa draws on to such spectacular effect. Repeatedly, Śrī Harṣa weaves together act, mood, expression, and the world that renders them meaningful.

[59] *yena tanmadanavahninā sthitaṃ hrīmahauṣadhiniruddhaśaktinā /*
siddhimadbhirudateji taiḥ punaḥ sa priyapriyavacobhimantraṇaiḥ // 57.

[60] Tubb 2014. [61] Ibid., pp. 379–80.

[62] Ibid., p. 379ff. Tubb puts this in self-consciously funky terms, asking us to think of the glamorous brutality of Rāvana as his being in 'nightclub mode', wearing 'bling-bling jewellery' at a 'karaoke party', his playing of the *mṛdaṅgam* drum suggesting that he 'started a sort of conga line'.

A wreath of creepers—in an embrace so tight it hurt—their encircled arms were as the noose of the lord of hearts, as lotus stalks all golden.[63]

Or

She could not help but smile, that slender-waisted young woman, upon seeing her husband's lower lip, charming with a spot of her eyes' collyrium, as if it were a red *flor impia* blossom with a bee clinging to it.[64]

As the discussion of Bronner and Tubb shows, Śrī Harṣa is very much in the tradition of which he is such a significant heir, when it comes to the use of literary techniques that work back and forth between people and their environment, in order to point to the complex truth that not only the imagination of the reader, but also the life of the human subject within and without the text is ecologically constituted at all times. At some barely articulate level, the density of our subjective states is but the fullness of the world that makes us subjects at all. A state of body—an embrace, a smudged lip—is a state of living, and living is a subjective totality.

But Śrī Harṣa also moves away from the conventions he inherited and refashioned so boldly. He is bolder still in going where his predecessors (and successors) seldom go—to the bed itself, at the time of lovemaking itself. Bronner notes of Subandhu's work,

For all its fascination with love, the *Vāsavadattā* never actually depicts lovemaking as it happens. This, too, is true not just of this work. Sanskrit poets dwell at great length on the foreplay spat and on the aftermath of love, the emissaries exchanged between lovers, and the pining of the separated, but hardly ever on the way love is actually consummated. There are some obvious reasons for this, of course, including the fear of trespassing the boundaries of propriety. Then, there is the theory developed by Ānandavardhana some three centuries after Subandhu, according to which poetry is at its best only if it suggests, rather than explicitly narrates, emotional experiences such as love. Ānandavardhana believed that for a reader to be able to 'taste' *eros* in a poem, it would have to be intimated by things such as the setting... or the bodily gestures of the characters... as well as the description of their beautiful body parts... if, instead, the poet actually says such things as 'they fell in love' or 'they made love,' the psychoaesthetic effect is instantly destroyed.[65]

As we will see, Śrī Harṣa obviously thought the effect is not in the least destroyed. And when it comes to the full expression of erotic phenomenology, his frankness makes a crucial contribution, for it is in the intensity of lovemaking itself that we find the re-imagining of bodiliness and the percolation of subjectivity that this book has tried to find in other genres.

63 *bāhuvalliparirambhamaṇḍalī yā parasparamapīḍayattayoḥ /*
āsta hemanalinīmṛṇālajaḥ pāśa eva hṛdayeśayasya saḥ // 96.

64 *vīkṣya patyuradharaṃ kṛśodarī bandhujīvamiva bhṛṅgasaṃgatam /*
mañjulaṃ nayanakajjalairnijaiḥ saṃvarītumaśakatsmitaṃ na sā // 125.

65 Bronner 2016: 257–8.

Touch, Vision, and the Other Senses: The Erotic as Multimodal

Merleau-Ponty realized that the erotic was a critical demonstration of the bodily condition of phenomenology. '[W]hile erotic perception colors the world in the same manner as perception in general, it also colors the world quite differently by offering a privileged way of experiencing our being-in-the-world', says Lisa Käll in her reading of Merleau-Ponty.[66] By 'privilege', Käll appears to mean that the erotic sensation is what 'lays bare in the most manifest way' our 'lifeworld'.[67] The erotic, in other words, gives us more self-understanding of our being than any other type of perception. If ever there was a place where the notion of 'flesh' as a post-Cartesian ontology of being is to be expressed, it has to be in the erotic experience. Let us think again about how to understand 'flesh', in the words of Elizabeth Grosz. 'Flesh is being as reversibility, being's capacity to fold in on itself, being's dual orientation inward and outward, being's openness, its reflexivity, the fundamental gap or dehiscence of being that Merleau-Ponty illustrates with a favorite example—the notion of "double sensation," the capacity of one hand to touch another that is itself touching an object.'[68]

We must, however, remain mindful of the still-asymmetrical nature of the touch. Luce Irigaray and many of her readers invest a great deal in the significance of touch, but argue that touch can nevertheless be presented in a way that does not acknowledge its mutuality. Christopher Cohoon, for example, expresses suspicion at how touch might be used in men's depiction of the erotic relationship:

> Irigaray critically appropriates from 'Phenomenology of Eros' [in Emmanuel Levinas's *Totality and Infinity*]...the notion of the caress as a non-possessive mode of touching the other as other which, as Irigaray notes, Levinas conceives in a manner that one-sidedly positions the man as the active lover (*l'amant*) and the woman as the passive beloved (*l'aimée*).[69]

Cohoon goes on, in his reading of Irigaray's critique of Emmanuel Levinas,[70]

> Unlike visual perception, the touch of the caress is already intimate; since it is always localized across a surface of contact and is therefore incapable of taking place from a distance, it does not run the risk of totalizing the other in a comprehensive view...In positioning the feminine subject (*l'aimée*) as the passive object of the caress of the man (*l'amant*), Levinas seems to forget that, unlike vision, touch—contact!—is inherently reciprocal and intersubjective, which is perhaps why Irigaray suggests that Levinasian lovers do not properly touch...This basic corporeal reciprocity is precisely what is emphasized in Irigaray's appropriation of the concept of the caress: the touch of the caress is a 'call to co-exist'—a call to intercorporeality.[71]

If, however, touch is the erotic phenomenological mode par excellence, but the social ecology of the lovers imbues their contact with differential meaning, we must

[66] Käll 2012: 231. [67] Ibid., p. 230. [68] Grosz 1993: 44. [69] Cohoon 2011: 480–1.
[70] And here I offer no view of Levinas himself, or the accuracy of Irigaray's reading of him.
[71] Cohoon 2011: 485; quoting Irigaray: 1992/1996: 125.

acknowledge that bodily subjectivity continues to be inscribed with gendered normativity—that is to say, in the erotic as much as other more formal contexts such as the one we studied in the dialogue beween Sulabhā and Janaka. Perhaps only a woman (bracketing for this discussion the question of gender-formation) can present caress non-possessively; it is not clear in Irigaray what possibilities she extends to a man's capacity to represent touch non-possessively.

So we must ask how touch can function from within the specific social context of lovers: a context that throughout history everywhere has been saturated with the notion of the man as active lover, and yet become representative of that mutuality of touch that is the true mark of the erotic. Nala must follow the rules of touch if it is to carry the mutual charge of the erotic (as opposed to the merely lustful).

In beginning love's revelry, her beloved's hands—one here, and the other there—sought to clasp her strong, but for long she resisted, both hands against one; left no entry for him, pressing herself close against the bed.[72]

Śrī Harṣa here plays with the intersection between social normativity and the erotic. The former requires that touch be approached differently by the woman and the man, as he touches and she is touched. But the erotic is the erotic only when this difference is denuded, and the two people become mutual in their touching. This opens up a subtle distinction between the automatic mutuality of touch—to touch is to be touched—and its intentional mutuality—when both seek to transform the perceptual mechanics of touch into a true seeking of each other's touch.

Feigning curiosity in her engagement pearlstring, her husband brushed the base of her neck, coursing along her breasts.

He touched her perfumed breast then, putting his own necklace upon her; said, 'You decorated me with your garland in the *svayamvara* assembly; it is only proper that I in turn pay homage to you.'[73]

As we will think about in greater detail, Śrī Harṣa uses Damayantī's modesty in a complex way. Here, he seeks to describe a way in which the fact that Nala touches and Damayantī is touched is slowly transformed by Nala's suggestion that his apparent presumption of the social norm is in fact a mutual act: he is only belatedly responding to her touch at the wedding. Nala re-reads the meaning of the touch, hitherto loaded differentially with her modesty and his eagerness: he seeks its erotic charge to come from mutual homage. Or we can say, this is the full erotic 'colouring' of the 'double sensation' of the phenomenologist: the double sensation is not only between subjects,

[72] *vallabhasya bhujayoḥ smarotsave ditsatoḥ prasabhamaṅkapālikām /*
ekakaściramarodhi bālayā talpayantraṇanirantarālayā // 43.

[73] *hāracārimavilokane mṛṣākautukaṃ kimapi nāṭayannayam /*
kaṇṭhamūlamadasīyamaspṛśatpāṇinopakucadhāvinā dhavaḥ // 44
yattvayāsmi sadasi srajāñcitastanmayāpi bhavadarhaṇārhati /
ityudīrya nijahāramarpayannaspṛśatsa tadurojakorakau // 45.

it is also an intentional realization of mutual sensation and not just the asymmetrical touch of one subject upon the other.

Here we have the classical male poet yet somehow operating in such a way that, it seems to me, he strives to turn around the norms of his lifeworld within his realization of the erotic. This is brought home when we look at two further forms of touch with which the scene deals, the kiss and the nail-mark.

Now, the kiss is the heightened expression of the touch by which subjectivity constantly travels upon the surface of feeling. Śrī Harṣa is aware of the sensory operation itself and in its implication within a larger economy of socially normative feeling. In the early stages of their first lovemaking, Damayantī must behave within coded norms of feminine sexuality, under the sign of modesty, and her response to the heavy charge that touch has in the high society of classical India is indicative of that. The Merleau-Pontian notion of 'erotic dehiscence' of which Grosz talks is emblematically the kiss, the classic double sensation. So it is with the kiss that the erotic touch of the lovers is inaugurated.

She bent low with modesty and he kissed her on her forehead. She unbent a little and he kissed her on her cheeks. She was emboldened; he smiled and instantly kissed her mouth.[74]

Śrī Harṣa also presents touch as slipping erotically from the starting point of the active man to the active woman. The exact act is a culturally loaded touch that goes somewhat beyond the 'caress': a familiar feature of the love-mark from *kāmaśāstra*, the erudite science of pleasure, namely, the 'nail-mark'.

The erotic is the literal and figurative marking of each by the other's 'touch'. First, still using the trope of her modesty, Damayantī is said to require Nala's action. But we begin to see the breaking down of one-sidedness, literally, in touch, for his action is to have her touch break through his affective boundary.

She refused to mark him with her nails, even as he begged her; so he distracted her with talk, took hold of her hand to press against his chest, and delighted in piercing himself with her nails.[75]

This initial and partial subversion of one-sided touching marks the start of the erotic flow in which non-possessive mutuality swells up; for as they make love, the poet indicates the conscious way in which one-sidedness is subverted in erotic touch, and boundaries are breached together and of each other. As time goes by, Damayantī exclaims:

'I am a maid at your service. Here, I kiss you. Here, I scratch you with my nails. I hold you, I lay you upon my heart. I will not disobey you. Oh, but just let me be!'

74 *prāgacumbadalike hriyānatāṃ tāṃ kramāddaranatāṃ kapolayoḥ /*
tena viśvasitamānasāṃ jhaṭityānane sa paricumbya siṣmiye // 41.

75 *yācanānna dadatīṃ nakhakṣataṃ tāṃ vidhāya kathayā'nyacetasam /*
vakṣasi nyasitumāttatatkaraḥ svaṃ vibhidya mumude sa tannakhaiḥ // 72.

Through such teasing shyness in their lovemaking, she gave of herself, her kisses, and more; that disingenuous girl (she tricked her lover and tricked her shame). But then, what is beyond the reach of the artful mind![76]

Levinas argued about the caress that 'the intentionality of pleasure, directed purely and simply towards the future itself, and not an anticipation of any future event, has always been misrecognized by philosophical analysis'.[77] Irigaray responds that this means that, 'To caress, for Levinas, consists, therefore, not in approaching the other in its most vital dimension, the touch, but in the reduction of that vital dimension of the other's body to the elaboration of a future for himself.'[78] There may be a case that she is misreading Levinas; or she may be bringing to the surface precisely that masculine assumption of the male ego that she charges is hidden in him.[79] At any rate, it is entirely possible to think that if the caress were an egological pleasure directed to the male subject's own temporal concerns—and it is perfectly possible to think that conventionally, one might expect Nala to approach sexual pleasure in just the way that directs his own narrative—then there would be 'nothing of communion in pleasure', as Irigaray claims.[80] But the way Nala's active role slips away into a mutual, non-possessive breaching of boundaries suggests that he is in fact being drawn into a subjective space-time created by Damayantī's artful mind, which sees, as Bronner argues in the case of Subandhu's depiction of women, 'the female eroticized subject as the world's most powerful and creative force'.[81] As Cohoon points out, 'In *Elemental Passions*, speaking in the voice of a lover, Irigaray says,[82] "the internal and external horizon of my skin interpenetrating with yours wears away their edges, their limits, their solidity, creating another space—outside any framework".'[83] The skin is transformed from a 'hull' into a 'threshold'.[84] Śrī Harṣa asks us to imagine our way into the transformation of the lovers caused by Damayantī's formation of mutuality.

The significance of touch to erotic phenomenology has tended to problematize the role of vision, for vision needs radical revision if it is not be merely the objectifying gaze, as we saw in the chapter on the dialogue between Sulabhā and Janaka. Vision must be itself part of the visible, if it is not simply to incorporate into its own subjectivity that which is seen. Irigaray makes a typically sweeping claim (whose historical

[76] *cumbyase'yamayamaṅkyase nakhaiḥ śliṣyaseyamayamarpyase hṛdi /*
no punarna karavāṇi te giraṃ huṃ tyaja tyaja tavāsmi kiṃkarā // 90
ityalīkaratakātarā priyaṃ vipralabhya surate hriyaṃ ca sā /
cumbanādi vitatāra māyinī kiṃ vidagdhamanasāmagocaraḥ // 91.

[77] Levinas 1987: 89. [78] Irigaray 1990/1991: 179.

[79] It should not be thought that I have a generally critical position on Levinas—it should be clear here that we are only reading Irigaray's Levinas, and that too in order to elucidate some aspects of the erotic that pertain to my reading of the *Naiṣadhacarita*. For a sympathetic engagement with Levinas through Indic studies, in this case in the context of ethics in the Vedas, see Patton 2007a. A deeper engagement with Levinas on the erotic—a sensible suggestion made by an anonymous reader for the Press—would make for a somewhat different project, which I hope to undertake in my next book.

[80] Irigaray 1990/1991: 180. [81] Bronner 2016: 257. [82] Irigaray 1982/1992: 59.

[83] Cohoon 2011: 486–7. [84] Ibid., p. 489.

accuracy is less important to us than the philosophical concern she expresses): 'For Western philosophers such as Sartre or Merleau-Ponty, seeing is not a way of contemplating but of seizing, dominating and possessing in particular the body of the other. This transforms love and amorous life into a struggle between partners who want to master and possess the other.'[85] Hence, she claims, it becomes important to enter the erotic relationship through touch, which preserves otherness but blurs the boundaries between the two. But others in the tradition of Merleau-Ponty have long been aware of the need to not put vision in tension with touch. So Alphonso Lingis talked (some time before Irigaray's essay) about the eye that caresses, which 'no longer pilots or estimates... [but] moves, or rather is moved', and does not 'seek substances, the principles, the causes of the alien' but searches for 'the look of the other'.[86] Lisa Käll says about this notion, 'It depends on the look of the other for its own look and the desire to be seen is a desire also to see and to become seer-seen. Erotic perception... does not... originate in a detached perceiver but is instead given birth in the midst of the perceivable'.[87]

In short, without denying the peculiar reflexive mutuality of touch, and its consequent significance for the delineation of the erotic phenomenon, we must re-think vision so that its significance lies in its having the same interdependent symmetry. Only then can we assimilate vision into erotic phenomenology. But in fact we should ask why at all there has to be a particular tension between touch and vision to negotiate, and why one or the other has to function as the paradigmatic modality of the erotic. It seems, to be harsh for a moment, scarcely believable that the philosophical theorization of the erotic could have so escaped the commonplace familiarity of multimodal lovemaking.

Śrī Harṣa's depiction confines itself neither to touch nor to vision. We have already seen that he admits of an intensification of the erotic, a movement within desire, from hearing to seeing, when Nala compliments the goose on its personal message describing Damayantī, by saying that what he has heard from the goose has seemed as if he has seen her. Maya Tevet Dayan gives a sensitive analysis of the first time Nala sees Damayantī, in Canto VI, when he goes to her palace as the emissary of the gods, cloaked in invisibility. Tevet Dayan points out that her beauty, which Śrī Harṣa compares to both the day-lotus and (antithetically) the moon, while greater than both, also speaks in a 'heart-rending' way about how beauty itself is a mere reflection, an implication of a metaphysics of what is not real.[88] This implication of the uncertainty of the visual is mirrored at the start of Canto VIII, when Nala throws off his invisibility and reveals himself—but only as the messenger of the gods. Damayantī is immediately drawn to him—

> She felt fondness for him thinking him to be Nala, but in that very moment, wondering 'how can that be?', she withdrew her affection.[89]

[85] Irigaray 2004: 390. [86] Lingis 1983: 9. [87] Käll 2012: 241.
[88] Tevet-Dayan 2010: 74–7.
[89] *tasminnalo'sāviti sānvarajyatkṣaṇaṃ kṣaṇaṃ kveha sa ityudāsta* / VIII.5a.

It is not enough that he looks like Nala, there is more to Nala—and thus to her love—than how he looks. Despite acknowledging the pull of vision, Śrī Harṣa still qualifies its power.

Śrī Harṣa also explores the nature of the tension between vision and touch in Canto VI, when Nala seeks to reach Damayantī in the depths of the palace, while he is still invisible. He is so lost in thought of her, he imagines her everywhere in the palace, even when she actually walks in front of him. She, of course, cannot see him but is constantly thinking of him too. Then they bump into each other. She cannot see him although she is always thinking of him, while he sees her everywhere when looking for her; in these extremes of vision, they cannot make sense—literally—of their touching the other.[90]

> Seeing each other as somewhere else even when standing together, they embraced the other in reality even as they embraced in the pretence of their thoughts.
>
> Although Bhīma's daughter found him in her touch, she took him for an illusion, as she did not see him; and the king, although he saw her, stood stunned and could not take her touch.
>
> They knew the touch to be true for the joy it caused, but were checked by the error of their prehension. They were confounded: along the way they touched each other for real, and yet could have no faith in it.[91]

The effect is such that they cannot restrain themselves from this erotic game (VI. 54), even when taking it to be unreal—while it is real without their taking it to be so. Further inquiry into the role of imagination in erotic phenomenology would take us elsewhere. For the moment, let us note the balance of vision and touch—the one who sees cannot believe without touch, and the one who touches cannot believe without seeing; and yet, because touch and vision are present in a confoundment of knowing, unknowing, hope, and longing, the encounter is erotic.

Let us then turn to when touch and vision are present without confusion. Now that their withdrawal to the nuptial bed has brought touch into the centre of the erotic subjection of one to the other, not only vision but in fact the other senses also become involved in that play of otherness and togetherness that is the erotic phenomenon. Śrī Harṣa subtly brings out the powerful fact that the erotic is indissolubly multisensory. Early on in the bedchamber scene, he once more uses shyness to suggest the way vision can be made to mean both indirection and attainment on Damayantī's part. The manner in which the question of how a woman's vision is to grasp is answered teasingly, again drawing in the environment, richly endowed with bright materials.

[90] Tevet Dayan 2010: 87–93 approaches this incident from the viewpoint of a meditation on knowledge and illusion, favoured subjects of Śrī Harṣa the Advaita philosopher.

[91] *anyonyamanyatravadīkṣamāṇo parasparеṇādhyuṣite'pi deśe /*
aliṅgitālīkaparasparāntastathyaṃ mithastau pariṣasvajāte // VII.51
sparśaṃ tamasyādhigatāpi bhaimī mene punarbhrāntimadarśanena /
nṛpaḥ sa paśyannapi tāmudītaḥ stambho na dhartuṃ sahasā śaśāka // 52 ||
sparśāṭiharṣādṛtasatyamatyā pravṛtya mithyāpratilabdhabādhau /
punarmithastathyamapi spṛśantau na śraddadhāte pathi tau vimugdhau // 53.

She could not bring her husband within the range of her eyesight, nor place them without; she kept her eyes on whatever she could, the looking at which she could look at him as well.[92]

Then sound returns joyously, in as intimate a creation of mutuality as the original hearing had been a diffuse subjectivity stretching longingly across intractable distance.

When she arched her eyebrow as they made love, it was as if the love god had bent his bow. And then when she moaned, it was the hum of his discharged arrows.[93]

And why not taste—betel and camphor transmogrified—which surely is as significant for the performance of erotic intersubjection as that touch which is a plain kiss?

Making love, they became joyously drunk with the nectar of the other's lips astringent with an excess of betel, drenched with the camphorous fragrance of the 'rising sun'.[94]

But it is true, touch encompasses all, for in it is something more than the two human beings in all their passion, whether expressed or sated. Once more we see the formation of erotic phenomenology in its ecological, multimodal, subjectivity-mediating, boundary-crossing bodiliness, through Śrī Harṣa's imagery and naturalism.

In the joyful frenzy of climax, their fingernails dug into each other. It was piquant and sweet, like molasses juice with a sprinkling of red pepper.[95]

They held each other, put their lips together, thighs entwined, as if seeing in their dreams what they had done to each other, enfolded in their embrace, holding on tight. And they slept.[96]

So we return to touch (but we do not forget the other senses). But that first sleeping together of what the audience knows will be of a life-long commitment, is not exactly a return to what was before. They have been altered, and the way their skin remains in touch is the sign of their changed subjectivity, a sharing that is of both but yet requires both to be something else. This 'something else' is not necessarily subversive in a social sense. Depicting that would require looking at literary characters in other contexts, where difference in social status, or belonging to opposite sides of a political divide, might lead lovers into other kinds of transformations. Nala and Damayantī offer no scope for the writer to express such changes.

The subversive nature of the erotic here is a phenomenological one—the touch changes what a bodily being feels; it permits the lovers to find their bodies making

92 *nā'nayā patiranāyi netrayorlakṣyatāmapi parokṣatāmapi /*
vīkṣyate sa khalu yadvilokane tatra tatra nayate dadānayā // 54.

93 *yadbhruvau kuṭilite tayā rate manmathena tadanāmi kārmukam /*
yattu huṃhumiti sā tadā vyadhāttatsmarasya śaramuktihuṃkṛtam // 93.

94 *pūgabhāgabahutākaṣāyitairvāsitairudayabhāskareṇa tau /*
cakraturnidhuvane'dharāmṛtaistatra sādhumadhupānavibhramam // 103.

95 *āsta bhāvamadhigacchatostayoḥ saṃmadeṣu karajakṣatārpaṇā /*
phāṇiteṣu maricāvacūrṇanā sā sphuṭaṃ kaṭurapi spṛhāvahā // 118.

96 *miśritoru militādharaṃ mithaḥ svapnavīkṣitaparasparakriyam /*
tau tato'nu parirambhasaṃpuṭaiḥ pīḍanāṃ vidadhatau nidadratuḥ // 152.

sense to them now. In that way it can upset and upend hitherto explanatory senses of oneself, and thereby make it open to the possibilities of feeling otherwise. Before we finally do leave Nala and Damayantī asleep, we will turn to look more extensively at how Śrī Harṣa takes us through the many ways in which lovemaking sensitizes us to the percolation of subjectivity across boundaries.

Lovemaking as Questioning Oneself

As we make our way deeper into the Canto, and further into the description of their lovemaking, we follow Śrī Harṣa's acute, but seldom serious observations on how Damayantī's and Nala's sense of themselves—the assumptions that inform their fleeting thoughts and the emotions that have accompanied them up to this point—shifts and flows in the erotic spaces in-between. From within the tradition of *kāvya* literature, Śrī Harṣa cannot help his literary perspective being outside the lovers' phenomenology (there is no scope for the first-personal voice of the writer); but his skill as an aesthetician lies in drawing us into that indeterminate space where the theorists debate whether the essence lies in the characters, the poet or us.[97] There, the lovers, in being themselves, change the way the other has been. What Eleanor Godway says of phenomenology in general is brought out powerfully in the erotic:

> [T]ruth is not something already fixed and immutable, available to an 'absolute observer,' yet it is not therefore an illusion, to be abandoned when we have to recognize that what we 'know' is relative to our situation. While there is no 'accurate blueprint of all perspectives,' there is your perspective and mine, and to the extent that they differ, and exactly to that extent, we have a chance of learning more, of widening our horizons. What matters is our capacity to let our own perspective be put in question. This, if anything is the practical (lived) meaning of 'objectivity,' the re-orienting experience of 'I thought I knew,' which has been the blind spot of so much epistemology.[98]

The erotic brings sharply into focus this putting of one's perspective into question. It is what the vulnerability of being-with does to the lovers.

Damayantī and Nala are now in the bedchamber, and the completeness of their intimacy dawns upon them. When the gods had cunningly asked Nala himself to be their emissary to Damayantī, and he had had to conceal his identity in order to be faithful to this high duty, she had rejected all of them, and declared that she loved only Nala. To a messenger, to a third party of neutral status, much could be said frankly. Furthermore, she is ambivalent about the implications of her having chosen him in public. This latter, of course, is the recurrent theme of the *svayaṃvara*: the tension between the containment of the woman to the conventional demands of marriage and

[97] For a critically precise outline of the historical development and intellectual contours of the debate over where the essence of the aesthetic experience—rasa—lies, derived from the magisterial translation of a wide array of texts, see Pollock 2016: Introduction.

[98] Godway 2007: 81.

the flash of agency available in the theatrical performance of choice.[99] Now, it strikes Damayantī, Nala would see this woman before him quite differently from the demure bride with her desires veiled in the fashion of well-bred royalty; he would see her as the woman who had openly declared herself for him! As we will soon see, Śrī Harṣa makes frequent use of the trope of the high-status woman's modesty, only to make us question our assumptions about the lovers, even as they question themselves.

> She thought of when she had made him listen to her—her indecorous language!—back then when he had been a messenger. Now in heightened shyness she asked herself, what am I to do?
>
> She had taken the Naiṣadha at the assembly, shamelessly, swiftly, all by herself. Thinking back on her quicksilver conduct, she could not look Nala in the eye.[100]

But then Śrī Harṣa switches our focus to what happens to Nala, a change to the character of the self-possessed male, pleasingly misunderstanding his bride in a way that makes him question himself: indeed, he displays a suspension of any reasonable epistemology of self-awareness.

> He suspected a lack of love in her—she who looked away only in blushful shyness. Then recalling her feelings for him, discovered when a messenger to her, he did away with his alarm.[101]

Only who she is—her desire, her words, her conduct—can make him re-read her aright, and find the answer to the question that had arisen in his misreading of her initial disquiet.

Percolating Subjectivity: Modesty and Other Bodily States

In the ecological view that I have been espousing, the nature of this intersubjectivity should be understood in a holistic and complex way, not as an abstract transformation of an interiority but as given across the whole range of one subject's presence to another. To make this point concrete, let us go through a leitmotif of this lovemaking scene, where Śrī Harṣa draws on the conventional depiction of the young woman's modesty/shyness/bashfulness. Śrī Harṣa is by no means an anachronistic and gender-bending poet of sexual non-normativity. What is interesting precisely is that, original though he may be in many respects, he writes from within a civilization with highly elaborated

[99] Scholars continue to disagree on the historical origin of the practice by which the royal woman chose her husband. See, e.g., Chatterjee 1961; Schmidt 1987; and Brockington 2006. Also, Brodbeck 2013, to which I owe the original references.

[100] *dūtyasaṃgatigataṃ yadātmanaḥ prāgaśiśravadiyaṃ priyaṃ giraḥ /*
taṃ vicintya vinayavyayaṃ hriyā na sma veda karavāṇi kīdṛśam // 31
yattayā sadasi naiṣādhaḥ svayaṃ prāgvṛtaḥ sapadi vītalajjayā /
tannijaṃ manasikṛtya cāpalaṃ sā śaśāka na vilokituṃ nalam // 32.

[101] *hrībharādvimukhayā tayā bhiyaṃ sañjitāmananurāgaśaṅkini /*
sa svacetasi lulopa saṃsmarandūtyakālakalitaṃ tadāśayam // 38.

codes of conduct. (These are codes perhaps global and persistent to this day: '[C]ultural representations tend to "enclose" subjects in "well-defined forms," imposing upon them certain identities—for example, woman as delicate, submissive, caretaking, and merely corporeal, and man as thick-skinned, aggressive, breadwinning, and supra-corporeal—and ultimately pushing them well beneath the raw sensitivity of their bodies' boundaries, determined in their own becoming and restricted to well worn or unjust possibilities for intimacy with others.'[102]) We have already seen that his view is subtly at odds with the restrictive nature of that depiction: first, the description of Nala's abashment at the possibility that the world will find out that he has fallen in love demonstrates Śrī Harṣa's willingness to depict this peculiarly reflexive and implicitly judgemental emotion as a general human possibility even for heroic men. Second, Damayantī's shyness has the particular erotic function of driving both of them into an intensity of interaction, where her casting it aside implies that it is not a morally irreducible aspect of being a woman. What I point out below is that he appears to have had the imaginative freedom within his cultural context to play with the slipperiness of cultural representations of gendered subjects without extending it to gender itself.

In this process, we have two interlocking ecological points to make. One is that the manifestation of a cultural representation of gendered subjectivity—in this exemplary instance, the peculiar (and peculiarly specific) emotion of shyness—is not to be understood in any dualistic way as being about the interiority of the subject or the physical body, but rather holistically. The other point is that the manifestation and transformation of such states of bodiliness should be seen as instances of the percolation of subjectivity between the lovers. So we begin with her modesty and its structuring of her erotic subjectivity, and note that modesty is a performance of her whole being, not an inward or an outward resistance on its own, but a circumspection of longing that only increases its erotic charge.

In beginning love's revelry, her beloved's hands—one here, and the other there—sought to clasp her strong, but for long she resisted, both hands against one; left no entry for him, pressing herself close against the bed.[103]

The king, smiling, looked at the silken gauze upon his bride's thighs. Overcome with shyness, she covered herself with its fringe, as if she had been naked before.[104]

The god of love did not permit the doe-eyed girl to look away from Nala, but modesty stopped her from looking at him. So her look ran towards her husband, but turned back its course, again and yet again, filled with shyness.[105]

[102] Cohoon 2011: 486, drawing on Irigaray 1982/1992: 104.

[103] *vallabhasya bhujayoḥ smarotsave ditsatoḥ prasabhamaṅkapālikām /*
ekakaściramarodhi bālayā talpayantraṇanirantarālayā // 43.

[104] *sa priyoruyugakañcukāṃśuke nyasya dṛṣṭimatha siṣmiye nṛpaḥ /*
āvavāra tadathāmbarāñcalaiḥ sā nirāvṛtiriva trapāvṛtā // 47.

[105] *nāvilokya nalamāsituṃ smaro hrīrna vīkṣitumadatta subhruvaḥ /*
taddṛśaḥ patidiśācalannatha vrīḍitāḥ samakucanmuhuḥ pathaḥ // 53.

But now his response is not an exclamatory masculinity, nor even a self-contained sureness. Rather, he offers a gendered mirroring—at once similar and different—of her restrained longing, now when no restraint appears necessary. (But, in fact, it is, for it is the catalyst for the erotic tension to reach a higher pitch before the disappearance of restraint has an even greater effect on their union.) He is submissive, he is as gentle as she.

'I will drink just the once of your lips; I will beg nothing more of you.' He murmured in submission, yet inevitably, necessarily, held her tight and tasted her lips.

'I am your servant, who has drunk of the wine of your lips. Now I have another duty to do: let me work on your thighs.' And he gently placed his tender-leaved hands upon them.[106]

His dependence on her pleasure shifts the focus away from the still-present cultural norms to the mutual expression of desire. The fulfilment of her desire is his, but again, not as triumph but as contentment: a surprisingly easeful emotion for so intense a description of pleasuring:

Then did she have a contest, a plenitude of resistance and curiosity; there was sweating and shuddering, dread, desire and gratification; as too pleasure and playful pain.[107]

That when he kissed her she did not turn away her face was manna showered on her husband's heart. How contented he was, that when he placed his hand upon her breast she did not push it away.[108]

Once more, the point is made that intersubjectivity is intersubjection of the means of pleasure to each other; once more, that a gendered trope can remain in function only to upend our expectation of its purpose.

Being masterful, he could (if he had willed) conquer the scarf of the lovely-browed damsel, that outward screen of her heart; but he was no master in removing the inward screen of her maidenly modesty.[109]

Thereafter, modesty having brought them to the point it is no longer needed, we have a sweeping back and forth, as each one takes the other, in a mutuality that dissolves resistance because it occurs through an outspreading of each subjectivity. From her perspective:

106 *anyadasmi bhavatīṃ na yācitā vāramekamadharaṃ dhayāmi te /*
ityasisvadadupāṃśukākuvāksopamardahaṭhavṛttireva tam // 59
pītatāvakamukhāsavo'dhunā bhṛtya eṣa nijakṛtyamarhati /
tatkaromi bhavadūrumityasau tatra saṃnyadhita pāṇipallavam // 60.

107 *astivāmyabharamastikautukaṃ sāstigharmajalamastivepathu /*
astibhīti ratamastivāñchitaṃ prāpadastisukhamastipīḍanam // 62.

108 *cumbitaṃ na mukhamācakarṣa yatpatyurantaramṛtaṃ vavarṣa tat /*
sā nunoda na bhujaṃ tadarpitaṃ tena tasya kimabhūnna tarpitam // 70.

109 *sa prasahya hṛdayāpavārakaṃ hartumakṣamata subhruvo bahiḥ /*
hrīmayaṃ tu na tadīyamāntaraṃ tadvinetumabhavatprabhuḥ prabhuḥ // 73.

There was no proud eminence, no liquid ocean, no grove, no hard rock, no husbandly domain, no heavenly abode, where she did not play with him; there was no manner in which she did not have him.[110]

And from his:

Looking at her and looking at her, he looked at her once more and yet more in joy. Holding her and holding her again, he yet held her more; he kissed her but eager, kissed her again. But they never found it enough.[111]

But, of course, the perspective from the one is also from that of the other. This is the intricacy of erotic subjectivity. It is true that the coming together of the lovers requires 'a conjunction of radical otherness and autonomy on the one hand and desire and intimacy on the other', as Irigaray notes.[112] Yet surely, this is only one part of the intricacy. The conjunction is neither paradox nor contradiction, but the rendering of a phenomenological condition—the sense of oneself as distinct, as the giver and the recipient of attention—into an erotic relationship. It is about being with another in a way that makes the sense of oneself indistinct. It may perhaps look problematic if we read this ontologically—if there are two entities who are distinct, how can they be made one? But throughout the course of our studies, I have resisted making close phenomenological description a mere passage to metaphysical closure.

What we have is the sense of distinctiveness, together with a dialectic with intimacy's questioning of such distinctiveness. The poet wisely chooses to conjure up the undergoing of this experience indirectly, through metaphor; any attempt at the literal disclosure of the subjective merely results in an arbitrary ontological configuration, perhaps of two selves, or one self, or even the loss of self. But such determination would add nothing to the experience.

The circle of her pearl string upon her swelling breasts broke apart in the dance of their love play, but the lovely girl—those breasts now strung with beads of sweat—took no notice.[113]

Then there was just the one necklace of pearls, his. But reflected within that string of sweat-beads upon her bosom, it became another ornament, to replace the one torn away.[114]

They held each other; and the gap between each delighted thrill appeared to be a league, the moment between each interlocked gaze an aeon.[115]

110 *na sthalī na jaladhirna kānanaṃ nādribhūrna viṣayo na viṣṭapam /*
krīḍitā na saha yatra tena sā sā vidhaiva na yayā yayā na vā // 84.

111 *vīkṣya vīkṣya punaraikṣi sā mudā paryarambhi parirabhya cāsakṛt /*
cumbitā punaracumbi cādarāttṛptirāpi na kathaṃcanāpi ca // 106.

112 Irigaray 1984/1993: 13.

113 *chinnamapyatanu hāramaṇḍalaṃ mugdhayā suratalāsyakelibhiḥ /*
na vyatarki sudṛśā cirādapi svedabindukitavakṣasā hṛdi // 107.

114 *ekavṛttirapi mauktikāvaliśchinnahāravitatau tadā tayoḥ /*
chāyayā'nyahṛdaye vibhūṣaṇaṃ śrāntivāribharabhāvite'bhavat // 109.

115 *yojanāni parirambhaṇe'ntaraṃ romaharṣajamapi sma bodhataḥ /*
tau nimeṣamapi vīkṣaṇe mitho vatsaravyavadhimadhyagacchatām // 113.

The Contingency of the Heterosexuate

There can be no question that an erotic phenomenology requires detail; a textual study such as this requires a specific narrative. Now, Hillary Chute notes about Luce Irigaray's own project, 'A new sexuality invested with mystery works against the idea that sex is a base "corporeal particularity," yet Irigaray desires an erotic ontology of sexual difference whose foundations are not solely in the abstract.'[116] As the over-confident prudery of past critics of the *Naiṣadhacarita* shows, it is all too easy to let a queasy misunderstanding of the carnal masquerade as a judgement about taste.[117] Equally, an abstract theory of the erotic is not likely to open up the imagination to the shifting perspectives required for locating the phenomenologist within the erotic life. Nonetheless, it is unclear why Irigaray thinks that the result should be an 'ontology' of the subject that, because erotic, requires fixing the sexual identity of the lovers. Chute rightly points out that Irigaray's notion of *mixité* extends to mixed-religion and multicultural couples, but they are all heterosexual. 'Her conceptualization of a solution to the dilemma of subjectivity and community—that "being I" and "being we" become instead simply "beings-in-relation" (yet with "I" and "you" still individuated, singular)—is seductive, but her strong emphasis on the relation *between* the genders as "the privileged place for the creation of horizontal relations" leaves much unanswered.'[118] Here, what is not clear is why Irigaray's notion of 'carnal sharing' cannot be an exploration of the subjective richness and ethical potential of erotic phenomenology without also becoming an ontology predicated on sexual difference. Christopher Cohoon rightly observes in this regard, 'The wonder that sparks *eros* is evoked not by the otherness of the other sex per se (as Irigaray seems to assume), but rather by an other who is sexed, that is, an other who could be of the same sex as oneself. Indeed, no sex or sexuality is precluded. To begin with, since sexual difference has no fixed reality outside its manifestations in embodied individuals, it makes sense that the object of erotic wonder be not sexual otherness itself, but the corporeal specificity of a concrete other, which is always sexed.'[119]

It seems sufficient to say that, in so far as subjects begin with a sense of pre-givenness in the erotic relationship, and may feel transformed in their subjectivity in its course (and in future, with or without that relationship), their sexuality is intrinsic to their inter/subjectivity. Their sexuality is the salience by which their whole presence is engaged in this relationship (as opposed to others). The response to this criticism ought not to be the proliferation of ontological categories, but rather a matter of simply suspending the ontological urge when delineating the specific features of the erotic couple. Ecological phenomenology always seeks the exact if varying trajectories of

[116] Chute 2004.

[117] Hence Mortiz Winternitz holding that the text is often 'disgusting to persons of refined taste', and that, 'judging by modern standards, an impatient Western critic should stigmatize the work as a perfect masterpiece of bad taste and bad style!' in his *History of Indian Literature*, originally translated into English in 1927; quoted in Patel 2014: 33.

[118] Ibid., p. 33. [119] Cohoon 2011: 485.

the lines of affective relationship that run through and between the subject and its environment. In the case of the erotic, this requires paying attention to the human beings involved. If it were reflexive practice it would concern oneself and one's lover; in the case of a phenomenological description, I argue, it requires artistic richness, so as to not drift into an abstraction that stultifies the potential for other experiences to be presented in their other ways. The paradox of erotic presentation, then, is that inasmuch as it is specific, it does not seek universality, but rather, indicates how we could think of other specific relationships. This is a quality evident in Śrī Harṣa's evocation of these lovers, a royal couple located within the classical social, cultural, and literary tradition of India. Yet there is much that would be unexpected if we took that tradition to be a monotonic structure of fixed gender norms. But by now, the patient reader will not find the percolation of subjectivity across skin and across norms so very unexpected in Śrī Harṣa's poetry.

We will turn to their climax later, but first let us turn to Śrī Harṣa's description of Nala's post-coital dissolution, the presumption of the male gaze muted, transformed by his dependence on her happiness.

A drop of sweat on the tip of her nose, the red lac on her lower lip gone, the freckle on her cheek fading—her face brought joy to that Naiṣadha.[120]

He sunk into a liquid joy, seeing the sheen of her damp underarm, revealed when she threw back her arms to tie back her hair, now without its knot of flowers.[121]

Then Śrī Harṣa switches to the light-heartedness that is both insightful about passion fulfilled, and also artful about keeping the poem contained within its romantic frame despite all the foreboding about the future. Damayantī frowns playfully at the bruise on her lips and the nail marks on her breast.

Seeing his lover's face adorned with an expression of ire, he quailed and said, 'My lissom darling, I don't know who made you angry; tell me. I'll punish him!'[122]

He acknowledges that it might be he himself who needs punishment, for it is his nails and teeth that might have hurt her (133).

If it was indecorous of me to bite you with my teeth with passion, without compassion, my lady of the beautiful teeth! Why then, can you not take revenge for it by biting my lip in your turn?[123]

[120] *svedabindukitanāsikāśikhaṃ tanmukhaṃ sukhayati sma naiṣadham /*
proṣitādharaśayāluyāvakaṃ sāmiluptapulakaṃ kapolayoḥ // 121.

[121] *vītamālyakacahastasaṃyamavyastahastayugayā sphuṭīkṛtam /*
bāhumūlamanayā tadujjvalaṃ vīkṣya saukhyajaladhau mamajja saḥ // 124.

[122] *roṣarūṣitamukhīmiva priyāṃ vīkṣya bhītidarakampitākṣarām /*
tāṃ jagāda sa na vedmi tanvi taṃ kaścakāra tava koparopaṇām // 131.

[123] *ānanasya mama cedanaucitī nirdayaṃ daśanadaṃśadāyinaḥ /*
śodhyate sudati vairamasya tatkiṃ tvayā vada vidaśya nādharam // 135.

He guiltily lists three offences on his part, all taking up again themes that we have noticed before: his nails scratched her breasts, his teeth bit her lips, and his diadem lit the room while he removed her clothes. He corrects the first by fanning her breasts—with their rainbowed lines marked by his nails—and cooling them; and then he serves her again by caressing her feet (134). (It might be easiest to dismiss this startling action by saying that the sexual sciences (*kāmaśāstras*) allow for the inversion of gender norms, and the man may bow at the woman's feet in the bedroom whereas in ritual submission she would have to at his. But the—perhaps romantic—alternative is to ask whether the constrictive convention comes second, in a bid to control the erotic within the patriarchal; after all, there was lovemaking before there were laws, unless one thinks somewhat bleakly that it required laws for there to be love.)

With these tender words, he let his hair kiss the bed; so that the stream of his diadem's bejewelled light flowed on to the blushful lotus that were her feet.[124]

He bows low on the bed and pleads that she not be angry with him for having scratched her during their love-making:

Then that lady of the beautiful teeth gratified her masterful lover, holding and hiding her lotus-like feet with her lovely hands; her wounded pride assuaged by his tender obeisance, she showed her smiling face to his.[125]

If my argument holds, two things make sense simultaneously: on the one hand, Śrī Harṣa cannot but narrate from within the concrete context of his cultural world, about these two heterosexual people and what they convey about love and lovemaking. On the other hand, the emotional insights with which this passage is laden—the post-coital teasing, the shifts in roles and role-playing, the simulation of other emotions for the purpose of affirming their (temporarily) satiated longing—make sense to any two lovers, of whatever culture and whatever gender. The trick is to learn this lesson from artistic detail: leave any possible generalization as an indication of what humans can share of their phenomenology, and do not petrify it as a stipulation about what constitutes a human being.

The Sense of What Body Is: On Boundaries and Their Limits

The consistent presupposition of the modern existential puzzle over lovemaking has been that it is about subjects who have a peculiar relationship with a body. The puzzle then becomes as to what the erotic is (even in the narrow sense of sexual desire alone), given that the relationship now seems to be between one subject related to a body and

124 *itthamuktimupahṛtya komalāṃ talpacumbicikuraścakāra saḥ /*
ātmamaulimaṇikāntibhaṅginīṃ tatpadāruṇasarojasaṅginīm // 137.

125 *sātha nāthamanayatkṛtārthatāṃ pāṇigopitanijāṅghripaṅkajā /*
tatpraṇāmadhutamānamānanaṃ smerameva sudatī vitanvatī // 140.

another subject with a similar relationship to his/her own body. For is the erotic about subjects or their bodies? A telling example of this comes from a recent critique of Jean-Paul Sartre:

> Sartre understands sexual desire as the doomed attempt to confine the Other's subjectivity within the bounds of his or her body,[126] but what we believe to be happening in romantic *Eros* is very nearly the reverse: *the empowering of the body—the torso, the hands, the genitals—with the creative potential of a transcendence.* In romantic love the Other *chooses not* to 'transcend me on all sides', but rather to engage his or her transcendence with my own in the mutual shaping of a world, a shaping we can now conduct with our transformed flesh. In romantic sexuality my body and the body of my lover carry the full burden of our personhood. On this occasion only, our bodies become *who we are*... Rather, I have been inspired by his or her sexualized presence *to bring my subjectivity to the surface of my flesh*, to make my subjectivity congruent with my flesh, and I have done this in the hope of encouraging the same unfolding, revealing, divine transubstantiation in my beloved.[127]

What we have seen of Nala and Damayantī certainly points to an understanding of their erotic relationship as being about a mutual shaping of a world and a matching unfolding and revealing. But it is strange to see in this claim the tenacious persistence of a dualism of subject and body, where the erotic is presented as a particular bringing of subjectivity to the surface of flesh, as if by implied contrast there are other relationships in which a disembodied subject is able to flourish. I have sought to counter this problematic presupposition; that is why the study of the erotic ought to be continuous with the study of other areas of ecological phenomenology. The presence of the human subject is the presence of bodiliness, although precisely what is taken to be body changes with phenomenological context. It seems thoroughly misleading in light of our study to treat the category of body as the instrument (of a subject) through which an account of the erotic relationship can be generated. It is no wonder then that we are left in the passage above with a peculiar fetishization of body parts as the only explanation for how erotic subjectivity is at all possible.

In her celebratory phenomenology, whenever she is diverted from the stern ontological task of constructing the architectonic of the sexuate, Irigaray offers much the more intuitive sense of what happens with the sense of bodily boundaries when lovers meet. As Chute says, 'Irigaray's most fervent argument here is for the creative... integrity of what she memorably names "carnal sharing."... Irigaray's focus on the carnal emphasizes that carnal union can be a privileged place of individuation, an engaged practice even more rigorous than the renunciation of the flesh.'[128] In one of her own lyrical passages, Irigaray makes a series of interrelated claims:

> [E]gological, solitary love does not correspond to the shared outpouring, to the loss of boundaries which takes place for both lovers when they cross the boundary of the skin into the mucous membranes of the body, leaving the circle which encloses... solitude to meet in a shared space,

[126] E.g., Sartre 1956: 389–91.
[127] Gordon and McKinney 2010: 20–3.
[128] Chute 2004: no pagination.

a shared breath, abandoning the relatively dry and precise outlines of each body's solid exterior to enter a fluid universe where the perception of being two persons [*de la dualité*] becomes indistinct, and above all, acceding to another energy...produced together and as a result of the irreducible difference of sex. In this relation, we are at least three...you, me and our work [*oeuvre*], that ecstasy of ourself in us [*de nous en nous*], that transcendence of the flesh of one to that of the other become ourself in us [*devenue nous en nous*]...of pleasure's neither-mine-nor-thine, pleasure transcendent and immanent to one and to the other, and which gives birth to a third, a mediator between us thanks to which we return to ourselves, other than we were.[129]

Again let us set aside the unmotivated ontological claim that this experience is 'a result of the irreducible difference of sex'. Instead, we must take note of two major aspects of carnal sharing. One is the sensation of the loss of the boundary of skin, and the consequent explosion into a fluid indistinction of subjectivity. The other is the description of this outpouring as a mediating *oeuvre* of subjectivity. We shall turn to a series of verses and their description of this carnal sharing, before concluding with some ideas of what all this implies for the accounting of erotic bodiliness, what it feels to be a body in love. First is the climax, carefully described as 'unsequenced', as coming and a coming together, with tāntric practice but also silly hilarity.

He saw that tender she, sought her climax in haste; to prolong her, he startled her, exclaiming—of his reflection upon the polished floor—'who is he?!', before, just at the right time, making her see that it was he.

At that moment too, he single-pointedly concentrated on the twelve-spoked sun [*īḍa*, right nostril] and the cooling moon [*piṅgala*, left nostril]; and thus he kept pushing back at too soon a coming.

He attended to their climax then, kissing the crook of her arm, his beloved's breast, her navel; they shared that pinnacle of pleasure, that delight which is the culminating secret of lovemaking.

Now, their limbs tiring, their eyelids fluttering, breathing heavily, with a sibilant soft whisper, goosepimpling all over, they came together, unsequenced.[130]

And later, after the tenderness of their post-coital teasing that we have already seen, there is the delicious mix of what will last and what cannot, the desire and the satiation:

Their love for each other an elixir, they sought to love each other again. But their wish remained unfulfilled, for short-lived was that malicious night.[131]

129 Irigaray 1990–1991: 180–1.

130 *vīkṣya bhāvamadhigantumutsukāṃ pūrvamacchamaṇikuṭṭime mṛdum /*
ko'yamityuditasaṃbhramīkṛtāṃ svānubimbamadadarśataiṣa tām // 114
tatkṣaṇāvahitabhāvabhāvitadvādaśātmasitadīdhitisthitiḥ /
svāṃ priyāmabhimatakṣaṇodayāṃ bhāvalābhalaghutāṃ nunoda saḥ // 115
svena bhāvajanane sa tu priyāṃ bāhumūlakucanābhicumbanaiḥ /
nirmame ratarahaḥsamāpanāśarmasārasamasaṃvibhāginīm // 116
viślathairavayavairnimīlayā lomabhirdrutamitairvinidratām /
sūcitaṃ śvasitasītkṛtaiśca tau bhāvamakramakamadhyagacchatām // 117.

131 *tau mitho ratirasāyanātpunaḥ saṃbubhukṣumanasau babhūvatuḥ /*
cakṣame natu tayormanorathaṃ durjanī rajaniralpajīvanā // 141.

Nala expresses clearly that 'privilege' of which Irigaray speaks—an individuation, but of their togetherness. This first, single act is not in itself the entirety of their giving themselves to the other; it began before, when she chose him above the gods (and again, we know that it will deeply influence how each chooses to show love for the other in times of terrible misfortune).

'What room is there for me to say, "Consider me indeed your own"? For, by discarding the king of the gods like a length of straw, you have bought me for the price of your compassion.'[132]

Of course, he does not literally think that he has won her pity and not her love; but he wants to express something deeper, albeit in a light-hearted vein. He wants to imply that he understands that her love was given entirely of her own accord. He does not want her to think that he has such a high opinion of himself that he presumes to think that she has come to love him solely because of his intrinsic qualities. She loves him of her accord; if it had been merely the qualities of a potential suitor that had attracted her originally, then Indra would have been a nobler choice than any human being. His understanding of the trueness of her love, then, comes from his not taking himself to be a man of kingly virtues. This sensory, emotional, even social swapping of their sense of themselves as individuals (the king seeing himself now akin to a length of straw, the demure bride the compassionate agent of togetherness) is part of the percolation of subjectivity. What is the notion of bodiliness that emerges from this essay in erotic phenomenology?

It seems that an ontological account of body neither informs nor is particularly furthered by attention to the representation of the erotic relationship; it is a wheel that does not engage with any sensitive account of love/making. Moreover, if we do try to develop such an account, we end up constructing problems in such a framework, oscillating between incompatible pictures of the body in reality, asking if it is a stable material with boundaries or a fluid collection of entities (just as in a post-Cartesian programme we ask if the body is different from the subject or the subject is merely reducible to body). But it is not so puzzling nor seemingly dichotomous to rephrase our analysis as a pure methodological inquiry: what can we say about the shifts that occur in our sense of bodiliness within erotic phenomenology?

There is a core to the experience of lovemaking: a dialectic between a bounded, reflexive givenness of subjectivity that seeks to express desire in a mutual engagement with the beloved other, and a total sensation of becoming open to, accepting of, and critically being changed by the presence of what was hitherto distinctly other. This dialectic is intensely felt for a time, and more pervasively but less acutely later, as a substantive commonalization of subjectivity, in which the self/other indexing of experience fades back and a shared field of awareness, neither self nor other, is foregrounded in awareness. This substitution of otherness by mutuality is expressed in different dimen-

132 *dhīyatāṃ mayi dṛḍhā mameti dhīrvaktumevamavakāśa eva kaḥ /*
yadvidhūya tṛṇavaddivaspatiṃ krītavatyasi dayāpaṇena mām // 146.

sions of our sense of ourselves. When subjectivity—its feeling of distinctive identity, its opening up to otherness, and its experience of a new sharedness—is about thought and sensory changes, emotion and proprioception, words and affect, it no longer seems useful to think of the subject in some particular metaphysical relationship to a body. Subjectivity simply is bodiliness (so the body is not the subject reduced away); we just need to have an expansive and pluralistic acceptance of what that means in different contexts.

With this in view, I read Śrī Harṣa's poetic description of lovemaking as the feeling of changes to bodily boundaries, so that the field of erotic subjectivity shifts over time and experience. Accordingly, there are changes in what one counts as one's body, where that bodiliness ends, and how it feels as a bounded entity. Although Jonna Bornemark writes of the erotic relationship as specifically the encounter of bodies bound by their skin, what she says about the skin has nevertheless a wider phenomenological significance for erotic ecology as I have presented it: 'It would be only the limit between you and me.' This limit is 'the border between us, [it] no longer only separates us but also connects us. The limit is what we share.'[133] She clarifies further, 'The body is a limit in this experience in three ways: first, it is a limit as the maximum of bodily experience; second, it is the border of my body as a field next to yours, and finally, it is a limit that both divides us and binds us together.'[134] I would qualify the second and third points of this insightful readings of 'limit'. Regarding the second point, the limit is in fact the field of intersubjectivity, calling into question precisely the sense of the skin as boundary of body. The limit is where the sense of a pre-constituted bodiliness is required in order to undergo a sense of being mutually constituted by the other. That is why it is the limit in the third sense: It is thus the condition for the possibility of both otherness and something new between oneself and other. This applies to what it means to talk of 'the limit as maximum experience', because this applies to all the organs of subjectivity, not just the senses but such things as imagination and emotions.

So we should be careful to not be misled by the obviousness of skin to make the limit a palpable material fact alone. In terms of sensation, of course skin does operate as the limit in the act of making love. In fact, more carefully, we should say the volumetric limit is the plane of touch between the skin of the lovers. That plane of affect is where subjectivity is simultaneously separated and united. For one to feel oneself is to feel the other, and to feel the other is to feel more than oneself. But the limit operates in ways other than through skin in propinquity. The sharply remembered first meeting, the bed, and the windows and the birds seen together, the oblique affection carried by gently teasing words, the interpretation of the past and expectations for a future—all these one carries with all of one's organs of subjectivity, the senses, emotions, mind, and whatever other analytic categories we have to hand to describe ourselves. But one also finds them imbued with their character only because of the

[133] Bornemark 2012: 262. [134] Ibid.

presence of the lover. This is what is hinted at in the penultimate verse, which we have encountered before:

They held each other, put their lips together, thighs entwined, as if seeing in their dreams what they had done to each other, enfolded in their embrace, holding on tight. And they slept.[135]

Here Śrī Harṣa doubtless relies on his audience to think about the philosophical nature of dreaming and sleeping as espoused in the system of Advaita Vedānta to which he belongs. Dream sleep and deep sleep have implications for the nature of subjectivity: the former raises questions about the presumption of the subject–object distinction that is intrinsic to phenomenality (since dreams also have this distinction and yet are not veridical in relation to waking experience), and points to the Advaitin's interrogation of our assumptions about the status of ontological difference. The latter temporarily blurs the subject–object difference and indicates, according to the Advaitin, the underlying non-duality of consciousness.[136] Here, Śrī Harṣa seems to rephrase this wide-ranging and radical metaphysics playfully, as if it were really an insight into the transformation of erotic subjects in the compellingly ordinary state of post-coital sleep.

So our subjectivity in romantic love is one where our bodiliness is felt as a bounded and pre-given presence uniquely available to us, that has now been shaped afresh in critical ways (that will become evident only through the narrative of our lives). This re-constitution is not a loss of an originary sense of self but of changes to it, across different dimensions of subjectivity: which dimensions they are will depend upon the contingencies of who one is and who exactly the lover. The changes will concern the way one makes judgements, responds to favourite songs, handles the demands of work, views one's physical makeup, takes a particular moral course, and so on. This making afresh happens critically through lovemaking, when the whole range of what I call the organs of subjectivity form the limit with those of the other. Bodiliness then feels at its limit, neither in its pre-given stability nor in its future trajectory, but now—in the state where both human beings begin and end simultaneously. It is the core of erotic phenomenology, from which we may draw out the motive power of a love story.

We can end with the concluding verse, which goes to that core. When the goose had first reported to Damayantī about Nala's love, it had said (III.118) that Nala's accomplished artistry in drawing would eventually be perfected on Damayantī's swelling bosom alone. It had then foretold how their skins would show the mark of their fungibility to each other's presence.

'During your festival of passion, let the pictures drawn on your breast be erased by Nala's lotus hands thickly coated with the waxy sweat of arousal, so that they are reabsorbed into the very hands from whence they came.'[137]

135 *miśritoru militādharaṃ mithaḥ svapnavīkṣitaparasparakriyam /*
tau tato'nu parirambhasaṃpuṭaiḥ pīḍanāṃ vidadhatau nidadratuḥ // 152.

136 Indich 1980: chapter 4, for a clear outline of how dreaming and sleep are part of the standard Advaitic theory of consciousness.

137 *sattvasrutasvedamadhūtthasāndre tatpāṇipadme madanotsaveṣu /*
lagnotthitāstvatkucapattralekhāstannirgatāstaṃ praviśantu bhūyaḥ // III.123.

Now that had come to pass in an even more dramatic way:

> Their lifebreath was inseparable, declared by an intermingled suspiration, all rapid flow; breathing brought about by the languor of making love, lovemaking betokened by sighing breath. Their two hearts had become one, it could be seen: the elephants and dolphins—once saffron-painted upon her lovely breasts—were now signs imprinted upon the chest of the king. This was the couple that slept in happiness.[138]

The erotic is not quite a destruction of the border between you and me,[139] but the recreation of our two separate borders as the limit between us, a plane that is simultaneously and necessarily both of us. The perforation of skin occurs when the sense of two borders is sought to be overcome mutually. But once the touching skin and membranes have formed the erotic limit, then the percolation of subjectivity does not require breaking down defences; it simply is the phenomenal feature of the limit as the plane of common presence. The transfer of Damayantī's saffron drawings on to Nala, the mirroring of sweat and pearl beads, the intermingling of breath—all these are evocations of something shared that partakes of both and yet is more than either. It is about the lovemaking but it is also about the love that does not cease after the sweat and saffron are gone.

[138] *tadyātāyātaraṃhacchalakalitarataśrāntiniśvāsadhārājasravyāmiśrabhāva-sphuṭakathitamithaḥprāṇabhedavyudāsam /*
bālāvakṣojapatrāṅkurakarimakarīṃ mudritorvīndravakṣaścihnākhyātaikabhāvobhayahṛdayamayād-dvandvamānandanidrām // 153.

[139] As Bornemark 2012 argues, p. 266.

Conclusion

Lessons from the Chapters

In the first chapter, the first objective was to show that a medical text does not have a self-evident idea of the body that is the object of its attention. As we followed the text's self-conscious exploration of the patient's body, we saw that its concern to understand health and illness in fact took it into a holistic consideration of what it is to be the person to whom the physician attends. The interdependence of patient and physician in accurate diagnosis, the complex aetiology of disease and the experience of illness, and the social-moral regimen for a normatively prescribed healthy life, all go to show that medical phenomenology is deeply ecological. What makes for a patient is, in fact, what makes for a person—a materially bound being whose subjectivity is composed through diverse, changing lines of influence acting upon and within and between humans. Body is thus contextually understood in this text, varying with the purpose at hand. It is, of course, predominantly the specific anatomical details and theorized physiological functions firmly bounded by skin; yet at other points, it is a composite entity of qualities both constituting and being constituted by agentive conduct in a social and intersubjective environment.

The second chapter was perhaps the one that least needed to make the basic case that to be human is always to be at the intersection of multiple forces that construct bodily identity, for that has been a critical and foundational argument of feminism. Nevertheless, I tried to show that—whatever the unknown authors of this text exactly intended when they deliberately represented a woman as the wise ascetic victorious in debate with a powerful king—the arguments the almswoman Sulabhā makes together amount to an original outline of gendered phenomenology. Some familiar lines of debate—about the biological and the constructed, agency and structural constraints, body and rationality—are seen in fresh light because of the way Sulabhā is represented, and given as arguing about how she is formed by her context and how she re-forms it. As such, the ecology of gendered phenomenology is presented not only as what always and continuously forms intersectional identity, but also as what agentive self-awareness re-configures it. In particular, the apparently insuperable problem of the sexual character of body in the construction of gender is treated in a way that I suggest has not been seen in the contemporary literature.

The third chapter, like the first, had at least one initial, negative objective: to show that the rigorous contemplative practices taught by Buddhaghosa do not cleave to an inside–outside and mind–body distinction. Although I did not spend time on critical engagement with a flourishing literature that treats practices of disciplined attentiveness (popularly termed 'mindfulness') in a highly mentalistic way about some sort of 'inner' transformation, I sought to make the positive case that Buddhaghosa's teachings locate such attentiveness in a rich environment of natural surroundings and social interaction. Equally, I did not seek to refute the conventional view that his practices of sharp focus on the constitution of the human being draw a dualistic map of mind and body.[1] Instead, a careful reading of his practices of understanding resulted in a modular, multi-perspectival analysis. Together, the various practices showed the experience of being human—seen through the magnifying glass of disciplined meditative analysis by a monk—as ecological, constantly reworking the constitution of bodiliness through shifting foci of phenomenological analysis.

The final chapter was more experimental, a reading of a narrative that does not declare itself to be offering a view of bodiliness. Nevertheless, the richly layered and lyrical depiction of lovemaking licenses us to think creatively about what love is and how it is made. Śrī Harṣa's poetry has us see erotic phenomenology as deeply ecological: everything from word-constructed image to a joint climax, from lavish palace decoration to the evocativeness of courting birds, from socially constructed shyness to wild and carefree moans, from locked vision to arousing nail-marks, form and re-form bodily boundaries. Subjectivity percolates through these lines of affect that run across and through the limit of bodiliness that must both separate and fuse experience.

The key thought in all this is that, in an ecological phenomenology, the human subject is conceived as what is found to itself within the infinite nodes of an ecology of being. The delineation of body is arrived at by working back phenomenologically from the entire world of experience, with the robust acknowledgement that the point of arrival—a conception of what counts as body—is dependent upon the motivation for attending to experience, the areas of experience attended to, and the expressive tools available to the phenomenologist. (It would take another, more perilous undertaking to defend this contention, but I may as well say for heuristic purposes that this is the opposite of traditional bracketing: it is not that the world is left out in order to pursue the subject but that it is in going out to the world that the subject is found. And the living body is not the pre-given spark for an ontological mystery but the contingent description arrived at after a phenomenological quest.)

If this book has a large unifying claim, it is that phenomenology undertaken as a disciplined methodology to interrogate experience shows us three interrelated things:

(i) Body as a philosophical category is integral to the sustained study of experience;
(ii) at the same time, it must always be clear that the understanding of body is contingent upon the context of and motivation for study; and

[1] But see Heim and Ram-Prasad 2017 [Early Release]/2019 for such a discussion.

(iii) such understanding requires an account of 'bodiliness'—the human being as that which is a subject through and as 'body'—in terms of the interactive relationships between a dynamic range of contextualizing aspects of the world of the subject.

Coda: Thinking Cross-culturally

In looking at representations of experience presented in contexts free from the historical Western trajectory that prompted the formation of Phenomenology as a self-naming discipline, while also engaging with that very tradition (in several of its manifestations), I have of course made this book an oblique commentary on phenomenology across cultures. But I have quite deliberately kept away from making any metatheoretical points about something like 'cross-cultural phenomenology'. None of the Western material studied here, nor indeed the foundational analyses of Husserl or Heidegger, generally sought to frame the philosophical enterprise of phenomenological analysis as being one about a culturally circumscribed subject. (I set aside here Heidegger's specific considerations about history, which are acutely focused on the West.) I take these classical Indian texts to be equally concerned about human beings as such, as being intrinsically about the human condition. If humanity is indeed indivisible (as Mahatma Gandhi put it[2]), then questions about what humans are should be communicable, interpretable, and understandable conceptually across the specific cultural boundaries that the contingencies of history have thrown up. Naturally, such communication needs contextualization, a mutual lexicon, and mutual respect.

It is up to the reader familiar with Western traditions of thought to judge whether this book has provided the requisite contextualization and lexicon. But these are procedural issues, and I want to confine myself to them. It may be that this is a naïve attitude to take, but I believe that it is not only a separate but also wrong-headed undertaking to justify why one might develop a cross-cultural philosophical project in the first place. What really matters is to ensure that such a project is neither hegemonic in silencing cultural difference nor apologetic in pleading for such difference.

I have framed the cross-cultural comprehensibility of ecological phenomenology as an engagement between a thematic of modern Western thought—phenomenology—and a sophisticated Indic literary exploration of the bodily nature of humanness. This makes for a specific sort of mutual illumination. The modern Western Phenomenological tradition articulates as a theory a profound way of examining experience in order to understand the nature of human subjectivity, but it does so primarily as a response to an elaborately developed metaphysical problem. Yet it has struck some thinkers that the methodology of examination is significant in itself without being saddled with a metaphysical teleology.

[2] See Parekh 2006: 340ff.

The Indian materials I look at offer a dazzling variety of ways of examining experience and subjectivity, and do so in exactly this methodologically scrupulous manner, without directing it at the determination of a metaphysical truth. This is not because metaphysics is not at the heart of Indic thought, but because the materials I study show how phenomenological study—once it is brought out as such—is not metaphysical in orientation. This results, therefore, in an approach to the Indic that is thematized through the modern West, but an analysis that shows how the Indic materials can lead to rich and productive consideration of experience. Within this framing, I therefore have not looked at how these texts have been studied by native commentators: they have many wonderful things to say, but they do not articulate the nature of bodiliness in health, gender, contemplative discipline, and erotic intersubjectivity through the theme of phenomenological analysis. The cross-cultural here is folded into the conceptual whole, and is not a higher-order statement of programme.

In the end, then, ecological phenomenology as it is presented in this book has taken the particular cross-cultural path it has because of the range and limitations of my expertise and interests. It is perfectly possible that working through some other angle between and across the textual traditions of different cultures might throw up quite different focal points of analysis and rather different ways of configuring human experience. If the idea of ecological phenomenology as a way of thinking about the nature of experience and its analysis has emerged with any plausibility from this book, then that would be the most encouraging sign that thinking across cultures (rather than always defending why and how one might and should) is comprehensible and worth undertaking.

Bibliography

Primary Texts

Chapter 1

Caraka Saṃhitā. Text with English Translation and Critical Exposition Based on Cakrapāṇi Datta's Āyurveda Dīpikā 1976–2001 Ram Karan Sharma and Vaidya Bhagwan Dash. Six volumes. Varanasi: Chowkhamba Sanskrit Series.

Chapter 2

Mahābhārata, Śāntiparvan. 1999 Electronic text, Bhandarkar Oriental Research Institute, Pune, India. Text entered by Muneo Tokunaga et al., revised by John Smith. http://gretil.sub.uni-goettingen.de/gretil/1_sanskr/2_epic/mbh/mbh_12_u.htm (accessed 30 January 2018).

Chapter 3

Buddhaghosa *Atthasālinī* (*Dhammasaṅgaṇī-aṭṭhakathā*), Chaṭṭha Saṅgāyana Collection, Vipassana Research Institute, Dhamma Giri, Igatpuri, India; www.tripitaka.org (accessed 30 January 2018).

Buddhaghosa *Visuddhimagga* Vipassana Research Institute, Dhamma Giri, Igatpuri, India. www.tripitaka.org (accessed 30 January 2018).

Chapter 4

Shastri, Devarshi Sanadhya 2002 *Naiṣadhīyacaritam of Mahākavi Śrī Harṣa with the Jīvātu Sanskrit Commentary of Mallinātha and the Candrikā Hindi Commentary.* Varanasi: Krishnadas Academy.

Secondary Literature

Adams, Robert Merrihew 2013 'Consciousness, Physicalism, and Panpsychism', *Philosophy and Phenomenological Research* LXXXVI 3: 728–35.

Albahari, Miri 2011 'Nirvana and Ownerless Consciousness', in D. Zahavi, Mark Siderits, and Evan Thompson (eds), *Self, No-self?* Oxford: Oxford University Press, 217–38.

Allen, N.J. 1996 'The Hero's Five Relationships: A Proto-Indo-European Story', in Julia Leslie (ed.), *Myth and Myth-Making*. London: Curzon.

Alter, Joseph 2004 *Yoga in Modern India: The Body between Science and Philosophy*. Princeton: Princeton University Press.

Atherton, Margaret 1993 'Cartesian Reason and Gendered Reason', in Louise M. Antony and Charlotte Witt (eds), *A Mind of One's Own. Feminist Essays on Reason and Objectivity*. Colorado: Westview Press, 19–34.

Baker, Robert 1997 'Review of Hans-Georg Gadamer's *The Enigma of Health*, (Oxford, Polity Press, 1996)', *Medical History* 7: 397–9.

Barbaras, Renaud 2005 *Desire and Distance*. Stanford: Stanford University Press.

Barbaras, Renaud 2011 'The World of Life', Leonard Lawlor (trans.), *Philosophy Today* 55: 8–16.

Barnes, Michael 2014 'Narratives of Detachment: Meister Eckhart and Buddhaghosa on Personal Transformation', *Medieval Mystical Theology* 23/2: 102–15.

Bauer, Nancy 2001 *Simone De Beauvoir, Philosophy and Feminism*. New York: Columbia University Press.

Beauvoir, Simone de 1949 [1972] *The Second Sex*. Howard Madison Parshley (trans.). Harmondsworth: Penguin.

Bhikkhu Bodhi 2011 'What Does Mindfulness Really Mean? A Canonical Perspective', *Contemporary Buddhism* 12/1: 19–39.

Black, Brian 2007 *The Character of the Self in Ancient India*. Albany: State University of New York Press.

Böhler, Arno 2011 'Open Bodies', in Axel Michaels and Christoph Wulf (eds), *Images of the Body in India*. New Delhi: Routledge, 109–22.

Bond, George D. 1988 'The Arahant: Sainthood in Theravāda Buddhism', in Richard Kieckhefer and George D. Bond (eds), *Sainthood. Its Manifestations in World Religions*. Berkeley: University of California Press, 140–71.

Bordo, Susan 1987 *The Flight to Objectivity: Essays on Cartesianism and Culture*. Albany: State University of New York Press.

Bornemark, Jonna 2012 'The Erotic as Limit-Experience. A Sexual Fantasy', in Jonna Bornemark and Marcia Sá Cavalcante Schuback (eds), *Phenomenology of Eros*. Södertörn: Södertörn Philosophical Studies, 247–66.

Brockington, John L. 2006 'Epic *svayaṃvaras*', in Raghunath Panda and Madhusudan (eds), *Voice of the Orient (A Tribute to Prof. Upendranath Dhal)*. Delhi: Easter Book Linkers, 35–42.

Brockington, Mary 2001 'Husband or King? Yudhiṣṭhira's Dilemma in the *Mahābhārata*', *Indo-Iranian Journal* 44/3: 253–63.

Brodbeck, Simon 2006 'Ekalavya and *Mahābhārata* 1.121–28', *International Journal of Hindu Studies* 10/1: 1–34.

Brodbeck, Simon 2013 'The Story of Sāvitrī in the *Mahābhārata*: A Lineal Interpretation', *Journal of the Royal Asiatic Society* 23/4: 527–49.

Bronner, Yigal 2010 *Extreme Poetry: the South Asian Movement of Simultaneous Narration*. New York: Columbia University Press.

Bronner, Yigal 2014 'The Nail-Mark that Lit the Bedroom', in Yigal Bonner, David Shulman, and Gary Tubb (eds), *Innovations and Turning Points. Towards a History of Kāvya Literature*. New Delhi: Oxford University Press, 237–62.

Bronner, Yigal, David Shulman, and Gary Tubb (eds) 2014 *Innovations and Turning Points. Towards a History of Kāvya Literature*. New Delhi: Oxford University Press.

Bruzina, Ronald 1990 'The Last Cartesian Meditation', *Research in Phenomenology* 20/1: 167–84.

Bryson, Cynthia B. 1998 'Mary Astell: Defender of the "Disembodied Mind"', *Hypatia* 13/4: 40–62.

Bucknell, Roderick S. 1993 'Reinterpreting the *Jhānas*', *Journal of the International Association of Buddhist Studies* 16/2: 375–409.

Bullington, Jennifer 2013 *The Expression of the Psychosomatic Body from a Phenomenological Perspective*. Springer DOI: 10.1007/978-94-007-6498-9_2.

Burley, Mikel 2007 *Classical Sāṃkhya and Yoga: An Indian Metaphysics of Experience*. London: Routledge.

Burwood, Stephen 2008 'The Apparent Truth of Dualism and the Uncanny Body', *Phenomenology and Cognitive Science* 7: 263–78.

Cadenhead, Raphael 2013 'Corporeality and Askesis: Ethics and Bodily Practice in Gregory of Nyssa's Theological Anthropology'. *Studies in Christian Ethics* 26/3: 281–99.

Callanan, J. 2011 'Making Sense of Doubt: Strawson's Anti-scepticism', *Theoria* 77: 261–78.

Carman, Taylor 2008 *Merleau-Ponty*. London: Routledge.

Carr, David 2003 'Transcendental and Empirical Subjectivity', in Donn Welton (ed.), *The New Husserl*. Bloomington: Indiana University Press.

Cassell, Eric J. 2004 *The Nature of Suffering and the Goals of Medicine*. Oxford Scholarship Online, November 2011. DOI: 10.1093/acprof:oso/9780195156164.001.0001; p. 129.

Cerulli, Anthony 2012 *Somatic Lessons. Narrating Patienthood and Illness in Indian Medical Literature*. Albany: State University of New York Press.

Cerulli, Anthony and U.M.T. Brahmadathan 2009 '"Know Thy Body, Know Thyself": Decoding Knowledge of the *Ātman* in Sanskrit Medical Literature', *eJournal of Indian Medicine* 2: 101–7.

Chakravarti, Uma n.d. 'Of Meta-Narratives and 'Master' Paradigms: Sexuality and the Reification of Women in Early India'. http://www.cwds.ac.in/wp-content/uploads/2016/09/OfMeta-NarrativesMonograph.pdf.

Chatterjee, Heramba 1961'*Svayaṃvara*, the Ninth Form of Marriage', *Adyar Library Bulletin* XXV: 603–15.

Chattopadhyaya, D.P., Lester Embree, and J.N. Mohanty (eds) 1992 *Phenomenology and Indian Philosophy*. New Delhi: India Council of Philosophical Research/Motilal Banarsidas.

Chute, Hillary L. 2004 'Irigaray's Erotic Ontology: Review of Luce Irigaray's *Between East and West: From Singularity to Community*. New York: Columbia UP, 2002', *Postmodern Culture* 14/2, January. https://muse-jhu-edu.ezproxy.lancs.ac.uk/article/55200.

Clark, Andy 1997 *Being There. Putting Brain, Body, and World Together Again*. Cambridge, MA: MIT Press.

Cohoon, Christopher 2011 'Coming Together: The Six Modes of Irigarayan Eros', *Hypatia* 26/3: 478–96.

Collins, Steven 1998 *Nirvana and Other Buddhist Felicities: Utopias of the Pali Imaginaire*. Cambridge: Cambridge University Press.

Comba, Antonella 1987 'Carakasaṃhitā, Śārīrasthāna and Vaiśeṣika Philosophy', in G. Jan Meulenbeld and Dominik Wujastyk (eds), *Studies on Indian Medical History*. Delhi: Motilal Banarsidass, 39–55.

Cousins, Lance S. 1989 'The Stages of Christian Mysticism and Buddhist Purification: Interior Castle of St Teresa of Avila and the Path of Purification of Buddhaghosa', in Karel Werner (ed.), *The Yogi and the Mystic. Studies in Indian and Comparative Mysticism*. London: Curzon Press, 103–20.

Cousins, Lance S. 1994–96 'The Origin of Insight Meditation', *The Buddhist Forum*, IV: 35–58.

Dasgupta, Madhusraba 2000 'Usable Women. The Tales of Ambā and Mādhavī', in Mandakranta Bose (ed.), *Faces of the Feminine in Ancient, Medieval, and Modern India*. New York: Oxford University Press, 21–32.

Dastur, Françoise 2000 'World, Flesh, Vision', in Fred Evans and Leonard Lawlor (eds), *Chiasms: Merleau-Ponty's Notion of Flesh*. Albany: State University of New York Press, 23–49.

Davidson, Arnold I. 1990 'Spiritual Exercises and Ancient Philosophy: An Introduction to Pierre Hadot', *Critical Inquiry* 16/3: 475–82.

Davis Jr., Donald 2005 'Being Hindu or Being Human: A Reappraisal of the *Puruṣārthas*', *International Journal of Hindu Studies* 8/1–3: 1–27.

Derrida, Jacques 2005 *On Touching—Jean Luc Nancy*. Christine Irizarry (trans.). California: Stanford University Press.

Dhand, Arti 2008 *Woman as Fire, Woman as Sage. Sexual Ideology in the Mahābhārata*. Albany: State University of New York Press.

Doniger, Wendy 2002 'Transformations of Subjectivity and Memory in the Mahābhārata and the Rāmāyaṇa', in David Shulman and Guy G. Stroumsa (eds), *Self and Self-Transformation in the History of Religions*. Oxford: Oxford University Press, 57–72.

Engel, G. L. 1977 'The Need for a New Medical Model: A Challenge for Biomedicine', *Science* 196: 129–36.

Evans, Fred and Leonard Lawlor (eds) 2000 *Chiasms: Merleau-Ponty's Notion of Flesh*. Albany: SUNY Press.

Evdokimov, Paul 1998 *Ages of the Spiritual Life*. With Michael Plekon and Alexis Vinogradov (eds), Sister Gertrude (trans). Moscow: St Valdimir's Seminary Press.

Fagerberg, David W. 2013 *On Liturgical Asceticism*. Washington, DC: Catholic University of America Press.

Fasching, Wolfgang 2011 '"I am of the Nature of Seeing": Phenomenological Reflections on the Indian Notion of Witness-Consciousness', in D. Zahavi, Mark Siderits, and Evan Thompson (eds), *Self, No-self?* Oxford: Oxford University Press, 217–38.

Filliozat, Pierre-Sylvain 1993 'Caraka's Proof of Rebirth', *Journal of the European Ayurvedic Society* 3: 94–111.

Fink, Eugen 1995 *Sixth Cartesian Meditation: The Idea of a Transcendental Theory of Method*. Ronald Bruzina (trans.). Bloomington: Indiana University Press.

Fitzgerald, James 2003 'Nun Befuddles King, Shows *Karmayoga* Does Not Work', *Journal of Indian Philosophy* 30: 641–77.

Flood, Gavin 2006 *The Tantric Body: The Secret Tradition of Hindu Religion*. London: I.B. Tauris.

Foucault, Michel 1978 *The History of Sexuality*, vol. 1. London: Allen Lane.

Foucault, Michel 1986 *The Care of the Self*. New York: Vintage.

Foucault, Michel 1998 *Technologies of the Self. A Seminar with Michel Foucault*. Luther H. Martin, Huck Gurman, and Patrick H. Hutton (eds). Amherst: University of Massachusets Press.

Foucault, Michel 2005 *The Hermeneutics of the Subject*. Frédéric Gros (ed.), Graham Burchell (trans.). New York: Picador.

Frauwallner, Erich 1984 *History of Indian Philosophy Vol. II*, V.M. Bedekar (trans.). Delhi: Motilal Banarsidass.

Fuchs, Thomas 2005 'Overcoming Dualism', *Philosophy, Psychiatry, & Psychology* 12/2: 115–17.

Gadamer, Hans-Georg 1996 *The Enigma of Health: The Art of Healing in a Scientific Age*, J. Gaiger and N. Walker (trans.). Stanford: Stanford University Press.

Gallagher, Shaun and Dan Zahavi 2014 'Phenomenological Approaches to Self-Consciousness'. *Stanford Encylopedia of Philosophy:* http://plato.stanford.edu/entries/self-consciousness-phenomenological/#BodSelAwa (last accessed 31 January 2018).

Gatens, Moira 1991 *Feminism and Philosophy. Perspectives on Difference and Equality*. Cambridge: Polity Press.

Gatens, Moira 1996 *Imaginary Bodies: Ethics, Power and Corporeality*. London: Routledge.

Gethin, Rupert 1986 'The Five Khandhas: Their Treatment in the Nikāyas and Early Abhidhamma', *Journal of Indian Philosophy* 14: 35–53.

Gill, Christopher, 2010 *Naturalistic Pscyhology in Galen and Stoicism*. Oxford: Oxford University Press.

Godway, Eleanor 2007 'Phenomenology, Intersubjectivity and Truth: Merleau-Ponty, de Beauvoir, Irigraray and *la conscience métaphysique et morale*', *Journal of French Philosophy* 17/2: 70–85.

Gokhale, Pradeep P. 1992 *Inference and Fallacies as Discussed in Ancient Indian Logic*. Delhi: Satguru Publications.

Gordon, Jeffrey and Audrey McKinney 2010 'Love and Lust: A Phenomenological Investigation', *Journal of the British Society for Phenomenology* 41/1: 8–32.

Griffiths, Paul 1981 'Concentration or Insight: The Problematic of Theravāda Buddhist Meditation-Theory', *Journal of the American Academy of Religion* 49/4: 605–24.

Grosz, Elizabeth 1993 'Merleau-Ponty and Irigaray in the Flesh', *Thesis Eleven* 36: 37–59.

Grosz, Elizabeth 1994 *Volatile Bodies. Towards a Corporeal Feminism*. Bloomington: Indiana University Press.

Gunaratna, Henepola 1985 *The Path of Serenity and Insight: An Explanation of the Buddhist Jhānas*. New Delhi: Motilal Banarsidass.

Gupta, Bina 1998 *The Disinterested Witness: Fragments of Advaita Phenomenology*. Evanston, Ill: Northwestern University Press.

Gupta, Bina 2003 *CIT: Consciousness*. New York: Oxford University Press.

Hacker, Paul 1995 *Philology and Confrontation. Paul Hacker on Traditional and Modern Vedānta*. Wilhelm Halbfass (ed.). Albany: State University of New York Press.

Handiqui, Krishna Kanta 1965 *Naiṣadhacarita of Śrī Harṣa*. Poona: Deccan College. 3rd Edition (original edition 1934).

Harvey, Peter 1993 The Mind–Body Relation in Pali Buddhism', *Asian Philosophy* 3/1: 29–41.

Hatfield, Gary 2014 *The Routledge Guidebook to Descartes' Meditations*. London: Routledge.

Heim, Maria 2014 *The Forerunner of All Things*. New York: Oxford University Press.

Heim, Maria forthcoming, 2019 *Voice of the Buddha: Buddhaghosa on the Immeasurable Words*. New York: Oxford University Press.

Heim, Maria and Chakravarthi Ram-Prasad 2017 [Early Release]/2019 'In a Double Way: *nāma-rūpa* in Buddhaghosa's Phenomenology', *Philosophy East and West* (forthcoming 69.1, January 2019).

Herrmann, Fritz-Gregor 2013 'Dynamics of Vision in Plato's Thought', *Helios* 40/1–2: 281–307.

Hiltebeitel, Alf 2000 'Draupadī's Question', in Alf Hiltebeitel and Kathleen Erndl (eds), *Is the Goddess a Feminist? The Politics of South Asian Goddesses*. New York: New York University Press, 113–22.

Hubbard, Kyle 2011 'The Unity of Eros and Agape: On Jean-Luc Marion's Erotic Phenomenon', *Essays in Philosophy* 12/1: 130–46.

Husserl, Edmund 1960 *Cartesian Meditations*, D. Cairns (trans.). The Hague: Martinus Nijhoff.

Husserl, Edmund 1989 *Ideas Pertaining to a Pure Phenomenology and a Phenomenological Philosophy. Second Book*. R. Rojcewicz and A. Schuwer (trans.). Dordrecht: Kluwer.

Indich, William M. 1980 *Consciousness in Advaita Vedānta*. Delhi: Motilal Benarsidass.

Ingalls, D.H.H. 1965 *An Anthology of Sanskrit Court Poetry. Vidyākara's 'Subhāṣitaratnakoṣa'*. Cambridge, MA: Harvard University Press.

Irigaray, Luce 1982/1992 *Elemental Passions*. Joanne Collie and Judith Still (trans). New York: Routledge.

Irigaray, Luce 1984/1993 *An Ethics of Sexual Difference*. Carolyn Burke and Gillian C. Gill (trans.). Ithaca, New York: Cornell University Press.

Irigaray, Luce 1985 *Speculum of the Other Woman*. Gillian C. Gill (trans.). Ithaca, New York: Cornell University Press.

Irigaray, Luce 1990/1991 'Questions to Emmanuel Levinas', Margaret Whitford (trans.), in *The Irigaray Reader*, ed. Margaret Whitford. Oxford: Blackwell.

Irigaray, Luce 1992/1996 *I Love to You: Sketch of a Possible Felicity in History*. Alison Martin (trans.). New York: Routledge.

Irigaray, Luce 2004 'To Paint the Invisible', *Continental Philosophy Review* 37: 389–405.

Irigaray, Luce and Eleanor H. Kuykendall 1988 'Sorcerer's Love: A Reading of Plato's Symposium, Diotima's Speech', *Hypatia* 3/3: 32–44.

Irrera, Orazio 2010 'Pleasure and Transcendence of the Self: Notes on "A Dialogue Too Soon Interrupted" between Michel Foucault and Pierre Hadot', *Philosophy and Social Criticism* 36/9: 995–1017.

Jamison, Stephanie W. 1996 *Sacrificed Wife / Sacrificer's Wife: Women, Ritual, and Hospitality in Ancient India*. New York: Oxford University Press.

Jani, A. N. 1957 *A Critical Study of Śrīharṣa's Naiṣadhacaritam*. Baroda: Bhandarkar Oriental Research Institute.

Jani A. N. 1996 *Śrīharṣa*. Delhi: Sahitya Akademi, Makers of Indian Literature Series.

Käll, Lisa Folkmarson 2012 'Erotic Perception: Operative Intentionality as Exposure', in Jonna Bornemark and Marcia Sá Cavalcante Schuback (eds), *Phenomenology of Eros*. Södertörn: Södertörn Philosophical Studies, 225–46.

Kapstein, Matthew 2013 'Stoics and Boddhisattvas: Spiritual Exercise and Faith in Two Philosophical Traditions', in Michael Chase, Stephen R. L. Clark, and Michael McGhee (eds), *Philosophy as a Way of Life: Ancients and Moderns. Essays in Honor of Pierre Hadot*. New York: John Wiley & Sons, Inc.

Karunadasa, Y. 2010 *The Theravāda Abhidhamma. Its Inquiry into the Nature of Conditioned Reality*. Hong Kong: Centre of Buddhist Studies, The University of Hong Kong.

Kushf, G. 2013 'A Framework for Understanding Medical Epistemologies', *The Journal of Medicine and Philosophy* 38/5: 461–86.

Kuznetsova, I., J. Ganeri, and C. Ram-Prasad (eds) 2012 *The Self: Hindu and Buddhist Ideas in Dialogue*. Aldershot: Ashgate.

Lamb, Sarah 2000 *White Saris and Sweet Mangoes: Aging, Gender and Body in North India*. Berkeley: University of California Press.

Larson, Gerald 1987 'Āyurveda and the Hindu Philosophical Systems', *Philosophy East and West* 37/3: 245–59.

Latour, Bruno 2004 'How to Talk about the Body? The Normative Dimension of Science Studies', *Body and Society* 10/2–3: 205–29.

Le Doeuff, Michele 1989 *The Philosophical Imaginary*. Colin Gordon (trans.). London: Athlone.

Leder, Drew 1984 'Medicine and Paradigms of Embodiment', *The Journal of Medicine and Philosophy* 9: 29–43.

Leder, Drew 1990 *The Absent Body*. Chicago: University of Chicago Press.

Levinas, Emmanuel 1981 *Otherwise than Being or Beyond Essence*. Alphonso Lingis (trans.). The Hague: Martinus Nijhoff.

Levinas, Emmanuel 1987 *Time and the Other*, Richard Cohen (trans.). Pittsburgh: Duquesne University (*Le Temps el l'autre*, 1979).

Lewis, Michael and Tanya Staehler 2010 *Phenomenology: An Introduction*. London: Continuum.

Lingis, Alphonso 1983 *Excesses: Eros and Culture*. Albany: State University of New York Press.

Lloyd, Genevieve 1984 *The Man of Reason: 'Male' and 'Female' in Western Philosophy*. Minneapolis: University of Minnesota Press.

Maas, Philipp A. 2008 'The Concepts of the Human Body and Disease in Classical Yoga and Āyurveda', *Vienna Journal of South Asian Studies* 51 125–62.

Maiese, Michelle 2014 'How Can Emotions Be Both Cognitive and Bodily?' *Phenomenology and Cognitive Science* 13: 513–31.

Malamoud, Charles 1981 'On the Rhetoric and Semantics of Puruṣārtha', *Contributions to Indian Sociology* 15/1–2: 33–54.

Malamoud, Charles 2014 'Shadows', in Yigal Bonner, David Shulman, and Gary Tubb (eds), *Innovations and Turning Points. Towards a History of Kāvya Literature*. New Delhi: Oxford University Press, 550–62.

Malinar, Angelika 2007 'Arguments of a Queen: Draupdadī's Views on Kingship', in Simon Brodbeck and Brian Black (eds), *Gender and Narrative in the Mahābhārata*. London: Routledge, 79–96.

Marion, Jean-Luc 2002 'The Unspoken: Apophasis and the Discourse of Love', Arianne Conty (trans.). *Proceedings of the American Catholic Philosophical Association* 76: 39–56.

Mary Astell [1694, 1697] 1970 *A Serious Proposal to the Ladies*, Part I, II. New York: Source Book Press.

Matilal, Bimal 1986 *Perception: An Essay on Classical Indian Theories of Knowledge*. Oxford: Oxford University Press.

Matthews, Eric 2002 *The Philosophy of Merleau-Ponty*. Montreal-McGill-Queen's University Press.

McClintock, Sara L. 2010 *Omniscience and the Rhetoric of Reason. Śāntarakṣita and Kamalaśīla on Rationality, Argumentation and Religious Authority*. Boston: Wisdom Publications.

McHugh, James 2011 'The Incense Trees the Land of Emeralds: The Exotic Material Culture of Kāmaśāstra', *Journal of Indian Philosophy* 39: 63–100.

McIntosh, Mary 1991 'Review of [Judith Butler's] *Gender Trouble*', *Feminist Review* 38: 113–14.

McIntyre, Ronald and David Woodruff Smith 1989 'Theory of Intentionality', in J. N. Mohanty and William R. McKenna (eds), *Husserl's Phenomenology: A Textbook*. Washington, DC: University Press of America, 147–79.

Meerbote, R. 1989 'Kant's Functionalism', in J. C.Smith (ed.), *Historical Foundations of Cognitive Science*. Dordrecht: Reidel.

Mehta, Neeta 2011 'Mind–Body Dualism: A Critique from a Health Perspective. *Mens Sana Monographs* 9/1: 202–9.

Merleau-Ponty, Maurice 1962 *Phenomenology of Perception*, Colin Smith (trans.). London: Routledge (1945 *Phénoménologie de la Perception*. Paris: Galimard).

Merleau-Ponty, Maurice 1965 *The Structure of Behaviour*. A. L. Fisher (trans.) London: Methuen.

Merleau-Ponty, Maurice 1968 *The Visible and the Invisible*, Alphonso Lingis (trans.). Evanston, Ill.: Northwestern University Press (1964 *Le Visible et l'Invisible*. Paris: Gallimard).

Meulenbeld, G. Jan 1999–2002 *A History of Indian Medical Literature*. 5 volumes. Groningen: Egbert Forsten.

Michaels, Axel and Christoph Wulf (eds) 2011 *Images of the Body in India*. New Delhi: Routledge.

Milbank, J. 2007 'The Gift and the Mirror', in Kevin Hart (ed.), *Counter-Experiences: Reading Jean- Luc Marion*. Notre Dame, IN: University of Notre Dame Press, 253–318.

Mohanty, Jintendra Nath 1992 *Reason and Tradition in Indian Thought*. Oxford: Oxford University Press.

Moi, Toril 1999 *What Is a Woman?* Oxford: Oxford University Press.

Mrozik, Suzanne 2007 *Virtuous Bodies. The Physical Dimensions of Morality in Buddhist Ethics*. New York: Oxford University Press.

Nagel, Chris 2012 'Phenomenology Without "Body"?', *Studia Phænomenologica* XII: 17–33.

Ñāṇamoli, Bhikkhu 1973 *Mindfulness of Breathing (Anapanasati)*. Kandy: Buddhist Publication Society.

Ñāṇamoli 1975 Translation of *Buddhaghosa's The Path of Purification*, Kandy: Buddhist Publication Society.

Noë, Alva 2009 *Out of Our Heads*. New York: Hill and Wang.

Nyanaponika Thera 1985 [Fifth Printing] *Abhidhamma Studies. Researches in Buddhist Psychology*. Kandy: Buddhist Publication Society.

O'Sullivan, Susanne 2015 *It's All in Your Head: True Stories of Imaginary Illness*. London: Chatto & Windus.

Offen, Karen 2005 'Defining Feminism: A Comparative Historical Approach', in Gisela Bock and Susan James (eds), *Beyond Equality and Difference. Citizenship, Feminist Politics and Female Subjectivity*. London: Routledge, 62–81.

Olendzki, Andrew 2011 'The Construction of Mindfulness', *Contemporary Buddhism* 12/1: 55–70.

Parekh, Bhikku 2006 'Gandhi's Legacy', in Richard L. Johnson (ed.), *Gandhi's Experiments with Truth. Essential Writings by and about Mahatma Gandhi*. Lanham: Lexington Books, 334–50.

Patel, Deven 2014 *Text to Tradition. The Naiṣadhīyacarita and Literary Community in South Asia*. New York: Columbia University Press.

Patton, Laurie L. 2007a 'How Do You Conduct Yourself? Gender and the Construction of a Dialogical Self in the *Mahābhārata*', in Simon Brodbeck and Brian Black (eds), *Gender and Narrative in the Mahābhārata*. London: Routledge, 97–109.

Patton, Laurie L. 2007b 'The Fires of Strangers: A Levinasian Approach to Vedic Ethics', in Purishottama Bilimoria, Joseph Prabhu, and Renuka Sharma (eds), *Indian Ethics. Classical Traditions and Contemporary Challenges*. Volume I. Aldershot: Ashgate, 117–47.

Pekkarinen, Immo n.d. 'The Many Faces of Woman. The Place of Woman in Emmanuel Levinas's *Totality and Infinity*'. http://www.nbl.fi/~nbl3145/elevinasa.htm (last accessed 31 January 2018).

Pereboom, Derk 2011 *Consciousness and the Prospects of Physicalism*. New York: Oxford University Press.

Piantelli, Mario 2002 'King Janaka as a Male Chauvinist Pig in the Mahābhārata', in Alessandro Monti (ed.), *Hindu Masculinities Across the Ages: Updating the Past*. Turin: L'Harmattan Italia, 35–55.

Pollock, Sheldon 1998 'Bhoja's *Śṛṅgāraprakāśa* and the Problem of Rasa: A Historical Introduction and Translation', *Asiatische Studien/Études asiatiques* 70/1: 117–92.
Pollock, Sheldon 2016 *A Rasa Reader. Classical Indian Aesthetics*. New York: Columbia University Press.
Preisendanz, Karin 2009 'Logic, Debate and Epistemology in Ancient Indian Medical Science – An Investigation into the History and Historiography of Indian Philosophy', *Indian Journal of History of Science* 44/2: 261–312.
Preisendanz, Karin 2015 'Between Affirmation and Rejection: Attitudes towards the Body in Ancient South Asia from the Ṛg Veda to Early Classical Medicine', in Gert Melville and Carlos Ruta (eds), *Thinking the Body as a Basis, Provocation, and Burden of Life*. Oldenboug: De Gruyter, 113–44.
Prets, Ernest 2000 'Theories of Debate, Proof and Counter-Proof in the Early Indian Dialectical Tradition', in Piotr Balcerowicz and Marek Mejor (eds), *On the Understanding of Other Cultures*. Warsaw: Oriental Institute, Warsaw University, 369–82.
Ram-Prasad, Chakravarthi 1995 'A Classical Indian Philosophical Perspective on Ageing and the Meaning of Life', *Ageing and Society* 15.1, March: 1–36.
Ram-Prasad, Chakravarthi 2001 *Knowledge and Liberation in Classical Indian Thought*. Basingstoke: Palgrave Macmillan.
Ram-Prasad, Chakravarthi 2002 *Advaita Epistemology and Metaphysics: An Outline of Indian Non-realism*. London/New York: RoutledgeCurzon Press.
Ram-Prasad, Chakravarthi 2005 *Eastern Philosophy*. London: Weidenfeld & Nicolson.
Ram-Prasad, Chakravarthi 2007 *Indian Philosophy and the Consequences of Knowledge*. Aldershot: Ashgate.
Ram-Prasad, Chakravarthi 2011 'Situating the Elusive Self of Advaita', in D. Zahavi, Mark Siderits, and Evan Thompson (eds), *Self, No-self?* Oxford: Oxford University Press, 217–38.
Ram-Prasad, Chakravarthi 2013 *Divine Self, Human Self: The Philosophy of Being in Two Gītā Commentaries*. New York: Bloomsbury.
Ramakrishna Rao, K. B. 1962 'The Sāṃkhya Philosophy in the *Caraka Saṃhitā*', *Brahmavidyā, Adyar Library Bulletin* 26/3–4: 193–205.
Rowlands, Mark 2010 *The New Science of Mind. From Extended Mind to Embodied Phenomenology*. Cambridge, MA: The MIT Press.
Rozemond, Marleen 1998 *Descartes's Dualism*. Cambridge, MA: Harvard University Press.
Salamon, Gayle 2012 'The Phenomenology of Rheumatology: Disability, Merleau-Ponty, and the Fallacy of the Maximal Grip', *Hypatia* 27/2: 243–60.
Sartre, Jean-Paul 1956 *Being and Nothingness*, Hazel Barnes (trans.). New York: Gramercy Press.
Schermerhorn, R.A. 1930 'When Did Indian Materialism Get Its Distinctive Titles?' *Journal of the American Oriental Society* 50: 132–8.
Schmidt, Hanns-Peter 1987 *Some Women's Rites and Rights in the Veda*. Poona: Bhandarkar Oriental Research Institute.
Selby, Martha Ann 2000 *Grow Long, Blessed Night. Love Poems from Classical India*. New York: Oxford University Press.
Shankar, S. 1994 'The Thumb of Ekalavya: Postcolonial Studies and the "Third World" Scholar in a Neocolonial World', *World Literature Today* 68/3: 479–87.
Sharma, B. N. K. 1981 *History of the Dvaita School of Vedānta and its Literature*. Delhi: Motilal Banarsidass.

Sinha, Debabrata 1955 *Metaphysic of Experience in Advaita Vedanta: A Phenomenological Approach*. Delhi: Motilal Banarsidass.

Sinha, Debabrata 1985 'Human Embodiment: The Theme and the Encounter in Vedantic Phenomenology', *Philosophy East and West* 35/3: 239–47.

Smith, A. David 2007 'The Flesh of Perception: Merleau-Ponty and Husserl', in T. Baldwin (ed.), *Reading Merleau-Ponty: On* Phenomenology of Perception. London: Routledge, 1–22.

Spivak, Gayatri 1988 *In Other Worlds*. New York: Routledge.

Strawson, Peter F. 1959. *Individuals: An Essay in Descriptive Metaphysics*. London: Methuen.

Strawson, Peter F. 1966 *The Bounds of Sense: An Essay on Kant's Critique of Pure Reason'* London: Methuen.

Strawson, Peter F. 1985 *Scepticism and Naturalism: Some Varieties*. New York: Columbia University Press.

Stroud, B. 1968. 'Transcendental Arguments', *Journal of Philosophy* 65: 241–56.

Svenaeus, Frederik 2000 'Hermeneutics of Clinical Practice: The Question of Textuality', *Theoretical Medicine and Bioethics* 21: 171–89.

Tevet Dayan, Maya 2010 *Divine Language Incarnate. The Poetic Metaphysics of Śrīharṣa Naiṣadhīyacarita*. PhD Thesis, Faculty of Humanities, Tel Aviv University.

Toombs, S. Kay 1987 'The Meaning of Illness: A Phenomenological Approach to the Patient–Physician Relationship', *The Journal of Medicine and Philosophy* 12: 219–40.

Toombs, S. Kay 1992 *The Meaning of Illness: A Phenomenological Account of the Different Perspectives of Physician and Patient*. Boston: Kluwer Academic Publishers.

Tubb, Gary 2014 'Something New in the Air: Abhinanda's *Rāmacarita*', in Yigal Bonner, David Shulman, and Gary Tubb (eds), *Innovations and Turning Points. Towards a History of Kāvya Literature*. New Delhi: Oxford University Press, 357–94.

Van Den Berg, J. H. 1955 *The Phenomenological Approach to Psychiatry*. Springfield: Charles C. Thomas.

Vasseleu, Cathryn 1998 *Textures of Light. Vision and Touch in Irigaray, Levinas and Merleau-Ponty*. London: Routledge.

Vogt, Henrik, Elling Ulvestad, Thor Eriksen, and Linn Getz 2014 'Getting Personal: Can Systems Medicine Integrate Scientific and Humanistic Conceptions of the Patient?', *Journal of Evaluation in Clinical Practice* 20: 942–52.

Wadley, Susan (ed.) 2011 *Damayanti and Nala. The Many Lives of a Story*. New Delhi: Chronicle Books.

Warnke, Georgia 2001 'Intersexuality and the Categories of Sex', *Hypatia* 16/3: 126–37.

Wayman, Alex 1976 'Regarding the Translation of the Buddhist Technical Terms *saññā/saṃjñā, viññā/vijñāna*', in O. H. de A. Wijesekera (ed.), *Malalasekera Commemoration Volume*, Colombo, 324–36.

Whatley, Shawn D. 2014 'Borrowed Philosophy: Bedside Physicalism and the Need for a *Sui Generis* Metaphysic of Medicine', *Journal of Evaluation in Clinical Practice* 20: 961–4.

White, David G. 1996 *The Alchemical Body: Siddha Traditions in Medieval India*. Chicago: University of Chicago Press.

Wijeratne, R. P. and Rupert Gethin 2002 (trans.) *Summary of the Topics of Abhidhamma and Exposition of the Topics of the Abhidhamma*. Oxford: Pali Text Society.

Wildberger, Julia 2014 'The Epicurus Trope and the Construction of a "Letter Writer" in Seneca's *Epistulae Morales*', in Jula Wildberger and Marica Colish (eds), *Seneca Philosophus*. Berlin: De Gruyter, 431–66.

Wollstonecraft, Mary 1975 [1792] *A Vindication of the Rights of Woman*. Harmondsworth: Penguin.

Wujastyk, Dominik 2003 *The Roots of Ayurveda*. London: Penguin Classics.

Wujastik, Dominik 2004 'Medicine and Dharma', *Journal of Indian Philosophy* 32: 831–42.

Wujastyk, Dominic 2009 'Interpreting the Image of the Body in Pre-Modern India', *International Journal of Hindu Studies* 13/2: 189–228.

Young, Iris Marion 1980 'Throwing Like a Girl: A Phenomenology of Feminine Body Comportment, Motility and Spatiality', *Human Studies* 3: 137–56.

Yu, Jiangxia 2014 'The Body in Spiritual Exercise: A Comparative Study between Epictetan Askēsis and Early Buddhist Meditation', *Asian Philosophy* 24/2: 158–77.

Zaner, Richard M. 1981 'The Other Descartes and Medicine', in Stephen Skousgaard (ed.), *Phenomenology and the Understanding of Human Destiny*. Washington: University Press of America, 93–119.

Zaner, Richard M. 2010 'At Play in the Field of Possibles', *Journal of Phenomenological Psychology* 41: 28–84.

Zimmermann, Francis 1979 'Remarks on the Conception of the Body in Ayurvedic Medicine', *South Asian Digest of Regional Writing* 8: 10–26.

Zimmermann, Francis 1987 *The Jungle and the Aroma of Meats: An Ecological Theme in Hindu Medicine* (original French publication 1982). Berkeley: University of California Press.

Zimmermann, Francis 2004 'May Godly Clouds Rain For You!: Metaphors of Well-Being in Sanskrit', *Studia Asiatica* V: 1–12.

Zimmermann, Francis 2006 'The Conception of the Body in Ayurvedic Medicine. Humoral Theory and Perception'. http://ginger.tessitures.org/terre-des-vivants/fluides-vitaux-et-physiologie/humoral-theory-and-perception/.

Index